Investigative Reporting

Investigative Reporting

A study in technique

David Spark

Focal Press

OXFORD   AUCKLAND   BOSTON   JOHANNESBURG   MELBOURNE   NEW DELHI

Focal Press
An imprint of Butterworth-Heinemann
Linacre House, Jordan Hill, Oxford OX2 8DP
225 Wildwood Avenue, Woburn, MA 01801-2041
A division of Reed Educational and Professional Publishing Ltd

℞ A member of the Reed Elsevier plc group

First published 1999

British Library Cataloguing in Publication Data
Spark, David
    Investigative reporting: a study in techniques
    1. Reporters and reporting
    I. Title
    070.4'3

Library of Congress Cataloguing in Publication Data
Spark, David
    Investigative reporting: a study in techniques/David Spark
    p. cm. – (Media series)
    Includes bibliographical references and index.
    1. Investigative reporting   I. Title   II. Journalism media journal
    PN4781.S69 1999
    070.4'3–dc21   99–044776

ISBN 0 240 51543 9

Composition by Genesis Typesetting, Rochester, Kent
Printed and bound in Great Britain by Biddles Ltd, www.Biddles.co.uk

Contents

Contents

Contents

Illustrations

Figure 2.1 A *News of the World* football investigation: the 'Toongate' exposé at Newcastle United

Figure 2.2 Investigator who was murdered: Veronica Guerin, pictured on the front cover of Emily O'Reilly's biography (Vintage, 1998), rattled Dublin's major criminals by confronting them in their homes

Figure 3.1 The Insight way: teamwork is still the secret of the *Sunday Times* Insight investigations which set an example in investigative journalism from the 1960s

Figure 9.1 The Sotheby's affair: investigator Peter Watson outside the premises of the fine art auctioneers (picture Channel 4)

Figure 11.1 Jonathan of Arabia: Cabinet minister Aitken (right) with his daughter Victoria on April 10, 1995, the day *The Guardian* and *World in Action* published their allegations about him and his Middle Eastern friends (picture Martin Argles, *The Guardian*)

Figure 13.1 A sale that never was. In the autumn of 1990 publishing tycoon Robert Maxwell was eager to reduce debts by selling assets. He was also keen to show he was doing so. Maxwell Communications Corporation issued this press release on October 7 announcing a sale raising £60 million. However, when Mark Killick of *Panorama* enquired, he was told no sale had taken place

Figure 13.2 Aftermath of the Maxwell affair: investigative journalist Tom Bower's devastating indictment in the *Daily Mail* seven years later

Figure 14.1 A reader service: the *Evening Mail*, Birmingham, campaigning against shoddy and swindling builders, investigates a roofer who started jobs, then left them unfinished

Preface

In examining the techniques used in investigative reporting I have been fortunate to be able to draw upon the experience of many well known journalists working in the field, who have given me unstintingly of their time during the preparation of this book. I thank them for their help and append their names below.

My aim has been to define for the young journalist what investigative reporting is and what qualities it requires and to identify the common factors and the special circumstances involved in a wide variety of investigations.

Investigative Journalism examines how opportunities for investigations can be found and pursued, how informants can be persuaded to yield needed information and how and where this information can be checked. It stresses the dangers and legal constraints that have to be contended with and shows investigators at work in two classic inquiries: concerning the mysterious weekend spent in Paris by Jonathan Aitken, then Minister of Defence Procurement, and the career of masterspy Kim Philby.

The book looks at such fields for inquiry as company frauds (including those of Robert Maxwell), consumer complaints, crime, police malpractice, the intelligence services, local government and corruption in Parliament and in overseas and international bodies.

It points to several conclusions of value in general reporting as well as in investigations. It advises young journalists to:

- Get to the facts at the heart of an issue – don't be content with spokesmen's comments.
- Explain difficult concepts – don't write around them.
- Don't just echo the views of your main source – find other sources with other views.
- Speak to as many relevant people as possible.
- Ask the simple and obvious questions which open out the subject.
- Don't take everything and everyone at their face value.
- Remember that everyone, every organization and every event has a history which may have a bearing on what is happening now.

I am grateful to those involved with investigative reporting who have talked to me about their work and experience. I should like to thank, in particular, Sam Bagnall, Martin Banks, Antony Barnett, David Bell, Richard Bettsworth, David Birkbeck, Chris Blackhurst, Alastair Brett, Tom Bower, Jimmy Burns, Mike Calvin, Duncan Campbell (of *The Guardian*), David Charter, Bernard Clark, Tony Collins, Roger Cook, Nick Davies, Richard Donkin, Ian Dowell, Geoff Elliott, James Evans, Ray Fitzwalter, Paul Foot, Michael Gillard, Jo-Ann Goodwin, Paul Halloran, Phil Hammond, David Hencke, Christopher Hird, Godfrey Hodgson, Chris Holby (Redbridge), Mark Hollingsworth, Terry Kelleher, Mark Killick, Paul Lashmar, Joe Layburn, David Leigh, David Leppard, Ann Leslie, David Lloyd, Garry Lloyd, Sue Lloyd-Roberts, Mazher Mahmood, Peter Marsh, Martin McGlown, Donal McIntyre, Maurice McLeod, Claudia Milne, Chris Mullin MP, Dave Murphy, Paul Nuki, Helen O'Rahilly, Bruce Page, Charles Raw, Bob Satchwell, Jonathan Smith, John Stonborough, Jan Tomalin, Stewart Tendler, John Ware, Peter Watson and Chris White. I refer to them in greater detail in an appendix to this book. One or two wished not to be named.

I should also like to thank those who have given me permission to quote from their work or their publications: Paul Foot, Matthew Parris, Geoffrey Goodman, editor of the *British Journalism Review*; Bloomsbury Publishing plc (for quotations from *Sotheby's: Inside Story*, by Peter Watson), Jonathan Cape (*A Hack's Progress*, by Phillip Knightley), Chatto & Windus (*Dark Heart*, by Nick Davies), HarperCollins (*Maxwell, the Final Verdict*, by Tom Bower) and the Orion Publishing Group Ltd (*Good Times, Bad Times*, by Harold Evans).

David Spark

1 What is investigative reporting?

ESTABLISHING THE FACTS

In only nine paragraphs, a correspondent told in *The Times* in October 1997 how three named retail groups had secretly helped fund an alliance campaigning to stop Sainsbury's building a store in North London. To corroborate the allegation, the correspondent had a document from the Stop the Store Alliance, plus admissions from all three groups. Here was a neat demonstration of investigative journalism, not only making an allegation but producing conclusive evidence and reporting it clearly and simply.

It is worth considering how the story might have run if there had been no document from the alliance. If run at all, it would probably have been an allegation-and-denial story, leaving readers to decide who to believe. Allegation-and-denial stories are quite attractive for newspapers. They enable complaints to be aired while saving time on research and minimizing the risk of a libel action, provided a good deal of space is given to the denial.

Investigative reporting goes beyond allegation and denial to establish facts which, if possible, decide the issue one way or the other.

A heated meeting at Portsmouth University in 1994 produced a range of allegations. Geoff Elliott, editor of the local evening paper, *The News*, asked his education reporter, David Charter, to establish some facts.

As a result, *The News* reported with documentary evidence that the university's then vice-chancellor, Neil Merritt, had exploited a concession concerning travel expenses on visits to Egypt and Malaysia. The concession was that, instead of travelling club class, as he was entitled to do, he could buy two economy class tickets for himself and his wife.

He accordingly bought economy tickets to Egypt and Malaysia but he claimed on expenses for a club class ticket for each journey. He drove to Heathrow to buy, claim for as expenses and later return, club class tickets costing £1,457 more than he paid for the economy tickets he actually used. The vice-chancellor, speaking to staff, admitted errors of judgement and said he had declared the £1,457 surplus as taxable income. After *The News*'s report, he resigned.

Investigative reporting is thus not impartially balanced between allegation and reply. It expresses a judgement based on the facts unearthed. (Though the collection and presentation of evidence must be even-handed, not slanted, and reporters must be prepared to revise their judgement in the light of the facts.)

Tony Collins, investigative reporter at *Computer Weekly*, says: 'A lot of graduates come out of university with the feeling that journalism is about sitting in the middle of issues.'

But Roger Cook said of his *Checkpoint* radio programme, predecessor of *The Cook Report*: 'This is and always will be a biased programme.' It was biased, he said, against fraud, criminality and injustice.

Checkpoint was revolutionary for the BBC. Instead of standing back with traditional impartiality, the BBC was looking into complaints and taking up the cudgels on someone's behalf.

Many journalists would argue this is no big deal.

Bruce Page, who worked on the thalidomide, Philby and DC-10 airliner stories for the Insight team at *The Sunday Times*, argues that all reporters should do what so-called investigative reporters do: check facts, never take anything on trust, never take anything on trust from people who have an interest in pushing a particular view.

Investigation, he says, is what journalism is about. What makes the contents of a newspaper different from those of an advertising brochure is that they say something which the newspaper staff have discovered by their own efforts. Journalism is not about asking important people what happened. It is about finding out yourself. Page feels it is dangerous to saw this off from the rest of reporting and call it investigation. There is nothing called investigative journalism, in his view, which is not just journalism as he learned it at the *Melbourne Herald*.

In an article in the *British Journalism Review* in September 1998 he calls this low journalism, as opposed to the high journalism expounded by Charles Moore, editor of *The Daily Telegraph*.

Moore wrote in *The Guardian* in April 1997 that he admired much of *The Guardian*'s work over corruption but there was a higher aspiration: to tell people the news and interpret it in a way they found interesting, honest and helpful.

Bruce Page replied in his article that reporting the news is higher than investigation only in the sense that a building is higher than its foundations. Investigative technique is the foundation on which everything in journalism rests.

NEWS: THE HIDDEN AREAS

What *is* the news? Is it what people say it is or are there hidden facts? Bruce Page writes that sources of news may be corrupt, so the evidence behind a news story must be critically analysed. Reporters should not simply be a conduit for material shaped by others.

Tom Bower, in the introduction to his book *Maxwell: The Final Verdict* (Heinemann/Mandarin, 1993), writes of *proper journalism* as opposed to straightforward reporting or the columnists' self-righteous sermonizing.

Michael Gillard of *The Express* says: 'Clever men hire public relations people to plant stories and they pay lawyers to threaten those who don't believe them. Companies and individuals put out PR fronts about who they are. Most papers are only too happy to accept that. But let's go and find out.'

Inside Fraud Bulletin and other organizations held a seminar in October 1998 with the title *Finding the Truth*. The brochure carried the slogan: 'A lie is the truth to people who don't know better.'

The brochure critically analysed a statement by President Bill Clinton that 'there is not a single solitary shred of evidence of anything dishonest in my public life'.

The brochure commented: 'Most people hearing this would understand it to be a total denial of wrongdoing and Mr Clinton clearly intended this to be so. However, more careful reading shows that Mr Clinton did not deny acting dishonestly: merely that there was no evidence of it. His further qualification concerning dishonesty in his public life suggests that the denial did not apply to his private life.'

The *Finding the Truth* seminar's subjects included 'Spotting the Conman', 'Strategies for Interviewing' and 'Lies in Writing'. These are all important to journalists.

David Murphy in his book *The Stalker Affair and the Press* (Unwin Hyman, 1991) draws a useful distinction. While the bulk of reporting depends on official occasions and spokesmen, some depends on unofficial people. He gives an example.

A general had been questioned about alleged shoplifting at Woolworths. An officer, incensed that this was apparently being hushed up, rang a freelance who approached the Manchester office of *The Mirror*. A reporter mentioned this to a friendly senior policeman who was able to name the general and the store. The police officer's contact in the Ministry of Defence confirmed the story, anonymously, and gave more details. (Note that, because the confirmation was anonymous, it was not sufficient.)

Army and police spokesmen denied everything, but a London reporter got the exact location of the store from the Ministry of Defence contact, and the police finally confirmed that an incident had taken place. So a story could be published.

GENERAL, SPECIALIST AND INVESTIGATIVE REPORTING

This book will use the phrase 'investigative reporting' to refer to this kind of work. The dispute being investigated need not be between an unofficial complainant and an official body. It could be between two organizations. It might concern a long sequence of events, even a whole lifetime. The point is that journalists pursue the matter beyond allegation and reply. They seek to prove or disprove the allegation.

David Murphy points out that three levels of reporting can be discerned. At the passive level, reporters report public events and what is said there. At the next level, they seek to explain or interpret what is said. At the third level, they look for the evidence behind it. To put it another way, reporting can be general, specialist or investigative.

General reporters usually lack detailed knowledge of the subject they are reporting on. They are in a hurry. They work on stories chosen by their news desk from an agenda set by major news sources and media (local or national). They seek quotes from spokesmen: managing directors, police superintendents, public relations officers, secretaries of organizations and pressure groups.

Murphy says that this serves a dual purpose for the newspaper. It shows news reports to be relevant to the society of which readers are part. It also vouches for their accuracy. If the managing director says it, it must be right. General reporting thus bolsters the managing director and the police superintendent as authoritative figures in society.

Specialist reporters, for their part, have a detailed knowledge of their subject and seek to explain it. Like general reporters, they are expected to file stories regularly. To achieve this, they have contacts in their subject area, to whom they speak frequently. They know who to approach for information. Their specialist knowledge gives them their own perspective on events and on the people in the news. They receive good information because they are knowledgeable people worth offering it to.

A third group, **reporters with an investigative turn of mind**, may be either generalists or specialists. Whichever they are, they are prepared to listen to non-spokesmen. They don't take the managing director's or the pundit's or the contact's word for everything.

In particular, they listen to non-spokesmen saying things which spokesmen wouldn't want to admit. They step outside the routine news agenda. (And this is one of their problems. News editors, struggling with today's news, say: Why can't it wait till next week?)

5

Such reporters are interested not in what people say about themselves but in what other people say about them. They seek to see behind the public face of organizations. They are in less of a hurry than most reporters. They make time to build up a detailed knowledge of the subject they are studying.

While most general and specialist reporting bolsters established authority and organizations, albeit including unorthodox groups, investigative reporting often subverts them. General reporting accepts the chairman of whatever as reputable and likely to be right. Investigative reporting pursues the whisper that he could be wrong.

> Investigative reporting seeks to gather facts which someone wants suppressed. It seeks not just the obvious informants who will be uncontroversial, or economical with the truth, but the less obvious who know about disturbing secrets and are angry or disturbed enough to divulge them.

FIGHTING READERS' BATTLES

Reporters keen on investigative work side with the less powerful and the forgotten. Carol Sarlar wrote in the *Sunday Times Magazine* about a woman who lost her home and her peace of mind because she gave evidence against five boys who killed another lad. Daniel McGrory wrote in *The Times* about forgotten Britons, unfairly imprisoned abroad and still in jail while higher-profile prisoners have been released. 'Our job,' says Claudia Milne of the TV programme maker Twenty Twenty Television, 'is to raise things which people in power find uncomfortable.'

Investigative reporting has also been described as comforting the afflicted and afflicting the comfortable.

The investigative journalists of the 1970s were mainly on the political Left, though they annoyed the Left by exposing corruption in Labour council leaderships (see pages 208–12). They had been involved in the revolutionary politics of the 1960s. They wanted to expose the secrets of the Establishment. They wanted a more moral Britain and they wanted to use the power of the media to shift things in the right direction.

Fulcrum Productions, which contributes to Channel 4's *Dispatches* programme, takes its name from a boast of Archimedes, that with a lever, a fulcrum and a place to stand he could shift anything.

There are other motivations. Ian Dowell, editor of the *Evening Mail*, Birmingham, thinks campaigns and investigations are essential if his paper is to stay in business:

'We are often beaten on news breaks by local radio, local TV, satellites, the Internet. Our salvation will be that we fight our readers' battles. If they're worried about the closure of a school or factory or about pollution, we should be there. With a large staff, we can afford to have two or three people on investigations.

'We have most success when the public are on our side.'

The News at Portsmouth also has a reporter working much of the time on investigations. The editor, Geoff Elliott, says: 'It brings great credit on a paper if it's seen to be doing something no one else is doing. People like their newspaper to be the means by which what is really happening is exposed.'

Chris White of *The Parliament Magazine* in Brussels says: 'The job is first to expose and get a good story and, second, to keep the public informed and let people know of the dangers they face.'

WHAT AN INVESTIGATIVE REPORT NEEDS

David Lloyd says that, when he was commissioning editor for Channel 4's *Dispatches* series, he chose stories to pursue by looking at their relevance to people's lives. He looked for novelty, surprise, originality, a story people think they know about but which is actually different. It is not necessarily unmasking a terrible evil but demonstrating that, while a person or institution would like people to believe something, the facts are otherwise.

News is increasingly buffeted by people who spin, who clamour for a place in the news agenda. If the facts don't support their reading, it is important to show this.

A key question for *Dispatches* is: Who don't want the story told and how powerful are they?

The dictum of the Insight team at Harold Evans's *Sunday Times* insisted on hard-edged stories. It said: 'All stories are either "We name the guilty man", "The arrow points to the defective parts", or "Stop these evil practices now."'

The investigations which Tony Collins writes for *Computer Weekly* affect everyone because they draw attention to waste of government money. They are not arcane discussions about computers.

Investigative reporters need to be practical. They need to ask: can this story be pursued in the time available? Bernard Clark, who makes programmes for Channel 4's *Dispatches*, points out that anyone can do an investigation that takes ten years.

He also points out that the choice of stories raises questions of ethics. An investigation in a newspaper or on TV is a heavy weapon to use on someone. Is the sin great enough to warrant the full treatment?

If you do attack someone, you need to be sure you are right.

There is another consideration. It is more comfortable to do investigations which further your own beliefs and prejudices. But it could be more important to look into the justified complaint of someone with whom you heartily disagree.

2 The making of an investigative reporter

THE QUALITIES REQUIRED

An investigative reporter, says freelance writer Paul Halloran, needs luck. 'If you're not gifted with a considerable degree of luck, you'll have an upsetting time. You make your own luck; but that's true only up to a point.'

Jonathan Smith of *The News*, Portsmouth, puts it like this: 'There are hundreds of stories. You have to be there at the right time with the right person to tell you what you need to know.'

One way to improve your luck is to have an incisive mind which spots what is significant. Staff at the BBC knew they were vetted by the Security Service, MI5, but thought little about it until *The Observer* splashed the story.

Investigative reporters also find they need curiosity and persistence. Tony Collins of *Computer Weekly* says:

'It's lovely, through persistence, to be able to help people discover information they wouldn't otherwise have discovered. A lot of my stories come down to a campaign for freedom of information.

'There's the problem of colleagues saying: "Haven't you already done enough about that?" Some of the best stories come out over a long period and you have to stay with them, to the point of causing weariness among colleagues.'

The persistence of some investigative journalists is breathtaking. Tom Bower's biographies of Robert Maxwell and Tiny Rowland each involved interviewing about 350 people, many of whom were not sitting by a telephone waiting to be rung up. Bower rang one man a hundred times.

A *Guardian* man says: 'You need to be a bit of a train-spotter. You need the attitude of mind that you really want to get to the bottom of things. It helps to have a sense of politics and history, too, so you don't see things in a superficial light.'

Jo-Ann Goodwin, who writes for the *Daily Mail*, talks of 'an enormous desire to know'. She adds: 'You have to be prepared to be very, very unpopular. You have to face the fact that your friends and associates may think you're doing the wrong thing.'

David Murphy, a journalist turned university lecturer, recalls that, while working for a Manchester fringe paper, he and a colleague once spent a whole weekend finding five people. 'Everything we did was obsessive. I don't think you can do it unless you're obsessive.'

But not too obsessive. You have to know when you have got as much as you need. You can always go on gathering information, but it's no good going on for ever.

Perhaps investigative reporting is a matter of single-mindedness. Only the single-minded are likely to put everything else aside that they've planned and jump on a plane to pursue their story. (Investigative reporting can be bad news for private life. Roger Cook of *The Cook Report* says he used to be away from home ten months of the year.)

You have to be prepared to read. To get to the bottom of the Dundee urban development scams (see page 210), Ray Fitzwalter of ITV's *World in Action* read 18 years of council minutes twice.

Bruce Page, formerly of *The Sunday Times*, says: 'You need some idea of scientific method and how science works. Journalists tend not to be interested in science and technology. But it's hard to get things right unless you are at least interested.'

David Birkbeck's inquiry for *Building Homes* into the fire-resistance of chimney flues (see page 159) required a willingness to make sense of a network of building regulations and British and European standards.

Keeping going, however long the task and however many the frustrations, requires some sort of moral conviction. One reporter told me:

'You have to have a feeling of outrage about wrongdoing, about deception, and about individuals you don't approve of. You're always meeting blank walls. Unless you're motivated, you're not going to get round or over them. You need anger or emotion.

'It's very lonely and it's often very demeaning. There's nothing more dispiriting than being told by a snotty-nosed PR or executive to go away.'

Bernard Clark, who makes programmes for Channel 4's *Dispatches* series, says reporters doing investigations need to be determined enough to knock on the 16th door when it's raining and they're tired and the first 15 calls have got them nowhere. (He also says they need to be inconspicuous, so no one notices what they are up to.)

The payback is that investigative reporters, in the main, enjoy their successes.

Terry Kelleher, who made a film with Paul Foot about the men wrongly convicted in the Carl Bridgewater murder case, says: 'It's not just a job. It's a difficult job. There are many easier careers in print and TV. But there's a buzz. If you get it right, if you get somebody out of prison or the law changed or an inquiry set up, it's very exciting. There is this incredible personal buzz.'

Mazher Mahmood, investigations editor at the *News of the World*, brims over with enthusiasm for the task. It shows real panache to pretend, as he did, to be a rich foreign businessman, take a luxurious hotel suite and crawl Marbella's nightspots with two Newcastle United Football Club directors recounting their dissolute adventures and their views on Newcastle women, fans and striker Alan Shearer (Figure 2.1). A touch of showmanship and cheek helps to project an investigative story, particularly on television.

3-page special on Newcastle crisis

TOONGATE

THE STING

Inside story on NEWS OF THE WORLD investigation that shook soccer world

Picture: RAOUL DIXON

IT IS the story that stunned Britain—and continues to send shockwaves throughout the world of soccer.

The News of the World's revelations that a top club is run by two leering, cheating perverts rocked our national game to its roots.

Newcastle United chairman Freddie Shepherd and vice-chairman Doug Hall–pictured above–stand exposed as arrogant creeps who sneer at the very fans who make their disgraceful lifestyle possible.

We showed that this pair are not fit to set foot in the Tyneside club's famous St James's Park ground, let

By MAZHER MAHMOOD, Investigations Editor

alone swagger to the best seats in the directors' box. Now the News of the World can reveal HOW we were able to bring you the scoop of the year.

The most significant fact of all is that the tatty tycoons were turned in by fans from their own club!

We were tipped off six weeks ago by Tynesiders shocked by Hall's sessions with Marbella prostitutes.

One supporter told us: "He's a disgrace to the club. He's always bragging about his money and his power and he's doing it all on the backs of the fans."

Weeks of painstaking inquiries around the globe by News of the World investigators confirmed the shame-

ful secrets of Hall and his sleazy pal Shepherd. But when we were ready to target the pair at the heart of their vice playground it took only one phone call to start the braggarts condemning themselves.

After we exposed them Shepherd employed a high-powered legal team to accuse us of employing "gross deception" and "entrapment."

In reality, our reporters wanted to talk about football, but Hall and Shepherd couldn't wait to chat about sex. When our man mentioned business in Saudi Arabia, Hall piped up: "We spent two nights in Dubai trying to find girls. Where do they hide them?"

Turn to the following pages for our account of how the Toongate story unfolded day by day.

SEX, LIES ON VIDEOTAPE — CENTRE PAGES

Figure 2.1   A *News of the World* football investigation: the 'Toongate' exposé at Newcastle United

Paul Halloran, formerly with *Private Eye* and now freelancing, says investigative reporters tend to have a certain similarity of temperament. They're usually short-tempered and quirky and tend to be drawn to the murkier aspects of reporting. They have a high burn-out rate. A lot have gone on to feature writing or to be foreign correspondents.

However short-tempered they may be, they have to want people to like them. They have to be good at personal relations if they are to get reluctant witnesses to speak. It is also useful to know a lot of people. Bernard Clark thinks that, in investigations, middle-aged journalists have an advantage. Besides being likely to know more of the history of a subject, they are also more likely to know people who are running the country: they went to college with them.

Investigation takes courage. It involves putting tough questions to powerful people. It involves confrontations with angry people. It can involve real danger.

It also requires an open mind because it is about facts rather than opinions. It is not really for people with fixed views on politics and society. It is for people ready to accept that what they find hard to credit may be the truth.

Few journalists would have the flexibility of mind to pursue the allegations which led to some of the most important investigations outlined in this book. When the Bridgewater Four and the Birmingham Six were found guilty, scarcely any journalist doubted the verdicts. There was no understanding at that time of the public and media pressure on police and juries to put somebody away after a dreadful crime, however meagre the hard evidence.

An investigative reporter can thus find himself out of step with his colleagues. This is not a bad thing. It challenges the herd instinct. With the help of the odd nudge from Downing Street or elsewhere, the British media herd establishes a common view of who is to be flattered, who denigrated.

No one wants to be thought unfashionable. So down with motor cars (except ours, of course). Up with Mo Mowlam, the Secretary for

Northern Ireland; down with the Orangemen. Down with Gazza, when ex-football-hero Paul Gascoigne was rejected from the England squad; poor old Gazza when he entered a drying-out clinic. Down with whoever has just been found guilty in a trial.

It can be embarrassing for some when the herd, as over Princess Diana, suddenly changes direction.

Peter Hitchens of *The Express* once commented: 'The more united Fleet Street is, the more wrong it is likely to be.'

If you question what others unthinkingly accept, investigative reporting could be for you.

THE PATH TO INVESTIGATION

Some investigative reporters have simply slid over from other journalistic jobs or do the occasional investigation while mainly involved in other work. Bernard Clark says he started the BBC's *Watchdog* investigation series when he got married and didn't want to be out on the road.

A surprising number of people have taken up investigative reporting either straight from university or after embarking on other professions. Peter Watson, who investigated Sotheby's, was a psychiatrist. Christopher Hird of the TV company Fulcrum Productions was a stockbroker, former broadcaster John Stonborough a policeman. Paul Halloran, a New Zealander, went from Ruskin College to *Private Eye*. Sam Bagnall, who did Channel 4's investigation of the Marchioness riverboat disaster, joined Bernard Clark's TV company on work experience while studying magazine journalism at the London College of Printing.

Nick Davies of *The Guardian* says he was inspired by the scandal over the Watergate burglary, which brought down President Nixon. The scandal broke as he was leaving university. He decided he wanted to cause trouble for people who abuse power. 'That,' he says, 'involves investigation because they cover their tracks.'

Mazher Mahmood was needled by the fact that the *Evening Mail*, Birmingham, wouldn't give him work experience. He went out, got his first investigative story, about video piracy, and rang the *News of the World* which he ultimately joined.

Mark Hollingsworth, fed up with his first six months in journalism at the *Scunthorpe Star*, packed all his belongings into three suitcases and a rucksack and set out for London where he made his name with his first book, *The Press and Political Dissent*.

Roger Cook joined a radio station in Sydney to raise money for his studies to be a vet. Having decided radio was more fun, he also grew crosser about some of the news he had to read on air. He was particularly cross about a story concerning a group of aborigines with no work and a drink problem. The authorities were proposing to move them out to a reservation, though they had been in the city for five generations.

Cook spoke up for them. He likes to speak up for the victims of stalkers and abusers and anyone who is being badly treated.

Jo-Ann Goodwin intended to be a university teacher, became an adviser on arts and media to the Labour Shadow Cabinet, wrote a book with Tony Banks MP and decided to become a writer. She rang uninterested editors with ideas for articles, which, she says, was 'absolutely horrible'.

In the end, she came across the story of an illegal Brazilian immigrant so sick with Aids, tuberculosis and syphilis that he had to be taken off the plane which was to fly him home. In this infectious state, he had gone round nightclubs, telling people he had flu. It took her 18 months to sell the story, which was eventually accepted by the *Evening Standard*. But it opened the way to a contract with the *Daily Mail*.

Investigative reporting has attracted some unusual people such as the Irish crimefighter Veronica Guerin and the helicopter pilot Jonathan Moyle, both of whom were murdered on the job. Moyle was gripped by an old-style patriotism and morality which caused him to report on fellow university students as well as to confront a Chilean arms manufacturer.

For Veronica Guerin, investigative reporting, which she began with an Aer Lingus exposé when she was already 32, had a fatal attraction. She worked at it all day and every day, sometimes taking her small son with her. Contacts, probably through her connections with the Fianna Fail political party, gave her a head start on other reporters.

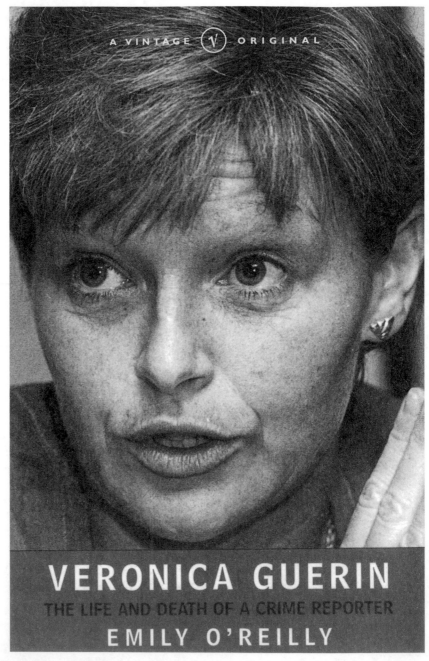

Figure 2.2   Investigator who was murdered: Veronica Guerin, pictured on the front cover of Emily O'Reilly's biography (Vintage, 1998), rattled Dublin's major criminals by confronting them in their homes

When she heard, early in her career, that a troubled beef producer had £25 million locked up in Cyprus, she got on a plane and went there. She never bothered about expense or expenses claims. Her first editor, for whom she worked as a freelance, told her biographer Emily O'Reilly: 'She had no real interest in doing the sort of mundane and pedestrian work that other rookie journalists do for years.' (*Veronica Guerin*, by Emily O'Reilly: Vintage, 1998)

BACK-UP FROM THE MANAGEMENT

For some editors, investigative reporting can be an irritant. John Stonborough recalls that, when he worked for the *East London Advertiser*, the editor used to go berserk. John's crime column meant aggro, the last thing he wanted in his Rotary club circle.

Alan Doig, who wrote *Corruption and Misconduct in Contemporary British Politics* (Penguin, 1984), suggests investigations are particularly unpopular at papers enjoying a monopoly. Such papers are part of the local Establishment and want to be seen as impartial. Investigations bring them down into the streetfighting.

There is the more mundane point that reporters spending days on investigations may be unpopular with colleagues doing less glamorous work.

Tom Bower writes in the preface to *Maxwell, the Final Verdict* (HarperCollins, 1995):

'*By nature anti-Establishment, the so-called investigative reporter finds himself working for newspapers which are increasingly pro-Establishment . . .*

'*Proper journalism is an expensive, frustrating and lonely chore. Often it is unproductive. Even the rarity of success earns the investigative reporter only the irksome epithet of being obsessional or dangerous. The final product is often complicated to read, unentertaining and inconclusive.*'

Successful investigations do require the enthusiasm and the critical eye of editors and, behind them, understanding proprietors. If the investigators are members of staff, then the editor needs to appreciate why they are writing nothing over a long period. Nick Davies, in *Dark Heart*, his investigation into British poverty and anti-social behaviour, thanks his editors at *The Guardian* for allowing him the time for his inquiries.

Investigative journalists need the trust of their employers. Bernard Clark made the first film about the 'dirty protest' by IRA prisoners in Long Kesh. The BBC, which then employed him, was not keen on the idea. Clark says: 'I told them, "What you are paying for is my judgement on the spot. The dirty protest is the biggest story in Northern Ireland at the moment."'

For preference, investigation needs to be part of a newspaper's image and policy, not something tacked on.

Tony Collins says *Computer Weekly* not only prints investigations. It is also the sort of paper which attracts the information he needs for writing them. It appeals to people who don't like incompetence and the waste of public money.

James Evans, lawyer at *The Sunday Times* in the 1960s, says:

'It is essential that any newspaper embarking on investigative work in a serious way has the backing of its management, so that it is able to commit resources and time without expecting something for immediate publication.

'The management must be prepared for the paper to become involved in litigation, which is expensive even if you win, as you do not normally recover your full costs, and it consumes much management time. What management has a right to expect is that, if litigation ensues, the paper will win: though, litigation being what it is, this can never be guaranteed.'

SPECIALISTS AND INVESTIGATIVE REPORTING

Investigative journalists working for TV or required to file copy regularly have little choice but to be non-specialist. Scarcely any speciality, apart from business, or the government's computer disasters, is going to produce a continuous stream of stories to investigate.

But doing an investigation without specialist knowledge can be hard work. Sam Bagnall found, when he looked into the sinking of the riverboat Marchioness, that he had to become knowledgeable enough to argue with the experts.

Maura Casey, an American journalist who campaigned about safety violations at a nuclear power station, makes a similar point. She writes that, if you make even a minor error, that will be used to throw doubt on the credibility of all your work. She had a list of nuclear engineers whom she consulted.

A Bangladeshi friend once asked me to find out what was happening to government money flowing into Tower Hamlets, East London, and – so far as an observer could see – disappearing with little trace. After a few weeks, I could describe the channels along which the money flowed. I could hazard no guess as to whether it was wasted or misappropriated. For that, I would have needed to be a specialist in East London affairs with a wide range of contacts there.

David Bell of the *Evening Mail*, Birmingham (see page 203), can acquire the information to write about abuses in Birmingham because he has covered the City Council for years.

Michael Gillard of *The Express* says: 'When I read the newspapers and someone is mentioned, I know about that person because of my knowledge of business affairs. I have never believed in being a generalist. Find something you enjoy and become expert. As a specialist, you have something to sell.'

Specialists are sometimes accused of becoming part of the scene in which they specialize. When Tony Collins wrote for *Computer News* in 1987 about the mysterious deaths of two programmers engaged in defence work, *The Sunday Times* offered to buy the story. When he went there, he found himself being grilled by defence correspondents. 'I told them,' he says, 'where to put their money.'

Michael Gillard agrees that a specialist can get co-opted by his sources of information. 'But there's no reason why your intelligence should be compromised. Have varied sources. A problem arises when there are a few sources who control correspondents, as in the parliamentary lobby.'

Christopher Hird of the Fulcrum Productions TV company says he finds his grasp of company accounts (as an ex-stockbroker) invaluable. He advises reporters keen on investigative work to take a first job not in local journalism but outside journalism or on a scientific, engineering, marketing or other specialist weekly. This will give them an expertise and foster their ability to marshal large numbers of facts.

Peter Watson has come to specialize in the art world. He says that to do investigations you have to be someone to whom people will leak information. That means you have to know what you are talking about.

Stewart Tendler, crime correspondent at *The Times*, says: 'It helps to know who to go to to unlock the door for you. Only a specialist has that knowledge. There are angles a non-specialist won't come across.'

There remains friction between specialization and investigation.

Investigative reporting has its cost for day-to-day reporting. Tony Collins says that his journal, *Computer Weekly*, was the only relevant magazine not invited when Health Minister Frank Dobson told the media about £1 billion of spending on information technology. Journalists from *The News*, Portsmouth, lost their privileges at the local football ground when the paper disclosed that a sale of the club's shares to former England coach Terry Venables had never actually gone through (see page 132).

Specialist writers need their contacts to help them with the next story. Investigative reporters may well produce stories critical of the specialists' contacts or the organizations they represent. Football writers didn't like *Panorama*'s exposure of Terry Venables' business dealings (Venables was disqualified as a director by the High Court in January 1998).

As Matthew Parris pointed out in a percipient article in *The Times*, journalists make friends. 'Of all the unseen but corrupting influences in journalism and politics, human kindness is the most corrupting. The webs of friendship, loyalty and acquaintance extend right across the political and media world.'

Peter Marsh wrote for the *Financial Times* a critical profile of Teflon Terry – Lord Burns, former Permanent Secretary at the Treasury. It broke with the convention that you do not discuss the policy-making role of civil servants. It helped, he said, that he wasn't part of the Treasury community of journalists. It is hard to be critical of someone who has been your host.

Stewart Tendler of *The Times* says investigative reporters can be ruthless. They have to get stories in print in spite of attempts people may make to get them not to write anything. If someone is a friend, they still run the story. At least they can say: 'You can give me your side of the story.'

As for specialists, says Tendler, 'one golden rule is that you shouldn't become a repository of secrets. You're paid to write.'

Specialists, too, sometimes become unpopular with contacts. Tendler says what he wrote about the Operation Countryman inquiry into London's police led to him being publicly condemned on the front page of a police newspaper. But 'the guy who condemned me still talks to me'.

Investigative reporters, for their part, cannot ride roughshod over everyone. Bernard Clark of Clark TV says: 'Never abuse the power of the press. The person you are unpleasant to, you will need next week'.

Stewart Tendler commends the idea of a specialist and an investigative reporter working together. This was the policy introduced at the *Financial Times* by Alain Cass when he was news editor. As investigative reporter he used Richard Donkin who had joined the *FT* from *The Yorkshire Post*. The new policy led to investigations into the lossmaking Midland International Trade Services, into the fall of the Bank of Credit and Commerce International and into Robert Maxwell. In the Maxwell inquiry, Bronwen Maddox, a specialist, produced a chart of the intricate web of public and private companies with which Maxwell cloaked his manoeuvres.

THE FREELANCE INVESTIGATOR

Paul Halloran and Mark Hollingsworth have run a successful freelance investigative partnership for years. Investigations by freelances commonly appear in colour magazines. Freelances have also set up successful TV production companies. It is possible to maximize income by using the same material for a TV programme, newspaper articles and a book.

However, doing investigations as a freelance is tough. David Northmore in his book *Lifting the Lid* (Cassell, 1996) shows that investigation does not have to cost much money. But it does cost time, which is money to a freelance. The story of the shoplifting general (see page 4) took as much time as a dozen or more straightforward reporting jobs.

Tony Collins of *Computer Weekly* says he could get commissions when he was freelancing; but 'you have to justify every hour and every day'.

Ideally, investigations require the backing of a well-funded organization. Investigative journalists need to be able to abandon an idea for which, despite great persistence, they can find no hard evidence. To publish an allegation without hard evidence is unjust. It is easier to do the right thing if it doesn't affect your income.

3 Insight and the development of techniques

Murray Sayle, from Australia, got his start in Fleet Street in the 1950s as understudy for *The People*'s crime reporter Duncan Webb. Webb was on the trail of the five Messina brothers, kings of London vice, but they stopped his inquiries by putting his picture on display in every brothel. So he recruited Sayle because, he said, 'I need someone who couldn't be me and couldn't be a copper. As a big woolman straight off the boat, you'd be perfectly convincing, Digger.'

Phillip Knightley tells the story in his book *A Hack's Progress* (Cape, 1997). Sayle, he says, recalled: 'Webb set a standard of honest reporting later to flower in various Insights, Daylights and other forms of group-grope investigative journalism which have since chewed up so many Finnish forests. But no one ever did it better or produced a worse set of bad guys than the Messinas.'

Whatever the exploits of Duncan Webb, reporting in Britain did move up a gear in the 1960s when Clive Irving introduced the Insight feature to *The Sunday Times*, then edited by Denis Hamilton. Professor Alan Doig has written in the *British Journalism Review* (Vol. 3, No. 4, 1992): 'Exposure journalism is as old as newspapers themselves. What was new, during the sixties, was its development by serious newspapers in looking at scandals *and* their contexts.'

THE INSIGHT METHOD

After the Profumo affair burst on the government in 1963, Irving's Insight team researched and published a detailed account of War Minister Profumo's adultery and downfall.

In doing so, they discovered and investigated a new story, not simply, as with Profumo, a news-background narrative. The name Rachman had cropped up alongside that of Mandy Rice-Davies on the fringes of Profumo. Clive Irving's colleague, Ron Hall, had a friend in the property business; and Insight found out how Rachman was winkling out supposedly secure tenants so he could sell their homes at a profit.

Another Insight journalist, Colin Simpson, formerly worked in antiques and knew about rings formed by dealers to acquire goods cheaply and re-auction them among themselves. He joined a ring which *The Sunday Times* exposed by sending reporters to interview its members simultaneously.

A celebrated Insight exposé followed the collapse of the Fire, Auto and Marine (FAM) insurance company, which was run by a Sri Lankan, Emil Savundra. An MP remarked to Harold Evans, then chief assistant to the editor of *The Sunday Times*: 'It's interesting about this Pakistani who's got away with all this money.'

Evans rang a Sri Lankan friend, who told him that Savundra had been in trouble for fraud before. Simpson obtained a list of share certificates which FAM claimed to hold. Harold Evans telephoned the chairmen of the companies listed to see if FAM's claim was genuine. It wasn't.

SHAKING UP THE QUALITY PRESS

The next year, Evans became editor of *The Sunday Times* and found in Insight an instrument ready to hand to shake up British quality newspapers. 'The quality press,' he wrote later in *Good Times, Bad Times* (Weidenfeld and Nicolson, 1983), 'practised invertebrate journalism. It recycled speeches and statements, and delivered stylish opinions on routine public affairs. It mistook solemnity for seriousness, and by seriousness I mean a serious scrutiny of institutions and activities which affect the lives, safety and happiness of millions of people.'

HELPING PEOPLE

While at his previous paper, *The Northern Echo*, Harry Evans had shown a ready sympathy with people in distress, such as the children

Figure 3.1
The Insight way: teamwork is still the secret of the *Sunday Times* Insight investigations which set an example in investigative journalism from the 1960s

damaged by thalidomide, and the victims of cerebral palsy who lived in a home near him.

He was a campaigning and cheekily innovative editor: the Dean and Chapter of Durham must have been startled when he stepped outside the normal boundaries of journalism and proposed to organise a *son et lumière* in their cathedral. But his *Northern Echo* campaigns were largely about making the North-East of England a better place. His national campaign for Timothy Evans, who had been wrongly convicted and sentenced to death, also had a limited aim since he could not bring him back to life.

But when Evans took over *The Sunday Times*, he made it clear that his parish, like that of a previous *Northern Echo* editor, W.T. Stead, was the world.

He first launched an inquiry into Philby, the shadowy friend of the spies Burgess and Maclean who had suddenly followed them to Moscow; and this led him into a story of deaths in Albania and into jousting with the government over secrecy.

After a DC-10 airliner crashed, he encouraged relatives to sue in the United States and this occasioned the first attempt by a British newspaper to claim the right to attend the taking of pre-trial depositions in an American court. (This was necessary because the case was likely to be settled before a full hearing.)

Efforts to help the families of children damaged by the drug thalidomide took him to the European Court of Human Rights, whose decision changed the British law on contempt of court. The issue of a writ no longer stops the British media from discussing a case. It becomes *sub judice* only when it is set down for trial (that is, enters a waiting list for a hearing).

> The lengthy inquiries into the DC-10 disaster and into thalidomide were not journalistic or political manoeuvres. They aimed to help people. It was also important that Roy Thomson, owner of *The Sunday Times*, was prepared to pay the bills.

Harry Evans wrote in *Good Times, Bad Times* (Weidenfeld, 1983): 'We did not seek trouble with the law; it happened because the journalism Roy Thomson made possible ran into conflict with arbitrary power. It was the power that is capable of building an airliner knowing it will fall out of the skies or of cheating small savers or concealing plans to rob communities of their railways or selling a deforming drug and refusing to compensate reasonably for the shattered lives.'

It is also interesting that Evans's *Sunday Times* was in at the beginning of the long-running media investigations into political sleaze. One of his earliest visitors was a man in a bowler hat carrying a judge's order to stop him publishing a report claiming that a British MP was working for the Greek government.

GETTING IT RIGHT RATHER THAN SIMPLY ON THE FRONT PAGE

The Evans *Sunday Times*, wrote Hugo Young, one of his lieutenants, preferred 'evidence over propaganda . . . asking questions rather than supplying a pattern of answers linked to an editorial line'.

Magnus Linklater, who later edited *The Scotsman*, recalled in *British Journalism Review* (Vol. 4, No. 2, 1993) that Insight enjoyed intellectual freedom:

'There was much point-scoring and no little intellectual arrogance but it produced some brilliant and above all unpredictable journalism . . .

'An Insight investigation might start with a theory, perhaps a myth to be challenged or a disaster to be explained, and then begin attempting to lure the facts towards it. If, at some point, the theory had to be abandoned, then another, more probable, was constructed to take its place . . .

'The knowledge that time was on your side, to get the story right and true rather than simply on to the front page, meant that the journalism was sustained by its own dynamic . . . Insight became not just a source of some of the most powerful investigations of its time but a by-word for integrity as well. The process of establishing the facts, of testing sources and, above all, discarding tempting but fallible theories was relentless.'

Insight's success inspired other national newspapers, including *The Daily Telegraph*, to set up investigative teams. Ray Fitzwalter of the *Telegraph and Argus*, Bradford, investigated John Poulson, the architect who corrupted local government. 'Alternative' papers, following the lead of *Private Eye* and *Time Out*, sprang up in Manchester, Liverpool, Leeds, Bristol and South Wales; and investigation of councillor-businessmen making a dishonest penny out of land and housing deals was part of their stock-in-trade.

Abroad, encouraged by the success of Carl Bernstein and Bob Woodward in driving President Nixon out of office in the United States, papers round the world have adopted the investigative approach. Vinod Mehta wrote in the *Financial Times* in 1997 that investigations have huge credibility with the Indian reading public. Indian politicians have faced charges in the press ranging from conspiracy to harbouring gangsters.

But in Britain, life for investigators became tough and lonely. Alan Doig in *British Journalism Review* quotes a *Times* reporter as saying: 'We burned our fingers badly over the bribery case [in 1969 when two *Times* reporters exposed police detectives taking bribes (see page 181)]. We don't want to do more stories like that.'

THE SWITCH TO BROADCASTING

The impetus provided by Insight flagged. *The Sunday Times*, after the Roy Thomson era, ceased to be the main force in investigative reporting. Broadcasting took over, with programmes such as Roger Cook's *Checkpoint* (broadcast on BBC radio from 1972) and television's investigations of miscarried justice in the cases of the Bridgewater Four, Guildford Four and Birmingham Six.

Cook came from Australian radio where his investigative reports so upset his superiors that they switched him back to newsreading. As soon as he could save the money, he left for Britain. Once there he persuaded Andrew Boyle and William Hardcastle to let him join Radio 4's *The World at One* and *The World This Weekend*.

The World at One got letters complaining about a Bristol company called Turret. Cook alleges it had sold people mortgages which were inappropriate or which they couldn't afford. Cook interviewed the complainants on tape and bearded the head of Turret in his den. 'What are your qualifications for running a financial organization other than being a heavyweight wrestler?' he asked.

The wrestler grasped Cook in a bearhug and threw him down the stairs. His tape-recorder, still running, recorded every thump. Nothing quite like it had been broadcast by the BBC before.

Thus began the style of interview for which Roger Cook became well known, though people came to realize in the end that physical attacks which could be broadcast on air did not help their case. Cook reckons he has been attacked about 20 times, most recently by the head of a multinational pharmaceutical company who struck him with a golf club. Cook had caught up with the man on a golf course.

Emboldened by success on *The World at One*, Cook and Andrew Boyle produced a pilot for a new programme called *Checkpoint*. Tony Whitby, controller of Radio 4, he says, was not keen to listen to anything so outspoken. Criticism on the BBC in the early 1970s was decorously expressed. Cook recalls: 'You didn't say "So-and-so is a crook and here's why."'

In the end, Boyle and Cook cornered Whitby in his office and waited for him to listen to the *Checkpoint* pilot. A secretary invited them in. Whitby was sitting at a table with a sheet of paper and an eraser. 'I want you to see what I'm doing,' he said. 'I am putting it in the schedules now.'

Cook's aim was to look into criminality, injustice and bureaucratic bungling. Unfortunately, Boyle dropped out and Cook had to spar with department chiefs who wanted *Checkpoint* to be less investigative, more of a consumer programme looking at complaints against mortgage and insurance companies. Cook was able to show that these complaints were often symptoms of a wider problem, the abuse of limited liability rules by dishonest company directors. These companies would trade and close down, leaving both suppliers and customers in the lurch. Then they would trade again under a slightly different name.

Reforms suggested by *Checkpoint* case histories figured in a report by the insolvency expert Sir Kenneth Cork which got the law changed. Under the new law, dishonest businessmen could be disqualified from being company directors.

At one stage, Cook was taken off the air. At that time the BBC was nervous about *Checkpoint* and its contentiousness. It received a voluminous complaint that Cook had been unfair and officious, and this complaint appeared to offer an excuse to end the programme. When asked to elaborate on the complaint, however, the complainer declined to do so. On second thoughts, he told the BBC, Cook was just doing his job.

Cook's problem with *Checkpoint* was not just with his department chiefs. It was also with radio's lack of resources, which were sufficient only for interviewing witnesses and collecting documents. To show crooks actually being crooked, he needed the resources of television. The BBC agreed to broadcast six *Checkpoints* on TV but it then decided to develop its consumer programme *Watchdog* rather than *Checkpoint*. Roger Cook switched to Central Television which, in the mid-1980s, began making *The Cook Report* for ITV. It was a spectacular success, winning an audience that reached 12 million.

Counting both *Checkpoint* and *The Cook Report*, Cook has done over a thousand investigations, which make him probably Britain's most productive investigative journalist.

INTO THE 1990S

The 1980s were the heyday of Granada TV's *World in Action* and Thames TV's *This Week*. In the 1990s the focus of investigative reporting has shifted. *The Guardian* took up the running with its stories of political sleaze. So, with its *Dispatches* series, did Channel 4, which had never attempted investigations in its early years.

The legal problems facing investigators have become more troublesome (see Chapters 6 and 10). Fighting libel suits is expensive in both time and money, though *The Guardian*'s successes in the law courts have brought it prestige.

Newspaper staffs today are smaller. Competition in the media means that cash is not so freely available as it was at Roy Thomson's *Sunday Times*. The paper's current Insight team produces stories most weeks and carefully gauges the effort which will be required to produce them. 'We have to do things quicker,' says Insight's editor, David Leppard. Investigation at the *News of the World*, too, is geared to weekly publication.

On television, the high salaries paid to presenters of current affairs mean less cash, it is suggested, for investigations. *World in Action*, like *This Week*, has passed into history.

TV producer Terry Kelleher says: 'People used to work months on a story. Now, if you spend time, it's your own.'

The fact is that most news in most newspapers is cheap. It is provided by people, from the Prime Minister downward, for whom someone else is paying. Even a modest investigative story is expensive by comparison. Investigative news, writes David Murphy, author of *The Stalker Affair and the Press*, is a marginal, minority, high-cost activity which is subsidized by other high-audience-appeal output.

Michael Leapman wrote an article in *The Times* in March 1998 headed: 'Is the BBC too mean to work with any more?' Leapman outlined Brian Lapping's difficulties in getting the money for his six-part historical investigation into the Arab–Israeli conflict *The 50 Years War*.

Nevertheless, historical series for which investigators interview everyone involved still get made. *Hostage*, shown in early 1999, told the story of the Western hostages held in Beirut in the 1980s and the intrigues aimed at freeing them. The BBC made an exhaustive series about the Cold War.

The Sunday Times still spends big money on Insight, and high fees are paid elsewhere for the right story. The media have prosperous corners which can afford full-time investigators, including *Computer Weekly* and some provincial papers. Such papers clearly believe there is a public demand for what they do. Tony Collins of *Computer Weekly* says: 'They hired me to get to stories that computer suppliers and users don't want us to print.'

Colour supplements print investigations on subjects outside the normal news agenda: false results in medical research, suicides in a Scottish prison for women. The year 1999 opened with three stories to whet the appetite of investigators: Salt Lake City's gifts to Olympic Games committee members; the European Parliament's stand against corruption and jobs-for-old-pals in the Brussels Eurocracy; and *The Mirror*'s exposure of frauds in candid television shows.

Brian McNair, reader in film and media studies at Stirling University, argues in *The Sociology of Journalism* (Arnold, 1998) that the relationship of journalism to the powerful in advanced capitalist societies is increasingly subversive rather than supportive. This results, he suggests, from both the amount of information available and the growing number of sources seeking to supply it.

McNair argues that the media marketplace offers rewards for exposure and revelation, particularly of the powerful. These rewards are increased circulation and profit. In other words, investigation may cost money but it can pay.

4 Finding the stories

Stories do not grow on trees. They have to be wrenched out of a reluctant and secretive society.
(Paul Foot in *The Journalists' Handbook*, October, 1997)

'All right,' Norton said. 'Now what do you know about Professor MacMahon ******* Ball?' I said I knew that MacMahon Ball was professor of international relations at Melbourne University, one of the few such departments in Australia. 'Well, I reckon he's a ******* Commo,' said Norton. 'And we're going to get him. I want you to do me a dossier on him. Everything you can find out. And then we'll ******* well crucify him in Truth.*'*
(from Phillip Knightley: *A Hack's Progress*, Cape, 1997)

CONTACTS AND TIP-OFFS

The best stories, says investigative reporter Mark Hollingsworth, come from people. After he covered the divorce case of MP's wife Elizabeth Jowett, she gave him hundreds of documents. She had been a director with her former husband, John Browne MP, of a private consultancy firm. It was the start of Hollingsworth's book *MPs for Hire* (Bloomsbury, 1991), which showed that many MPs were prepared to help companies, for a fee.

Stories come from public-spirited people, angry people, or simply friends and acquaintances. There are obvious exceptions such as BBC *Panorama*'s Maxwell exposé, set off by one of Maxwell's own handouts and a report to the Stock Exchange. The *Sunday Times* Insight team once got a lead from an obscure publication in Serbo Croat (see page 36). In the *Daily Mail*, Gaby Hinsliff wrote about MPs' repeated free trips to Cyprus after scanning the House of Commons register of interests.

But even some investigative stories which could have been found by reading documents have in fact needed someone to draw a journalist's attention to them. The problem is the vast quantity of reading material which might yield a story. A Conservative cabinet minister, according to Anthony Bevins, political editor of *The Express*, used to jest that the best way to hide something is to publish it.

So investigative stories, most often, come from people, and these people have their own reasons for supplying them. Paul Henderson, a managing director accused of supplying arms-making machines to Iraq, seems to have used *The Sunday Times* to warn the then government that, if prosecuted, he would speak about the nod and wink he believed he got from a minister (see page 133).

The tip for the story of MI5 vetting BBC staff came from Paul Greengrass, co-author with Peter Wright of *Spycatcher*, the book that disclosed what Wright was up to at MI5 in the 1960s and 1970s. Greengrass told Mark Hollingsworth who investigated the story for three months and then worked on it with David Leigh and Paul Lashmar of *The Observer*.

The germ of Paul Lashmar's film about an American air force general's breathtaking plan to win the Cold War (see page 39) came from the pilot who flew the first mission over the Soviet Union. The Mark Thatcher industry, interested in how Margaret Thatcher's son came by his wealth, started with a dinner party attended by the British ambassador to Oman: Thatcher was seeking work there for Cementation International when his mother visited the country. Mark Hollingsworth says a guest at the dinner told Magnus Linklater, who told David Leigh.

A STORY TO TELL

People with a story may select quite by chance the journalist they will give it to. Peter Watson worked with Ludovic Kennedy on a successful campaign to win a pardon for a man jailed for murder in Scotland. A little later, a Scot who had been in jail in what was then Rhodesia called on Watson. He asked for £20 and said he had a message from a cellmate, Kenneth McIntosh. The message suggested that Watson should visit McIntosh's brother-in-law in Aberdeen. The brother-in-law had documents from McIntosh outlining a scam by which the international sanctions against Rhodesia were being circumvented. The story won Watson a place on the *Sunday Times* Insight team.

Maurice McLeod of *The Voice* got in an even stranger manner the story of a sergeant-major planning to change sex. Using a friend's computer, he joined the America On Line Internet service because, he says, he wanted to download computer games. In joining AOL, he filled in a personal profile form, which meant that AOL included him in a list of journalists.

The sergeant-major, who called himself Joanne, feared he was about to be thrown out of the Army. Military rules stopped him speaking to the press, so he turned to the Internet. He decided to select a journalist from AOL's list and chose McLeod because he liked the film *Highlander* and thought someone called McLeod must be trustworthy.

Obviously it pays journalists to manoeuvre themselves into a position where they will receive such windfalls. Tapes of embarrassing radio transmissions between pit crews and drivers at the final grand prix motor race of the 1997 season were leaked to Mike Calvin, then of *The Times*. He and *The Times* were clearly chosen as being trustworthy and responsible.

Peter Preston, former editor of *The Guardian*, sent David Hencke to work at the House of Commons because he believed the House was a good place for tips about stories to investigate. Hencke says that, when you are known for investigations, people start telling you things that are not publicly known. He also says it is important to keep your name appearing in your newspaper, so people remember you.

Channel 4 received from an alert member of the public the tip that there was something odd in the pathologist's report on Yvonne Fletcher, the policewoman shot outside the Libyan embassy.

Mazher Mahmood of the *News of the World* says, however, that stories more often come from his contacts than out of the blue from the public.

Bernard Clark of Clark TV says you need contacts if you are to get stories in a secretive society like Britain's. He once addressed a roomful of water officials and asked them all for their phone numbers. As a result he got some excellent stories about water. He says:

'Old friends will give you things out of a pure love of gossip. But you have to phone them to keep in touch.

'And they must be able to reach you any time. I use a pager. I've got at least 25 stories because people knew they could always get me.

'The best contacts are people to whom you can give as much as they give you. They know you'd rather die than betray them. You have to do the story in such a way that your contact is the last person anyone would think told you.'

Donal McIntyre, of BBC Documentaries and formerly with *World in Action*, makes a similar point: 'Never forget your contacts: take them out to lunch. Make it clear you haven't just milked them for knowledge. Thank them for their contribution, canvass them for their opinions. They will come back to you over and over again with stories.'

WINDOWS ON HIDDEN PLACES

Mark Killick of *Panorama* says he acquires stories by going through windows of opportunity when they open. Court cases, company flotations and sales open windows on normally hidden areas of life. Losing lawyers says Killick, are a good source. They want to tell you why they should have won.

> A case before the General Medical Council in July 1997 opened a
> window on fraudulent medical research, and the *Sunday Times
> Magazine* went through it, aided by the editors of the medical
> journals. In November 1998, a contested election for the
> presidency opened a window on to the troubles of the International
> Amateur Boxing Association. Andrew Jennings took advantage for
> the *Financial Times*.

In a sense to talk of opening windows is a truism. Just about every
court report opens a window on someone's life. Just about every book
opens a window into the life of its author. Just about every big news
story opens a window on to its background.

The talent is to spot windows unnoticed by other journalists. Footnotes
in the prospectus for RJB Mining's bid for Britain's coal mines opened
for *Panorama* a window on the past of RJB's principal, R.J. Budge, so
that a programme about him could be made.

BETWEEN THE LINES

After Home Secretary Jack Straw spoke about solicitors coaching
people seeking asylum, a journalist at *The Sunday Times* spotted a
solicitor's advertisement (not written in English) in a journal for East
Europeans. As a result, a reporter who speaks Croatian went to the
solicitor's office, pretending to be seeking asylum. Even though the
reporter made it 110 per cent clear he didn't have a genuine case, the
solicitor egged him on. *The Sunday Times* published the story.

Paul Halloran, formerly with *Private Eye* and now freelancing, says he
finds stories in the more obscure corners of the *Financial Times* and
Lloyd's List. In the *FT* he found that Royal Ordnance had a contract to
clear mines in Kuwait. It hired Army sappers. Civilians were paid at
higher rates.

There are ideas to be found on the Internet. That was where a Liberal
Democrat peer, Lord Avebury, found in February 1998 a news report
about a British company providing arms to restore the exiled Sierra
Leone president to power.

Some investigations look at the social evils to which news reports draw attention: cowboy builders, drug dealers, gangland shootings. Two or three newspaper cuttings led investigator Terry Kelleher to inquire about the incidence of male rape. It is always possible that a group of cuttings, individually of no great interest, will draw attention to a hidden pattern in society.

Major controversies in the media can leave the public uncertain which side is in the right. They therefore attract investigative reporting.

A doctor in Cleveland decided a large number of children had been abused, and they were taken away from their parents for some time on the basis of this medical diagnosis.

Investigative journalist Bernard Clark says; 'I just thought it wrong that children were taken into care and there was no judicial hearing.'

One of the parents mentioned that a doctor in Basingstoke thought the diagnosis of abuse on the evidence given was rubbish. Clark rang the doctor. 'I have been waiting for a call,' he said. The doctor put Clark on to one of the Queen's specialists who said the diagnosis was wrong.

Clark proposed making a programme for Channel 4 but was turned down. He felt so strongly that he persuaded Thames TV and Tyne-Tees to take the idea up and gave them his work. The programme won a Royal Television Society award.

A NAME REMEMBERED

People who have been in the news can turn up there again, often in quite a new context. This is one reason why it is important to keep files.

Tom Bower wrote in the *Daily Mail* in 1998 about the previous involvement with Robert Maxwell of three people then in Tony Blair's government: Geoffrey Robinson, Helen Liddell and Lord Donoughue. He followed up with a two-page spread beside the *Mail*'s leader column accusing seven people and two professional firms of failing to blow the whistle on Maxwell.

The *Evening Standard* put together a rapid investigative report after a prominent Greek priest in London was murdered in Athens in 1997. A

Cypriot friend tipped off the *Standard* that, apart from being an inveterate womanizer, the priest had smuggled weapons for the Eoka guerrillas fighting the British in Cyprus in the 1950s and organized the defence of the Cyprus town of Larnaca against the Turkish army in 1974.

DOES IT MAKE SENSE?

Many people were puzzled when Ron Davies suddenly resigned as Welsh Secretary in October 1998. Being the victim of a crime seemed a trivial reason for stepping down. Was there something more behind it?

Around 1980, the profits claimed by Robert Maxwell and Asil Nadir seemed highly unlikely to sceptical journalists (see pages 130 and 138).

A question raised by business deals is whether people really have the money they say they have. Michael Gillard of *The Express* says he looks at what they own. If, like the Duke of Westminster, they own a lot, then, yes, they've probably got the money.

A businessman once announced plans for a £500 million trade centre in Liverpool. Everyone was delighted. But the *Liverpool Free Press* found he operated from his home, a smallish semi-detached in Kingston upon Thames. It seemed unlikely he could raise the money for the centre. He declined to name any of the office blocks he said he had built.

One of the silly season reports on television in August 1998 concerned Swampy Junior. A scarcely literate 11-year-old, with other protesters opposing a plan to chop down trees at Epsom, had won High Court permission to stay on the site. 'It all sounded too good to be true,' wrote Natalie Clarke in the *Daily Mail*.

She discovered that Swampy Junior didn't live, as suggested, in an Epsom tree house but in a council house at a nearby town where the family was unpopular with neighbours and the garden full of junk.

A LINK WITH THE PAST

So many events are reported in the media that the more historic, bringing about real changes, frequently fail to stand out. This makes the unnoticed events and unseen people of history a rich field for investigation.

One of the unseen people – unseen in Britain at any rate – was the American bomber commander of the 1950s, Curtis LeMay, profiled by Paul Lashmar in a *Timewatch* TV programme, *Baiting the Bear*. LeMay believed that, if he had enough bombers, he could defeat the Bear (the Soviet Union) with one strike. And, if he had the power to do this, he could dominate the Soviet Union and dictate the terms for ending the Cold War. He sought to keep his plans secret from the American government.

The CIA's unarmed U2 flights over the USSR, a Cold War shock-horror story, were the means by which President Eisenhower outflanked LeMay. The U2 flights assessed Soviet bomber strength – which both LeMay and Khrushchev sought, for their own reasons, to exaggerate – and they did this without using LeMay's bombers. So LeMay had no great effect on history, though he could have done under a less astute president.

From the point of view of investigative journalism, it is interesting that the real story of the U2s was very different from what it appeared to be at the time.

Contemporary history is full of mysteries which, as time passes, people become willing to explain. What happened 50 years ago can still be worth investigating. David Leigh argued in *The Wilson Plot* (Heinemann, 1988) that distrust of Harold Wilson among MI5 agents originated in his spell as President of the Board of Trade in the late 1940s. Leigh, by research into the public records, was able to show that there was nothing suspect about Wilson's efforts to promote trade with the Soviet Union at that time. Britain badly needed grain: buying it from Russia made sense.

One long-running historical story concerns the Russians and Yugoslavs sent home, many to their deaths, by the British Army in Austria and Italy in May 1945 at the end of the war. Some were not Soviet citizens and had the right not to go. Nikolai Tolstoy argued for years that they were victims of a conspiracy involving Harold Macmillan, at the time British minister in the Mediterranean, and a young brigadier Toby Low (who became Lord Aldington). In 1989, Aldington was awarded £1.5 million in libel damages against Tolstoy. This led in 1997 to two investigative books.

A Looking Glass Tragedy (Duckworth), by a journalist Christopher Booker whose sister had trawled through the 1945 documents, took

Aldington's side. He argued there was no conspiracy. The men had to be handed over because of the Yalta and other agreements, and given the need for smooth relations with the Soviets and Yugoslavs in the chaos of May 1945.

Ian Mitchell in *The Cost of a Reputation: Aldington versus Tolstoy* (Topical Books) argued the opposite case. So investigative journalism has not decided the issue. The historian Norman Stone, reviewing the books in *The Times*, agreed with Booker that there was no conspiracy. There didn't need to be. Too many of the Britons involved simply wanted a quiet life, and no trouble with the Soviets.

ONE THING LEADS TO ANOTHER

After *World in Action* broadcast *Business in Gozo*, one of its programmes about John Poulson, the Pontefract architect who corruptly obtained local authority contracts in the 1960s, a Dundee councillor rang the programme-maker, Ray Fitzwalter. 'You are the only people who can help us,' he said. This led Fitzwalter to uncover a long-running scandal in Dundee (see page 210).

When Claudia Milne made a film for Channel 4 about the conditions of mental patients on the Greek island of Leros, Greeks kept saying: What about your own hospitals in Britain? This led her to make a film about Ashworth special hospital on Merseyside which provides secure accommodation for mentally ill and psychopathic patients (see page 59).

Jo-Ann Goodwin, in pursuing her story (see page 15) about a Brazilian illegal immigrant too infectious to be sent home, discovered welfare agencies willing to offer help to illegal immigrants. She followed up by going to a state-funded London HIV centre with a friend and writing about the visit.

The friend posed as Dan, an HIV-positive illegal immigrant from Ghana. The centre, she reported in the *Daily Mail*, offered Dan help with housing and healthcare despite his illegal status, and gave tips on dodging immigration officers and the police. It also offered a free lawyer to sort out Dan's immigration problems, so he could claim benefit.

5 Pursuing inquiries: doing it right

THE AIM: TO DECIDE THE ISSUE

The object of a journalistic investigation is to establish facts which put the rights and wrongs of an issue beyond doubt. The BBC2 programme *Trust Me (I'm a Doctor)* in February 1999 looked at the tragic failure of some operations on small babies whose bile ducts do not function properly. The programme showed that such operations in specialist hospitals had a 65 per cent success rate. For hospitals carrying out only one such operation in a year, the success rate was only 17 per cent. The message was clear: these operations ought to be done in a specialist hospital, not the local general. The message was immediately accepted by the Royal College of Surgeons.

How do you set about establishing the facts which will enable you to clearly illuminate and resolve the issue you are investigating?

A POSSIBLE SUBJECT: HEROIN IN THE CITY

Here is one possible issue: does the City of London have a heroin problem? The *Financial Times* published in *Weekend FT* on November 21, 1998, an article entitled 'The Smackerati'. The accompanying illustration suggested that 'Guy', 'Toby', 'Rupert', 'Charles' and 'Jamie' were among an increasing number of raddled City gents taking heroin.

The article itself did not quite match the presentation. It was an illuminating and detailed interview by Simon Buckby with one particular young City smackerato pseudonymed Jarrett who spent most of his £85,000 a year on heroin injections. He alluded to other smackerati but they remained in the shadows. As the High Master of Manchester Grammar, Jarrett's old school, pointed out the following week, the *Weekend FT* article did not prove anything about drug culture at the school or in the City.

So the unmasking of Guy, Toby, Rupert, Charles and Jamie was left for another journalist or another day. Here clearly is a window opening on an explorable world. How might you explore it?

First, what is on record? There may be references to City smackheads in the cuttings; few stories are so new that no one has written about them before. There are certainly court cases: the pseudonymous Jarrett said he had been in court a couple of times. The number of courts to check on cannot be very great.

Court cases can yield traceable names and one of the names might talk to you and suggest others. This might lead you to dealers, like the squatters who supplied Jarrett. The court cases might also draw attention to knowledgeable police officers and others. A further lead in Jarrett's story is the clinic in Harrogate he said he attended.

Alternatively, you might get into the subject through conversations in City pubs. You could try canvassing City firms: have they ever had a problem with heroin-addicted staff? Do they have a policy on heroin? Most are likely to say nothing, but perseverance might just produce something useful: investigative journalism partly depends on luck.

Again, there are the doctors and hospitals covering the City. What is their experience? Does the drug control centre at King's College London's School of Life Sciences, or the National Addiction Centre at the Institute of Psychiatry, have useful material and useful people to talk to? Several agencies concerned with drugs are quite close to the City: the Association for Prevention of Addiction, the Standing Conference on Drug Abuse, Turning Point.

You will want to establish not just that there *are* heroin users in the City but how important this is: are there ten, a hundred, a thousand? How does it affect them? Is there or isn't there a case for saying: Stop this evil practice now?

DOING IT RIGHT

Most published work is judged on what is published. But investigative work may also be judged on how the work was done.

There are at least two reasons for this. First, if an investigation is not properly conducted, its conclusions may not be valid. This is as true for an investigation conducted by journalists as for an investigation conducted by the police.

Television has a particular problem. Programme-makers may fail to obtain all the pictures necessary to tell their story with the polish and realism that television requires. If they fill the gaps with acted scenes and this is discovered, their results could be questioned.

To be fully satisfactory, a journalistic investigation must unmistakably identify its villains and their involvement in wrongdoing. An ill-identified villain may not exist or, on TV, could be an actor.

Nick Davies in his book *Dark Heart* (Chatto & Windus, 1997) relates that, in 1969, the *News of the World* published an exposé of police malpractice in the Midlands. In the subsequent court case, the *News of the World*'s tape-recordings in which police officers appeared to incriminate themselves were ruled inadmissible as evidence. The defence submitted there was no proof that the voices on the tapes were those of the police officers accused.

Roger Cook says that, even before the broadcasting authorities drew up their codes of practice for investigative programmes, he and a colleague, David Perrin, drew one up for their radio programme *Checkpoint*. Its TV successor, *The Cook Report*, continues to abide by this code.

Cook and Perrin decided that, if they wanted to interview people about questionable conduct, they would give seven working days' notice, unless the people they were approaching were hardened criminals or liable to do a runner. They would also give notice of what areas they wanted to talk about, including file references to correspondence their quarry might have had with members of the public. They would not, however, submit a list of questions in advance, since that could rule out supplementary questions which would bring out the answers they were seeking. If given too much information, their targets might use it to pressurize witnesses or cover their tracks.

Other provisions in the Cook and Perrin code included always keeping an uncut tape of interviews. If someone refused to be interviewed, would not give notice of when they would nevertheless call on their quarry. This call would be at a business address, unless the home address was relevant, and they would make the call with as little fuss as possible. If they were offered salacious information about someone, they would not use it.

Roger Cook comments: 'If people made accusations against us, we wanted to be able to say: "This is how we behave."'

BRINGING IN THE LAWYERS

The second reason why it matters how you conduct an investigation is a legal one. Your investigation could lead to a lawsuit against your paper for libel or a complaint on invasion of privacy or other grounds to the Press Complaints Commission, the Independent Television Commission or the Broadcasting Standards Commission. If so, you want clear evidence to support what you have published. You also want to avoid any suggestion that you acted maliciously or took too little account of the codes of conduct.

An incautious statement even in a quite unconnected article could be construed as damaging evidence that you were prejudiced and therefore malicious. At least one investigative journalist was wary of what he was being quoted as saying in this book, for this reason.

Lawyers like to be consulted early in an investigation (though this may be affordable only for bigger media organizations). Jan Tomalin, head of legal services at Channel 4, says she advises not just on the content of programmes but on the making of them.

How a letter is phrased can be important. If journalists misrepresent their purpose, that can tell against them in a lawsuit.

Magazines and provincial newspapers which cannot afford to bring in lawyers at every stage of an inquiry must rely on pre-publication checks. A lawyer looks sentence by sentence at the text of an article and the evidence sustaining it. These checks may be essential to meet the terms of a libel-damages insurance policy. At £250 an hour, they can cost four-figure sums. There is an obvious temptation to avoid this expense by simply publishing, rather than investigating, complaints and following them with lengthy replies from whoever the complaints were made against.

NOTEBOOKS AND TAPE-RECORDINGS

Alastair Brett, a lawyer at Times Newspapers, says: 'Tape everything you can, every word you utter or is uttered to you.' When a solicitor complained he was 'grossly misled' by a *Sunday Times* reporter, *The Sunday Times* had their whole conversation on tape and was able to prove otherwise.

It is also important to date entries in a notebook. Get people to sign statements: this gives them more weight. If there is a libel action and your witnesses have died or gone abroad, their statements can be used in evidence.

Chris White of *The Parliament Magazine* in Brussels cautions against believing that only tape-recorded and documentary evidence are reliable: 'Once you have to bolster everything with tape-recording and documents, you can't move. You've got to be able to rely on traditional notes. There have to be points where you say your note is correct and you are believed.' (When the former England football coach, Glenn Hoddle, made an unfortunate remark about disabled people in 1999, the editor of *The Times*, Peter Stothard, backed his reporter's accuracy on the strength of his note.)

'Ideally,' adds White, 'you have a witness to everything.'

Notes versus tape-recording was a key issue in the controversy which followed *The Observer*'s cash-for-access exposé in 1998. On *The Observer*'s behalf, a journalist called Gregory Palast claiming to represent an American company went to see lobbyists in and around Westminster. Several boasted of the access they could provide to government information and to ministers, if the company became their client.

For the government, however, the really damaging paragraph was a chance quote attributed to Roger Liddle, an ex-lobbyist who had become Tony Blair's adviser on European affairs. Palast met Liddle at a party and quoted him as offering his help. Liddle said later, *The*

Observer reported: 'I did say "Give me a call" but I can't remember any more than that . . . It is complete and utter nonsense to suggest I was going around offering my services.'

Palast and Antony Barnett based *The Observer*'s front page lead story on what they described as 'taped telephone conversations and face-to-face meetings'.

The Observer was challenged to produce a tape-recording of Liddle's indiscretion. It did not have one. What it had was a note, written by Greg Palast on the back of Liddle's business card. Palast had gone to the party not knowing he was going to meet Liddle or even who Liddle was. Antony Barnett says that Palast wrote his note on the card after Liddle spoke to him.

Barnett had anticipated a possible problem. Before Palast went to see the lobbyists, Barnett suggested that he use a hidden tape-recorder. Palast was unwilling, not being comfortable in using this sort of gadgetry. He said he would take a friend, Mark Swedlund, to vouch for what was said. Swedlund was present at the meeting with Liddle.

Barnett points out that tape-recording is not always possible. It is easy to hide cameras and tape-recorders in the hotel rooms which investigative journalists often use for their scams. But there are impromptu occasions, a party for instance, where traditional note-taking has to be relied on.

One advantage of having tape-recorded evidence, says Barnett, is that it can be broadcast if controversy breaks out.

A court has reaffirmed the credibility of note-taking. When transport tycoon Richard Branson, who made a bid to run the National Lottery, received what he took to be an offer of a bribe, he dashed to the loo and made a note of what was said. In the subsequent lawsuit, the court accepted his note and found in his favour.

DISCOVERY OF DOCUMENTS

A key part of a lawsuit is the process of discovery. Each side can ask the other to disclose relevant documents: letters, notebooks, recordings, accounts. (This can be a strong disincentive to bringing a libel action, for anyone who has something to hide.)

As you take notes or make a recording, bear in mind that the other side may well see or hear it. So do not include the name of any contact you do not wish to disclose. Do not keep, longer than you have to, anything which will give away the contact's identity.

> If you are in the habit of adorning your notes with comments about the people you are speaking to, give up the habit. In court, a rude comment can be construed as showing your evidence-gathering was malicious, not even-handed. In a libel case, malice invalidates a defence of fair comment or a claim to privilege.

Incautious remarks are sometimes heard on tape. When undercover journalists in the US made a film for ABC TV about poor food-handling in the shops of a North Carolina grocery chain, they used swear words when staff followed correct procedure. This apparent lack of even-handedness may have contributed to ABC's $5.5 million bill for damages. (Interestingly the chain, Food Lion, did not sue for libel but for fraud. It accused the journalists of improperly obtaining jobs.)

Geoffrey Robertson, the QC defending *The Guardian* in a libel case brought by Neil Hamilton MP and the lobbyist Ian Greer (see page 213), expected his opponents to exploit the cynical humour in *Guardian* memoranda if the case had gone to court.

THE PROTECTION OF PRIVILEGE

Another reason for bearing libel in mind from the start of an inquiry is an important change in English law. In a case between Albert Reynolds, former Irish prime minister, and Times Newspapers in the summer of 1998, the Court of Appeal extended the scope of the defence of qualified privilege.

Under the Defamation Act, this defence covers a fair, accurate and unmalicious report of a public meeting or a statement by a government officer, providing a chance is given to explain or contradict what has been said. The Court of Appeal has extended this protection to defamatory statements on other matters of public interest provided:

1 The statement does not come from a political opponent, business rival or disgruntled ex-employee (or other axe grinder).
2 The person defamed has had the chance to rebut the statement.
3 The accuracy of the statement has, as far as possible, been checked.

This new defence puts a premium on evidence which cannot be dismissed as axe grinding. It also means that you should put allegations to whoever you are making them against. This has in the past been compulsory for television but optional for newspapers (see page 81).

INJUNCTIONS

What journalists fear is that, if they seek a response to allegations, the people concerned will seek to derail the investigation by threatening legal action or asking for an injunction to stop publication. Newspaper lawyer Alastair Brett says it is rare for people to seek injunctions unless they are genuinely innocent or there has been a serious mix-up over what the paper has been told. If there has been such a mix-up and the source is wrong, then it is as well for the story to be stopped.

People do, however, seek injunctions if they believe the allegations are based on confidential information which has been wrongly leaked to a newspaper (see page 101).

In 1999, publication of Jo-Ann Goodwin's second article on the Russell murder case (see page 93) was delayed after an intervention by lawyers for a prisoner. They did not want him to be named.

IN THE PUBLIC INTEREST

The principle underlying the Court of Appeal judgement on qualified privilege is that the public have a right to know about matters of genuine public interest.

The Court of Appeal said:

'The common convenience and welfare of a modern plural democracy such as ours are best served by an ample flow of information to the public concerning . . . matters of public interest to the community . . .

'In differing ways and to somewhat differing extents, the law has recognized this imperative, in the United States, Australia, New Zealand, as also in the jurisprudence of the European Court of Human Rights. It would be strange if the law in this country – the land of Milton, Paine and Mill – were to deny this recognition.'

The various press and broadcasting codes of practice similarly allow the public interest to override some of their provisions. Investigative journalists thus have some latitude provided they are acting in the public interest.

The Code of Practice of the Press Complaints Commission gives three examples of inquiries in the public interest:

1 **Detecting or exposing crime or a serious misdemeanour.**
2 **Protecting public health and safety.**
3 **Preventing the public from being misled by some statement or action of an individual or organization.**

The Broadcasting Standards Commission code adds a fourth:

4 **Disclosing significant incompetence in public office.**

6 Pursuing inquiries: getting it right

IS THERE A STORY THERE?

Perhaps you have an account of something that seems wrong but you don't know if the story you have been given is right. The real story may be different from what you were led to believe. Or the lead you have picked up, even if accurate, is not sufficient in itself. You need to know if other people have had similar experiences. Some things are bad enough in themselves to make a major story. Others become a major story only if they affect a lot of people.

John Ware of *Panorama* says the hard part of an investigation is getting it launched. You need a lot of energy to get up in the morning and go, not knowing if you are going anywhere:

'Half the battle is looking at information and saying: What does this all mean? What are the key questions? The trick is knowing the right questions to ask. Once you're confident you know the right questions, you can try one way to get an answer and, if that's blocked, try another.'

Channel 4's *Dispatches* series awards contracts in two stages. First, it awards a small sum to establish that there is a story that will stand up, a series of questions worth asking. Then it awards a larger sum for answering the questions and making the film. The essential aim is to establish a starting point and see a direction in which a logical and successful thread of inquiry can lead (see the Philby story, page 114).

Some stories are clear enough from the start. Others do not become clear for a long time. Others again are misconstrued. Bruce Page believes this happened with *The Sunday Times* inquiry (in which he took part) into thalidomide, the sedative given to pregnant mothers which caused children to be born with missing limbs.

When the effects of thalidomide became evident in 1962, its British makers, Distillers, argued that they were not to blame because no one then tested drugs on pregnant animals and no deformities would have appeared in rats and mice anyway. This was generally accepted at the time.

Dr Monty Phillips, the expert engaged by the parents in their fight for compensation, argued in reply that thalidomide belonged to an inherently dangerous class of drugs. So Distillers should have known it was dangerous. *The Sunday Times* took up his argument.

Neither Distillers nor Phillips was right. Drugs related to thalidomide were not necessarily dangerous. But, before thalidomide, leading drugs companies were already testing their products for effects on pregnant animals. Distillers was not a leading drugs company – it was a drinks firm seeking to enter the market for tranquillizers – and did not do the tests a leading company would have done.

As for rats and mice, they did show thalidomide's resorptive effect on foetuses but in a different way to humans. The rats and mice had smaller litters than usual.

Bruce Page soon discovered this when he became fully involved in the inquiry. So thalidomide did not require the lengthy and expensive investigation it had received. It was quite a simple matter once the question 'Was what Distillers said right?' was asked.

Another *Sunday Times* investigation concerned a DC-10 airliner which crashed near Paris with the loss of 346 lives after losing a cargo door. Harold Evans, in *Good Times, Bad Times*, asks why, after a previous warning, the door fastening had not been modified. Bruce Page points out that there was a wider question: Why did the loss of a cargo door bring down a DC-10?

The DC-10 was a wide-bodied aircraft able to carry several hundred people. Its competitors, the Boeing 747 and the Lockheed Tristar, were completely fresh designs. The DC-10 was not. Unlike the others, it had only two separate systems for controlling the aircraft. They were both knocked out when the cabin floor collapsed after the loss of the door. More DC-10s than Tristars, their direct competitors, were sold. The less safe DC-10 enjoyed a commercial advantage because it was designed afresh.

Whatever the story about thalidomide and the DC-10, there was no doubt a story existed. What if your story, however construed, simply doesn't run? In 1998, the news channel CNN retracted a report that American troops had used nerve gas during the Vietnam War. Also in the United States, the *Cincinnati Enquirer* apologized for an attack on the locally based fruit company, Chiquita Brands International.

In December 1998, in Britain the Independent Television Commission fined Central Independent Television £2 million for breaches of the ITC's programme code in a documentary called *The Connection*. The documentary sought to demonstrate a new route for running heroin into Britain. The ITC found no evidence of the route. It also found that so-called drug-runners were acting the parts, and that the 'heroin' shown was sweets. The ITC code says that a respect for truth is essential to all factually based programmes.

It is possible to report or film a story which isn't actually there, especially if it isn't actually there in some distant place. But the only honest thing to do with a story which doesn't stand up is to abandon it. If you've gone to the expense of travelling to Australia, say, you had better find a better story quickly.

> Programme-maker Bernard Clark warns against assuming too readily that someone is crooked and dangerous and then realigning the facts to support the case. 'You have to step back and say: "Is what I'm doing here fair?" It would be a better story doing it like this; but it isn't right.'

STANDING UP A STORY

Christopher Hird explains Fulcrum Productions' method of pursuing a story in this way:

1 Get everything we can anywhere in the public domain (libraries, Companies House and so on).
2 Establish a chronology of events. We often see connections not seen before.
3 Relentlessly look up everybody who might know something.

Most of the stories outlined in this book have been cracked by this approach, even if it has taken days of reading, door-knocking or telephone calls.

When making a television programme about the Hanson group, Christopher Hird listed 40 people who, at one time or another, had been directors of three subsidiaries. The programme team rang them all. Some had nothing to tell. Some wouldn't say anything. One in the North-West said: 'How interesting. I'll meet you at a service area on the M6.' He produced an important document.

Two TV programmes made by Fulcrum on share dealing by insiders led to Department of Trade inquiries.

One arose from the chance remark of a company secretary. He mentioned that, when a particular businessman bought shares in the company, other people bought at the same time. The businessman, it turned out, used to buy shares for himself, then for his company. Then he made a takeover bid, and the price of the shares he had bought earlier went up.

Fulcrum put together from *Financial Times* cuttings a list of companies in which the businessman's company held blocks of shares. Then they looked at the companies' share registers for the relevant periods.

Many shares were registered in the name of nominees. Fulcrum had a database of nominees. In addition, Hird asked to see company registers showing who the nominees represented. When the real buyers of shares were thus disclosed, he discovered some shares had been bought by the businessman personally.

The companies in which the shares were bought knew the exact time of purchase. The secretary at a Sheffield company produced his file. 'I couldn't believe my luck,' says Hird. Calls at two more companies produced similar results.

He was able to draw up a chronology of events. It showed that the businessman had profited personally from buying shares in companies which became his takeover targets.

FACTS FROM THE PUBLIC DOMAIN

In pursuing a story, get hold of everything you can in the public domain, says Christopher Hird. Where then do you look?

i)   Your office. Reference books, files, cuttings, phonebooks. It is important to keep good files. 'I file every letter that comes in,' says Tony Collins of *Computer Weekly*, 'every piece of paper and document.'

Other newspaper office libraries will vary in their willingness to help your inquiries. In writing this book, I found three newspapers' libraries helpful. One (which I used to work for) brushed me off. One wanted £5 per story, but pointed out I could access the material electronically at a public library. It is possible to consult the Press Association's cuttings library for a fee of £35 an hour (£45 if the PA Library does the research for you).

ii)   **The Internet.** More and more documents are posted on it.

iii) **Public libraries.** These may well have access to more material than you thought, including access to electronic databases other than the Internet and to back copies of national newspapers on CD-ROM:

a) Directories and registers. All professional people have to be registered, so they are listed in a register or directory. The best known directories will be in the public library. For the more obscure, you may have to ring the professional association. Well-known people could be in more than one directory, and each entry could tell you something more about them.

b) Yearbooks, for example Stock Exchange, Municipal (includes names and addresses of councillors), Health Services, Social Services.

c) Register of electors. Useful for finding people. Can be accessed electronically.

d) Books on the subject you're looking into. If they're not on the shelves, the library can probably get them for you.

e) Magazines. If the library doesn't have the one you need, it could help you find it. (The Science Reference Library in London files scientific journals: physical sciences 0207-412-7496; life, earth and medical sciences 0207-412-7288.)

f) Information on local societies.

g) Annual reports of companies.

h) Acts of Parliament and other government publications.

iv) **Local council offices.** Councils have to make a wide range of information available under the Local Government (Access to Information) Act and other Acts. It includes planning applications, registers of childminders, old people's homes, pollution data, fire precautions, food premises and sportsground-safety notices (see Appendix C).

v) **University libraries.**

vi) **Companies House** (see page 122).

vii) **Consumer protection organizations** (see page 160).

viii) **Regional offices of government ministries and agencies.** Health and Safety Executive, Environment Agency (covers rivers, pollution, waste).

ix) **Government ministries.** The government publishes vast numbers of reports and handouts. It also produces further documents which are less readily available.

David Hencke of *The Guardian* got interested in the work of the National Audit Office, which checks through government spending. He covered its report on British Aerospace's purchase of the nationalized Austin-Rover motor company (since sold on to BMW). The government was so anxious to have a British buyer that it made valuable concessions to BAe. The National Audit Office's report on these referred to an additional unpublished memorandum and, because of Hencke's coverage, he got a copy. This revealed £44 million worth of sweeteners given to BAe and not disclosed to the European Commission, which keeps an eye on subsidies that may give an unfair competitive advantage.

The present government has published a Freedom of Information Bill to open documents to the public. The Bill, however, has been strongly criticized because it gives government officers wide powers to keep documents secret.

John Major's government introduced in 1994 a code of practice with five undertakings:

1 To give facts and analysis with major policy decisions.
2 To open up internal guidelines about departments' dealings with the public.
3 To give reasons with administrative decisions.
4 To provide information about public services: costs, targets, performance, complaints, redress.
5 To answer requests for information.

As with local authorities, information is commonly refused because it is commercially sensitive. The Ombudsman can be brought in if information seems unreasonably refused. He backed *The Economist*'s request for the prices at which State assets were being sold.

For a fuller discussion of sources of information, see *Lifting the Lid: A Guide to Investigative Research* by David Northmore (Cassell, 1996).

7 Finding the people

TALK TO EVERYONE RELEVANT

A trawl through publicly available material will not necessarily produce anything for your investigation.

Mark Hollingsworth wrote in *British Journalism Review* (Vol. 6, No. 3, 1995) about his search for the sources of Mark Thatcher's wealth:

'From 1984 onwards, he was not a director or shareholder of any companies, apart from Emergency Networks Inc. He did not have an office except for two small rooms and a nameplate in Dallas. His firm, Grantham and Co., was not registered as a company but as a partnership. Business deals were conducted through intermediaries, bank accounts were offshore and shareholdings were held by nominees. Virtually no part of his commercial affairs was accountable to the public or regulatory authorities. Even a comprehensive Freedom of Information Act application in the United States failed to produce any relevant documents . . .

'What do you do when there are few documents or very little on the public record because of the subject's excessive secrecy? There remains one solution: personal connections. Investigative journalism is often perceived as highly specialized with the practitioners possessing magical and mysterious powers. But, in essence, the tools of the trade are relatively basic: the discovery and utilization of credible contacts.

'And even when there is substantial documentation, the key to success is ensuring the material is authentic and knowing how to acquire more. That can be done only through reliable sources.'

So an investigative reporter needs help from people. Once you have found some, ask them to recommend others. If time allows, speak to everyone who may have something relevant to say. You never know where something entirely fresh may turn up.

It can still be worth going to see someone, even if you think you've already got the story. Jo-Ann Goodwin, who writes for the *Daily Mail*, says that things which don't seem to be germane often turn out to be so.

After she had got her story about an infectious illegal immigrant (see page 15), she kept trying to see a woman he had stayed with before he was ill. 'I must have gone four, five, six times. She was never in. Finally I caught her. She told me how handsome he used to be, how many girlfriends he had. And she produced pictures of him.'

If you talk to everyone relevant that you can, this is also an insurance against error. In Phillip Knightley's autobiography *A Hack's Progress* (Cape, 1997), he tells how an earlier book involved him in a libel action. The book published in the late 1980s re-examined the case against Stephen Ward, an osteopath who introduced callgirl Christine Keeler to Secretary for War John Profumo, thus precipitating a scandal which rocked Harold Macmillan's government in 1963. Ward killed himself while on trial on charges of procuring and living on immoral earnings.

A police team of four were involved in his case. One had died. Knightley and his co-author Caroline Kennedy interviewed two more. The fourth, it seemed, had gone to Australia. They reasoned he had probably joined the police there and they checked every Australian force except the Commonwealth Police which he had in fact joined. They published the book without interviewing him, and he sued for libel.

FIND SOME EXPERTS

Among the people you seek to interview in your investigation should be some who are genuine experts in the subject. A university might yield these. They can lend authority to what you say and help you ask telling questions. The case for Sheila Bowler, cleared – after a retrial at the Old Bailey – of the murder of her 89-year-old aunt, was pressed by

Channel 4's *Trial and Error*; but it was supported by Professor Archie Young, an expert on the behaviour of old people. The key question was how the frail old woman came to be found in a river 500 yards from where her niece, seeking help with a flat tyre, had left her in their car. Young argued that, despite her frailty, she could have walked the distance.

When you have a list of the people you want to speak to, put it by the phone and ring them every day until you catch them. They won't all be immediately available. How best to speak to them is discussed in the next chapter.

What if there's a barrier between you and the people you want to find? You can't get to see them or you don't know who they are. One approach is to put a small story in the paper which will attract them. Or you can advertise. 'Did you take purple hearts in the 1950s?' inquired a Channel 4 advertisement on Euston Station. Once you have a few people, you can ask them to suggest others.

To make a film for Channel 4's *Cutting Edge* in 1991 about Ashworth special hospital, Merseyside, Claudia Milne approached lawyers acting for mentally sick people at mental health tribunals. Lawyers got the filmmakers in to see patients in Ashworth, from whom they learned about ex-patients.

Ashworth is one of Britain's special hospitals, which provide secure accommodation for people with psychiatric and psychopathic disorders. Some patients are sent there by the courts. Others are referred from other hospitals. Claudia Milne found that fewer than half the patients had criminal records. Her team found evidence of brutality and abuse of patients, including sexual abuse of women.

People making allegations on television are sometimes shown in silhouette or with jumbled faces or with backs to camera, so that they cannot be recognized. But, if their faces cannot be seen, it is hard for viewers to assess their credibility. Claudia Milne decided that people she had spoken to were making such serious charges they couldn't be shown in silhouette. It took her a long time to find enough who were prepared to let their faces be seen on camera.

The film led to an inquiry by Sir Louis Blom-Cooper who uncovered abuse of patients and recommended a change of culture to give therapy and treatment more of a chance. Blom-Cooper was principally concerned with patients who were mentally ill. Unfortunately, some patients with personality disorders took advantage of changes he inspired. This led to a disturbing report by Judge Peter Fallon in January 1999, and a tightening of security for these patients.

ACCESS BY INTERNET

Terry Kelleher faced a big barrier when he wanted to make a film about a series of RAF air crashes in 1996: he couldn't get on to airfields to talk to people.

David Lloyd of Channel 4 said to him: 'We don't simply want a programme about the cause being cutbacks and poor morale. It must demonstrate that certain crashes should have been avoided.'

The journalist who suggested the idea to Kelleher had been in the RAF. This was a help. But the Ministry of Defence refused to co-operate. It refused access to take pictures. It also refused interviews with senior officers. So how could a programme be researched, let alone made?

In point of fact, the ministry tried too hard to stop the programme. It sent notices twice to every air base saying that Channel 4 was investigating despite being refused co-operation. 'If contacted,' it said, 'report to your commanding officer.' Several people, alerted to the project, rang Channel 4 instead.

Terry Kelleher turned also to the Internet. He searched the net for technical information about a piece of equipment and the search led to the manufacturer.

He joined an Internet news group which, he says, 'is like going into a room and finding 10,000 people with experience. You ask: Have you experience with this kind of aircraft? You get five replies. Other people see them and then it cascades. You come up with contacts right round the world. Some anorak in Alaska or Mexico or Reading has the answer you seek and is delighted to help because it's his passion.'

Kelleher interviewed a Tornado pilot by e-mail. In the programme, the pilot's words were spoken by an actor.

WHISTLEBLOWERS AND AXE-GRINDERS

There is some information so sensitive you wouldn't want to know who it came from, in case you betrayed the source. Paul Halloran when he worked for *Private Eye* received copies of documents every few weeks from the Holiday Inn in St John's Wood, London. He never discovered who his informant was but it was clearly someone who disliked the arms dealers who then met at the hotel.

'Whistleblowers are an underrated species,' says Halloran. 'They are lonely and they risk everything. People who come with stories are really public-spirited. Perhaps they have been badly treated or there's a chance to get their own back.'

It is vital to protect sources of this kind if they don't want to come out into the open.

But, generally, investigative reporters need to be able to speak to whoever has sent information. They need contact with a real person, not just with an e-mail address, if they are to judge whether the information is true.

> If at all possible, informants need to be quotable. The accuracy of unattributed information can readily be challenged. Don't quote people if you don't know who they are.

The end result of any reporting will be no better than the information on which it is based. So can you trust your informants? Have they documents to back their story? *The Sunday Times* in 1995 suggested inaccurately that the former Labour leader Michael Foot had been a KGB contact. Foot sued. *The Sunday Times* withdrew, apologized and paid substantial damages.

Informants may be self-confessed crooks like the petty criminals who talked to Garry Lloyd and Julian Mounter about corrupt policemen (see page 181).

James Hodges, who took three suitcases of Sotheby's documents to Peter Watson, investigative journalist for Channel 4 (see page 67), was cleared of most charges he faced in court but convicted of two thefts and a forgery. So was he honest in what he said?

In the book *Sotheby's: Inside Story*, Watson reports a review by Antony Thorncroft of Channel 4's first Sotheby's programme, *Sale of the Centuries*. Thorncroft quoted a Sotheby's executive as complaining that 'a convicted felon' was being 'lionized'.

Informants may have an undisclosed purpose which they want you to serve. They may be axe-grinders. They might quite simply be mistaken.

They may be people you find unappealing. Perhaps they support some cause you oppose, or belong to a group you dislike. You would be only too glad to ignore what they say.

One approach is to ask: Did anyone else experience what you experienced? A second interview can corroborate the first, or show up uncertainties that need sorting out.

Garry Lloyd and Julian Mounter decided to believe their chief informant, Michael Perry, because he and his friends were prepared to sign statements. Perry also didn't seem like a fraud. He described being threatened with a charge of possessing gelignite. He said he went to *The Times* out of fear.

Concerning Hodges, Peter Watson explains that Hodges' Sotheby's documents were crucial:

'Writers and journalists are not unused to disgruntled or disaffected employees or ex-employees making allegations against their former companies. As often as not, they are a waste of time. About six months earlier, I had been approached by an ex-director of a large, Central London department store. He had a story to tell, he said, but he had no evidence to prove it . . . Hodges, however, claimed to have a small mountain of documents which supported his allegations' (taken from the book *Sotheby's: Inside Story* by Peter Watson, published by Bloomsbury Publishing plc in 1997).

Tony Collins of *Computer Weekly* says: 'A lot of people aren't on the level. They can't prove what they are saying. When someone has something solid, you ask for documents. You can't do anything unless they prove they will move heaven and earth to get information.'

He adds: 'Every story has a vested interest in it. I always listen to people who have an axe to grind so long as what they say provides a nugget of information when put into context. It doesn't matter how intemperately it's said so long as it can be proven.' He finds trade unions helpful concerning wastage of public money.

GO AND HAVE A LOOK

Searching the libraries and ringing everyone that anyone could think of were not sufficient to launch the *Sunday Times* inquiry into the Soviet agent, Kim Philby (see page 114). What did the trick was a visit to Cambridge where Philby went to university. The convention in cop shows on television is right: going and looking and talking to people pays off. A visit to a company's registered office can bring to light other companies it is connected with. A Liverpool journalist went to Kingston upon Thames and found that the developer who was supposed to be building a £500 million centre operated from a small semi-detached house. The formidable Irish investigator, Veronica Guerin, would travel miles to see someone rather than use the telephone.

Going to see may require imagination. How, for example, do you investigate pirates' attacks on shipping in the South-East Asian seas? Andrew Eames solved that problem by travelling with a travel firm. His article in *The Times* included a paragraph about the firm's holiday offer.

Tony Fernandes described in an article in *The Sunday Times* (July 1998) the search for his missing cousin Edgar.

No one knew where Edgar had gone on the holiday in Istanbul from which he didn't return. His relatives looked at what written material of his they could find: a 1994 guidebook and a bill listing two phone calls to Istanbul. The numbers matched the first two budget hotels in the guide. The family rang the numbers. One was now a shop. The person who replied at the other, still a hotel, hadn't heard of Edgar. The police said there wasn't a story. To be missing, you had to be missing for a month.

Searching and talking in London had got nowhere. So Edgar's brother and brother-in-law set off for Istanbul. They met a friend of the missing man and went to the hotel which had disclaimed knowledge of him. In a room they saw Edgar's bag and jacket. They now knew something had happened.

A Romanian woman remembered Edgar arriving on April 8 and meeting an Egyptian. According to the hotel register, the Egyptian stayed in the room till April 14.

The police still didn't think there was a story. But they had checked Edgar's Barclaycard spending. It was normal, they said. Then Edgar's relatives discovered that an Egyptian was using the card in Malta. Tony Fernandes joined the search in Istanbul, visiting a mortuary, prisons, hospitals, mental institutions. Then Interpol said that, around April 19, Edgar's passport had been used in Bulgaria and Greece. Fernandes and the other searchers were shown photographs of bodies at Istanbul's murder unit. They recognised Edgar's cross and watch.

They also found that Istanbul is a centre for trade in foreign passports: 174 Britons had disappeared in Turkey in ten years.

WHAT'S THE HISTORY?

Everyone and every event has a history. This history offers another route of inquiry. For the *World in Action* programme *Jonathan of Arabia*, David Leigh traced former Tory politician Jonathan Aitken's history from well before the mysterious weekend he spent in Paris when he was Minister for Defence Procurement.

Mark Killick's *Panorama* programme in November 1998 about Bernie Ecclestone's plan for a $2 billion bond issue faced the obvious problem that bond issues are of little interest to viewers. Mark made it interesting by tracing Ecclestone back to his days as a racing driver.

He showed how Ecclestone became the key figure in Formula One racing, with a 23 per cent share of its television revenue, and how the outcome of the bond issue related to a forthcoming ruling from the European Union about motor racing and its television rights.

8 Dealing with documents

Opponents of your investigation can argue with people you have spoken to. They can try to discourage them from appearing in a TV programme. If you're being sued for libel, your witnesses may no longer be around when the case is heard. If they *are* around, threats or an attractive offer may stop them turning up in court to give evidence. But it's more difficult to argue against or keep out of court an authentic, up-to-date document. Original documents are the hardest form of evidence, says investigative journalist and broadcaster Ray Fitzwalter. Photocopies are next best. (It may be necessary to bring evidence that they are indeed photocopies of the originals.)

Author Mark Hollingsworth says: 'People's memories aren't reliable, whereas if what they say is documented it's more reliable. It's also more difficult to get hold of. You have to get documents through people.'

John Ware says that, when he investigated for *Panorama* the case of Brian Nelson, who was infiltrated by the Army into a Northern Irish paramilitary group, he got all the relevant documents. 'Documents are the key to everything,' he says.

FAKES AND HOAXES

Even with a caseful of documents, however, investigative reporters are not necessarily home and dry. As in *The Sunday Times*'s thalidomide investigation, the real story may not be in the documents.

Documents get older as an inquiry continues, making it possible for people to argue that the situation described in the documents has changed. And documents can be faked. In 1977 the *Daily Mail* accused British Leyland of worldwide bribery. But it turned out that a letter, purportedly from Lord Ryder of the National Enterprise Board, had been forged by a former Leyland executive. A few years earlier, forged letters were used in a controversy over a land deal involving the brother of Harold Wilson's assistant, Marcia Williams.

Two documents about Mark Thatcher's business affairs showed up in 1989. They caused great excitement in the press. But they were both hoaxes.

So if people provide you with documents, you have to satisfy yourself that these documents are indeed what they say they are and prove what they seem to prove. Read with other documents, could they have a different interpretation from yours? Do they raise questions in your mind? Do they contain uncertainties which need to be probed?

CHECKING FOR AUTHENTICITY

Mike Calvin, who told in *The Times* how first, second and third places in a grand prix motor race were fixed, says you have to convince yourself that what you have been given is authentic. Your own and your newspaper's reputations are on the line.

Calvin's story in November 1997 was based on tape recordings of radio conversations between pit crews and drivers. He had received a telephone call asking if he had heard rumours of such tapes and inviting him to a chat. At the chat, he was given transcriptions but he insisted on the tapes themselves. 'I need to hear them,' he said.

When he heard the tapes, he recognized some voices. He also knew the circumstances of the race. He rang a couple of people to seek explanations of some of what was said, so he understood it all. Then he talked to his editor.

HOW PETER WATSON MADE HIS CHECKS

A detailed endeavour to check the authenticity of documents is described in Peter Watson's book *Sotheby's: Inside Story* (Bloomsbury, 1997). The book tells how he and Bernard Clark's TV company made two programmes for Channel 4's *Dispatches* series.

The first in November 1995 showed how thieves used mechanical diggers to open ancient tombs in Italy and obtain vases which were smuggled into Switzerland on their way to the London art market.

The second in February 1997 showed a Dutch member of Sotheby's staff in Milan making a deal the previous year to get an old painting to London, where it was auctioned. The programme also showed how Indian dealers got the figure of a goddess from a remote Indian village to London. The export of art objects over 100 years old from Italy and India is not legal. Since the programmes, two Indians who dealt in antiquities have been jailed. Sotheby's has ceased selling antiquities in London.

Watson shows that his whole investigation hinged on the genuineness of the documents which James Hodges, a former employee of Sotheby's, brought to him.

His first reaction was that the documents were indeed genuine. There were 3,000 or more. They were of many different types – originals, photocopies, handwritten notes, telexes. Some were signed by people whose signatures Watson recognized. Some referred to events he knew about. Many were mundane: no forger would bother to forge them. It took Watson two weeks to read them all.

To convince a publisher, he needed more evidence that the documents were right. There was a big complication: they were stolen. Sotheby's could seek an injunction for breach of confidence and get them back. Peter Watson had to corroborate the story they told without letting on that he had them.

He cross-examined Hodges three times. Then he sought to check the writing on handwritten documents. For comparison, he had letters from two Sotheby's people and, by chance, received one from a third. He and a friend of Hodges wrote to six more and got signed or handwritten replies. A handwriting expert said she was 90 per cent certain that the writing in the nine samples matched with the handwritten documents.

His next approach was to try to show that what the documents said happened did in fact happen. But his first attempt failed. Then he had a setback. Hodges had been accused of stealing a bowl and a helmet from Sotheby's. More charges were added, including forgery of two memos. This allegation of forgery put the authenticity of the documents back into doubt.

The increased number of charges, however, gave Hodges the chance to use more of the documents in his defence at the trial. This meant that more of them were tested there. Watson attended most of the trial and found that admissions by Sotheby's witnesses confirmed aspects of the art trade which some of the documents delineated. Sotheby's did not contest their authenticity. Watson decided to concentrate on these documents which had been used in court.

Watson's publisher, Bloomsbury, sought an opinion from George Carman QC. He said the problem was not whether the documents were genuine but whether they were complete. Would other documents change the picture? Sotheby's had not, however, introduced other picture-changing documents at Hodges' trial.

Peter Watson next tried some documents on Sotheby's, querying whether they might have been altered or create a false picture. Sotheby's commented only off the record but issued no denial of his story about the smuggling of antiquities.

Watson and Clark TV then returned to the question of whether what the documents suggested actually happened. Watson went to Apulia in Italy to investigate the theft of vases from ancient tombs. This led to the first Channel 4 programme.

A group of Hodges' documents concerned India. Photocopies showed that the figure of a goddess pictured in an Indian book had turned up in a Sotheby's sale in 1988. Sam Bagnall, producer of the Watson programmes, went to India to find Lokhari, the village near Allahabad from which the goddess figure had come. He and an Indian researcher vainly combed the Allahabad bookshops for a map with Lokhari on it. A bookseller, however, produced a copy of the 1990 census. It showed four Lokharis.

The bookseller suggested consulting a professor at Allahabad University. The professor was suspicious of an Englishman asking about antiquities but became helpful when Bagnall mentioned

Dr Chakrabarti, an expert the Watson team had consulted in Cambridge. The professor located the right Lokhari, and suggested a local archaeologist called Dubey to act as guide. He lived 'near the railway station at Bargarh'.

A Communist Party organizer at the hamlet of Bargarh took them to Dubey's house. And so they reached Lokhari 40 miles away where the headman was still angry at the loss of goddesses belonging to the village. The Watson team were able to establish the trade route from villages such as Lokhari to London.

RESPONSES AND SPOILING TACTICS

Investigative reporting is apt to provoke a reaction or spoiling tactics, so it is as well to be prepared.

A common response to an investigation is to criticize the evidence it has turned up, the people who have provided that evidence and the reporter who is writing it.

Freelance Paul Halloran also points out: 'Companies don't want people prying into what they see as commercially sensitive. They would like to know where we get documents. People search your rubbish bins to find out, so we have a shredder. They get private detectives to see who you rang.'

Or a company might bring in a media relations consultant to help with its defence. Roger Cook of *The Cook Report* says some people ought to have consultants, to persuade them to be open. However, he dislikes consultants who seek to denigrate and libel the reporters working on a story.

In the past, Cook ran into physical violence. In the worst case, when he was making a *Checkpoint* programme for radio, a man tried to run him down with a car. He suffered a fractured skull and awoke, he recalls, as in a B-movie, seeing a blurred vision of an Australian doctor bending over him.

Cook has also had death threats. One criminal, he says, admitted to police that he had been offered £20,000 'to get rid of me'. Cook adds: 'If you cave in to threats from the kind of people you are seeking to bring to book, they have won.'

One man found an ingenious way of stopping transmission of an investigative programme on Channel 4. He attacked a journalist and was charged by the police. This made the matter *sub judice* and the programme could not be shown.

Another response to an investigation is guerrilla warfare: write, or get a solicitor to write, detailed letters which require substantive replies before an article is published or a programme broadcast. Solicitors for the owners of the Bowbelle, the dredger which was in collision with the Marchioness pleasure boat, exchanged 35 letters with Channel 4 and its programme-makers before the *Dispatches* investigation into the accident was aired.

The law lends itself to the ingenious. Without wasting effort on a lawsuit, a Liverpool solicitor killed off the *Liverpool Free Press* by threatening to sue its distributors.

Tony Collins of *Computer Weekly* says that EDS, an information technology company much used by the government, threatened to take action on his past articles if he offended it again. 'We wrote a 16-page reply answering every allegation. We have continued to report on that company. They have sought good relations with us.'

Usually he gets responses to his stories from public relations people:

'A press officer won't necessarily lie,' he says, 'but will try to dampen faith in a story by coming up with facts you didn't know and questioning the accuracy of what you've done without actually telling you what's wrong. Perhaps you described something as a key site when, arguably, it's one of many. If you're told your story is a nonsense and they don't give good reasons, it's a sign there's something in it.

'Off-the-record briefers are dangerous because they can put you off. There's no accountability. If they give you facts which in retrospect prove not to be so, they know there is no comeback on them.'

Few journalists can have experienced the sort of sustained, though non-violent, campaign waged by business tycoon Robert Maxwell against Tom Bower (see page 144).

Garry Lloyd and Julian Mounter were interrogated for three weeks by the police after they exposed three corrupt policemen (see page 182).

They received menacing phone calls at night. They were unable to leave the country on reporting assignments. They had to give evidence in a trial where their reputation as well as the freedom of the accused was at stake. Garry Lloyd's promising career with *The Times* was brought to an end and he had to start again with the BBC.

REBUTTALS THAT DON'T REBUT

In a Kent lane in 1996, the Russell family were attacked by a man wielding a hammer. Six-year-old Megan and her mother Lin were killed. Nine-year-old Josie was left for dead but survived. In October 1998 a mentally unstable man called Michael Stone was convicted of the murders. A key witness against him was a prisoner who had occupied a cell next to Stone's.

Jo-Ann Goodwin in her investigation of the case against Stone (see page 93) mentions a report in the *Folkestone Herald* of a fracas outside this prisoner's home in which relatives berated him about his evidence. Goodwin writes that, when she asked Kent police about the incident, she was told no fracas had been reported. The police suggested that the story was spurious, that the story's writer had been sacked for making it up and that the former prisoner would sue if the story were repeated.

This response to Jo-Ann Goodwin's inquiries is on classic lines: deny the story, discredit the writer, threaten a lawsuit. 'All the nationals looked at this and dropped it,' she was told.

Goodwin found, however, that the editor of the *Folkestone Herald* stood by the story. The reporter who wrote it had parted company with the *Herald* but this was after he was promoted, not as a result of his account of the fracas. The *Daily Mail* later found a woman who witnessed the fracas.

In 1998 a firm defending the fire-resistance of its chimney flue liners ended inquiries from trading standards officers by providing a copy of a fax from an assessor for the British Standards Institution. The fax concerned a complaint which BSI had received. The assessor wrote:

I have reviewed the basis of the complaint, which was regarding the composition of your class I flue liners and the claim that they comply with the current building regulations. After consultation with a concrete technical expert within BSI and a detailed study of the supporting evidence, we have concluded that the complaint is unfounded.

This sounds like a comprehensive rebuttal of the complaint. But it has problems. First, the complaint did not concern building regulations but a British Standard. Second, the technical expert is not named nor are any details of the supporting evidence given.

Chris White, when he was freelancing for *The European* in Brussels, had painful experience of a rebuttal which was not a rebuttal. He had been inquiring into fraud in the European Commission's tourist unit and had been unexpectedly invited to interview Per Brix Knudsen, head of the Commission's fraud investigators. 'He kept asking me to switch the tape off,' White recalls. 'Then he would say things with the tape off.'

White reported the interview under the heading 'EC anti-fraud chief pledges "no cover-ups"'. Knudsen then wrote to *The European* as follows:

I did not make any comment whatsoever at the time of the interview on the subject of a 'financial control investigation' concerning the award of a 'tourism study contract' after a cruise. Furthermore, I am informed that no such investigation on this matter has taken place and that no such contract exists.

Having received this letter, *The European* closed White's fraud inquiry. White, for the reason explained above, had no taped record of Knudsen's remarks.

What Knudsen wrote in his letter referred to a paragraph deep down in White's article which read:

He [Knudsen] confirmed that a financial control investigation has recently reported that a Greek shipping organization which hosted a foreign ministers' meeting on a cruise ship was awarded a tourism study contract after Director General von Moltke [Heinrich von Moltke, director-general for tourism] took a second Greek island cruise with the same firm a month later.

Knudsen was strictly correct in denying that there had been a financial control investigation. There had been no investigation by the Commission's financial control department. But that did not mean there had been no investigation at all.

Knudsen was also strictly correct in writing that Von Moltke had not gone on a cruise. Rosemarie Wemheuer, a member of the European Parliament, later told White that Von Moltke had travelled to a Greek island on a ferry owned by a Greek cruise line. There had been a discussion about a contract. The contract was with a director of the cruise line.

So the devil is in the language. Chris White recalls an incident when he was working for the *Daily Mail*. He heard that the cooling equipment at a nuclear power reactor had broken down, and that staff had to play hoses on the roof. The press officer concerned, formerly with *The Daily Telegraph*, insisted on questions in writing and denied everything. White adds: 'I saw him months later. "Chris," he said, "you nearly had us. If you had asked one question slightly differently, we would have had to admit it all."'

9 Getting people to talk

YOU NEED TO BE NICE, HAVE AN INTRODUCTION, OR A FAVOUR TO OFFER, AND BE A GOOD TALKER

Talking to poorly educated, delinquent youngsters can be frustrating for any journalist. They have 99 reasons not to talk to yet another adult oppressor. So how did Nick Davies of *The Guardian* persuade several to tell him their tragic stories for his book *Dark Heart* (Chatto, 1997)?

'You have to put yourself in their place and thereby discover the one reason they might have for talking to you,' says Davies.

Wandering through Nottingham, he happened to see two boys hanging around a public lavatory in the middle of the fairground, looking for clients for what they called 'business'. He says: 'They were happy to talk to me because they thought I was a punter. But that was only for 30 seconds.'

They would have gone on talking for money, but Davies did not mean to give them any. The other thing he realized they wanted was food. 'Would you like to go for a McDonald's?' he asked.

Davies writes that, half an hour later, they looked like two boys on a family outing, blowing bubbles into their milkshakes and chewing on fistfuls of cheeseburger as they competed to explain themselves to him.

To delinquent lads in Leeds, Davies spoke about police corruption. They were engaged in a struggle with the police and, by talking to

Davies, they saw a way of doing the police some harm. Once he got talking with two lads, a further group joined in.

Nick Davies believes that persuading people to talk when they don't want to is the heart of journalism.

DON'T BE SHARP AND SMARMY

A niece of mine lost her job with a well-known firm where she had worked for 20 years. This resulted from something which wasn't her fault or even within her field of responsibility. She refused to talk to the first journalist who wanted to look into her case; but, five years after the event, she agreed to speak to author and campaigner Tom Bower. Why did she talk to Bower and not the other journalist?

The earlier one, she says, was much sooner after the event. 'He phoned me at work and I didn't feel comfortable with him. He was too sharp and smarmy. I said "No" but he kept thinking of new ways of asking the same question. This, he told me, was a chance to get even. But I wouldn't do that.'

Talking to Tom Bower, she said, was altogether more comfortable. He chose neutral ground for the meeting. 'I thought I might be nervous but I wasn't. He wasn't pushing. He asked good open questions. He would then wait till I finished. He also asked: "Do you know where this or that person is now?"'

If, as an investigative journalist, you want people to talk to you, you need to be nice to them. If possible, you need to be honest and straightforward in explaining why you want to talk to them and what you propose to do with the information. (The Broadcasting Standards Commission's code seeks fairness for contributors. They must be given a clear explanation of their contribution.)

Never take people for granted. Never give people the impression that you are using them. An interview should be a joint enterprise from which both sides gain something. You as interviewer get some copy. The person you speak to gets a fair and accurate expression of his or her views and knowledge.

People's reactions vary, as I discovered when researching this book. Most people were helpful, some enthusiastic. Some were suspicious of

75

the telephone in typically British fashion and wanted the request for an interview in writing. Two checked to make sure I was who I said I was. Some were too busy to meet me. One or two feared personal publicity. One brushed me off. One or two avoided me. One asked for a letter, then said he'd have to ask permission to talk to me and would ring back. He didn't.

Bernard Clark says: 'Most of the best stories depend on finding the right person. You have to win their friendship and gradually they begin to relax. You have to get the story but you also have to be yourself, a totally genuine person. People like to talk.'

TV producer Sam Bagnall says that in embarking on an inquiry you have to think first before you start speaking to people:

'Before you pick up the phone, you have to say to yourself: "Does this person want to talk to me? How do I explain what it is I am doing?" You can only persuade the persuadable.

'If it's going to do them damage, you've got to let them make the choice. It amazes me how many people will speak if they feel a burning sense of injustice. It gives you faith in humanity.'

He recalls a council employee in the Midlands who witnessed a misuse of force by police. He spoke on TV, even though his employer hadn't given him permission to speak. By doing so, he risked his job.

There is another consideration. Will this person tell someone else? 'You have to proceed with extreme caution,' says Bagnall. 'You don't want the story to leak. With TV there's such a gap before transmission. Newspapers can scoop you.'

Freelance Mark Hollingsworth once rang Gerry Long, the former head of Reuters and Times Newspapers (who died in 1998), to ask him about Rupert Murdoch, *The Times*'s owner. 'Why should I talk to you?' asked Long.

Hollingsworth adds: 'I didn't know what to say. He was living in France. Why should he talk to me?'

As a result, Hollingsworth is more circumspect about ringing people. He asks himself: Who is the best source? How am I going to get him to talk? Have I got an introduction? He says:

'If you are impatient and ring too quickly, people will put the phone down and you won't get a second chance. If you ring and say you know a friend, people are more likely to talk. People least want to talk if the subject is sensitive – intelligence, fraud, corruption. You need to know how human beings work and behave. Why might *they talk to you?*

'Sometimes they have a grudge or they know they will benefit financially at some stage. People do ask for money. A lot assume newspapers and TV will pay. If a story is true and accurate, chequebooks still come out.

'Some people, especially in America, just like talking. Businessman Gary Smith [who talked about Mark Thatcher's involvement in an abortive Nigerian oil deal] liked to talk. He liked to be involved. People like to be on the inside, involved in something exciting and mysterious.

'People will talk to further their own agenda. They may want revenge or publicity or to further the public interest, get something cleaned up.

'The British are private people. They don't talk to strangers. It's none of your business. They don't like or trust the press, unless you can help them with information or a favour.

'American journalists are too puritanical to make this sort of offer. They think everyone should talk to them anyway. They miss a lot of stories.

'Talking can be dangerous. The number of whistleblowers is so small.'

So, according to Mark Hollingsworth, it is useful to have an introduction or to have something you can offer in exchange for the information you hope to receive. TV programme-maker Christopher Hird says that a high-profile businessman was more willing to appear in a Fulcrum TV programme because Fulcrum was known to him as a result of work done by a sister company, Fulcrum Research, in the past.

Hird also says it can be more difficult to get some people to talk when you become better known. They know you're not going to ask them about their garden. Peter Middleton, former chief executive of Lloyd's, told a researcher: 'I don't want to discuss anything with Christopher Hird.'

Bernard Clark says that if you need to ring someone with a sensitive question it's better to ring them at home. Tony Collins of *Computer Weekly* says informants are often frightened to give you a steer, a hint. But 'I like people to tell me their suspicions.'

As my sacked niece's story shows, you cannot assume that, because people have been poorly treated, they will want to get even. However, a dispute commonly causes people to talk to journalists. British Biotech's disappointments and disagreements came into the news when its director of clinical research was dismissed.

Derrick Robins, former chairman of Coventry City Football Club, was irked that shares he sold were passed to his successor. This led him to disclose a correspondence with the then Paymaster-General, Geoffrey Robinson, over the shares, bought from him by Robinson's controversial offshore family trust.

All reporters have to be good listeners. Investigative reporters also need to be good talkers. They have to be able to keep a conversation going until something interesting is said. Peter Marsh of the *Financial Times* says it's towards the end of three hours, when you have got to know each other, that the interesting facts emerge. He also says it helps that the *FT* has a reputation for fair dealing.

When people are reluctant to say what they know, Bob Satchwell, who has done investigations for the *Lancashire Evening Post* and the *News of the World*, recommends trying amateur psychology and creating an atmosphere of revelation. Sometimes, if you keep talking to people and telling stories, they may be encouraged to top your stories by revealing their own.

> Don't neglect to ask the simple questions, even at the risk of appearing stupid and ignorant. TV interviewers intentionally ask simple, even stupid questions because they open up the subject.

Someone who has failed or refused to answer a question may answer it if you pretend you didn't notice and keep feeding it back into the conversation. I recall a Scottish journalist who, on a press visit, asked the same question over and over again. In the end, he got a reply.

If someone makes a remark about someone else, check it with the someone else. Since what people say is less reliable than documentary evidence, it is useful to have two people saying the same thing and thus corroborating each other.

It is always worth trying for an interview, since someone you never expected to say a word may agree to talk. Roger Cook once investigated a man seeking to take over a hot-dog-van empire by violence. The man leapt the counter of a van set up by *The Cook Report* and roughed up the staff. Then he rang up to offer an interview.

THE NINE RS OF INTERVIEWING

Across the Atlantic, a Chicago police expert called Steve Rhoads once spoke to a journalists' workshop and suggested nine Rs:

1 **Receive.** Ask open-ended questions. Don't interrupt. Receive as much information as possible.
2 **Relieve.** Be understanding. Relieve anxiety by changing the subject.
3 **Reflect.** Have you got the details right? You want the other person's view, not your interpretation of it.
4 **Regress.** Ask 'before that' questions, not just 'after that'.
5 **Reconstruct.** Going back to the scene can help, if only in the mind.
6 **Research.** By this stage in the interview, you should be on good enough terms to be able to ask the more stressful questions.
7 **Review.** Check the facts and quotes.
8 **Resolve.** Address any misunderstandings and discrepancies.
9 **Retire.** Give the other person a chance to add comments. Tell them how to contact you. End on a positive note.

Rhoads also suggests you should be wary if answers don't match the questions. Is the truth being hidden?

He suggests that a good approach to people reluctant to say much is to ask several non-threatening questions before the one to which you want an answer. 'You want to tell your side of the story, don't you? . . . So what did happen?'

One important consideration is whether people will allow their names and faces to accompany what they say. Television, in particular, needs faces. Some people would do almost anything to appear on television. Others are shy.

In both broadcasting and the press, names and faces lend a validity and credibility which unattributable copy lacks. You may also need people to give evidence in court. So you have to persuade people that you are doing something important which depends on their help.

Paul Lashmar made a programme for Channel 4 in 1997 about mistakes in cervical-smear testing at Canterbury. He says it made all the difference that the technician who sounded the alarm was prepared to appear in the film. 'It gave it so much greater impact.'

In the United States, a media council called the Minnesota News Council held a public hearing into a complaint by Northwest Airlines against a TV investigation. One reason why the TV station lost the argument was that the only person prepared to go on camera and talk about aircraft maintenance problems was a welder who was suing the airline after being fired. Twenty-five airline employees spoke to the TV station but wouldn't go on record. The station also failed to produce any independent experts.

If people refuse to be quoted or pictured, you have in the end to accept that and to make sure their identities are not betrayed. Some important sources will decline to say anything useful if they are going to be reported as having said it.

REACTION AND DENIAL

It is essential that you put allegations to whoever you are accusing. Even at the start of an inquiry when you have nothing firmer than allegations, you may find it worth approaching whoever the inquiry is about. It is courteous and it could save a lot of time.

But everything could be denied. You then have to decide whether you believe the denial and, if you don't, seek evidence elsewhere before returning with your case. What you hope is that you will get an admission in full or in part. For this you need the best possible grasp of the subject, so you are not fobbed off.

People who have been up to no good know precisely what no-good they have been up to. This inevitably gives them an advantage over investigating journalists who know only part of the story. The no-gooder's preferred course is to dismiss every allegation as inaccurate and say nothing more. 'Whatever you've heard, it's all lies.'

But the journalists have an advantage, too. A no-gooder doesn't know how much the journalists know and is probably curious to find out; since it is no use denying something which is going to be undeniable. Journalists may therefore be able to lure the no-gooder into a damaging conversation.

Even a denial can be interesting. Peter Watson tells in his book *Sotheby's. Inside Story* (Bloomsbury, 1997) how he and his colleagues tried to contact a man suspected of smuggling ancient vases from Italy into Switzerland. The man rang and said that, if they accused him of wrongdoing, he would take them to court for millions. But they hadn't said why they wanted to talk to him.

Michael Gillard of *The Express* says. 'You rarely get the full story but you can get close enough to be right. The way to get an admission is to make it clear that you know enough so they cannot mislead you or prevent publication of your article: an article which will be more damaging than if they co-operate. You hope that by showing what you do know you can bluff them into telling you the rest.'

They may complain about what you are doing, perhaps through a solicitor. 'If you are confident, you treat that as what it is, a bluff, and you publish.'

Television journalists face a more structured situation. The Independent Television Commission's code requires that, if serious allegations are to be put, prior warning must normally be given. It also says that, if someone declines to take part in a programme, care must be taken to give a fair account of the subject.

The Broadcasting Standards Commission code requires 'an appropriate and timely opportunity to respond'. It says that a contributor should 'be informed about the areas of questioning and, wherever possible, the nature of other likely contributions'.

> John Stonborough, who acts for companies assailed by investigative journalists, complains that, time and again, allegations have been sprung at the last moment, and people have been given little detail to respond to.
>
> Journalists, for their part, may well not want to give away their questions in advance and let people cover their tracks. As for disclosing other likely contributions, this could open the way for an approach to other contributors to persuade them to change their views. In the view of one leading TV executive, the fairness guidelines in the codes of conduct can be used to try to thwart good and justifiable journalism.

Roger Cook of *The Cook Report* drew up guidelines for his work so that he could answer allegations of unfairness should they arise (see page 43).

Chris White of *The Parliament Magazine* in Brussels says that, in putting allegations to people, it is best to say straight out who you are and to be forthright and direct. It is no good pretending not to be a journalist or pretending that you want information on something which you don't. If you are not sincere or do not convey sincerity, you won't get the interview. 'All such confrontations are like a lie-detector test,' says White. 'You have to pass it.'

Your only deception should be in distancing yourself from the allegations. You might say: 'I am here to talk to you on behalf of somebody else [your editor, for instance]. These allegations are being made. I don't know a lot about the matter but I would like to hear your side of the story.'

Once you have established a decent contact, you might say something like this: 'I will try in any way I can to put your case if you have one. But, if you tell me lies and I find out, I will write about it.'

White says that one reason why the direct approach can work is that people up to no good are often over-confident. They believe that, if they are crooked, they can hide it and gloss it over.

Also, says White, 'if you are up-front, it implies you know more than you are telling'.

He adds that in such situations 'silence is your friend'. Ask a direct question and wait for a reply. If you don't get one straightaway, don't babble on, because that gives the other guy thinking time; and if you're talking, he isn't. If you stay silent, he is the one under pressure to fill the silence.

INFORMATION THROUGH CONFRONTATION

For some journalists, including well-known TV and radio interviewers, confronting people is not just a possibly wearing requirement. They see it as essential that people under criticism should explain themselves. Roger Cook is not content with a written reply or a statement from a public relations man. He puts allegations in person, however elusive his quarry may be.

Other journalists seek their information through confrontation. Veronica Guerin in Ireland used to lay siege to the houses of the underworld figures she wrote about. In an interview published after she was murdered, she spoke about some kidnappers in whom her paper, the *Sunday Independent*, was interested. Who were these people? The paper's staff decided that the only way to find out was to meet them. This, she said, opened a new world to her.

Following the death of The General (a leading criminal called Martin Cahill), she wrote that he finally began to talk to her after she had delivered letters to his two Dublin homes every day for six weeks. Her biographer, Emily O'Reilly, says that sometimes Guerin would sit for hours outside a house, occasionally ringing her husband on her mobile phone for cigarettes and food.

Mark Thomas, on Channel 4 in 1997, made original use of confrontation in a programme protesting about the public's lack of a right to know about country estates to which there is public access. Under the Conditionally Exempt Land and Building Scheme, estate owners who give occasional access to the public receive a tax concession. But, since personal tax affairs are confidential, so is the fact that there is public access to the land. Thomas took a coachload of sightseers into one such estate. Also on Channel 4, in *The Mark Thomas Comedy Product*, he parked a tank outside the house of a Cabinet minister and asked him for advice on how to join the arms export trade.

Across the Atlantic, Maura Casey of *The Day*, a newspaper in Connecticut, campaigned about safety violations at a nuclear power station (to do so, she read the inspection reports, and also documents from workers who had been dismissed). After the mishandling of a valve leak, the station was forced to close. *The Day* then attacked and was credited with killing a Bill in the State legislature which would have put new money from the public into the troubled power company.

Maura Casey writes that she spent a day dropping in on government officials. The tactic rattled the cages of people involved and was more effective than making telephone calls.

GOING UNDER COVER

Former investigative reporter Bob Satchwell spoke, above (page 78), about creating an atmosphere of revelation. One way to do this and record damaging admissions is to pretend you are not a journalist at all but someone your quarry is glad to meet: a rich foreign businessman or a potential customer for electric-shock batons or the owner of an art collection or a recruit for extreme politics or even an asylum seeker.

Roger Cook of *The Cook Report* puts it like this: 'If we can persuade these guilty people to demonstrate what they do, we will have a more watchable programme and a second layer of evidence.' (The first layer of evidence is that from witnesses and documents.) Cook does not mind being an *agent provocateur* in this sense. What he would not do is seek to get people to do something dodgy outside their normal practice and character.

One obvious but important point is that a journalist attempting a scam must look and sound the part. The team for *The Cook Report*'s burglary programme in April 1999 included a former registered police informer. His grasp of Thames Estuary English made him sound entirely credible as a trusting and somewhat clueless small-time villain.

Paul Nuki, consumer affairs editor at *The Sunday Times*, seeks to expose manufacturers who dictate the prices at which their goods are sold. Such manufacturers are wary, and documentary evidence of such dictation is hard to find. He gets his evidence by pretending to be a new retailer who wants to handle their goods.

Undercover scams have also worked well for Mazher Mahmood in his investigations for the *News of the World*. They can provide the hardest possible evidence of wrongdoing. The crooks are to be heard convicting themselves out of their own mouths.

> In Britain, the Broadcasting Standards Commission requires that any secret recording should serve an overriding public interest and should not infringe the privacy of bystanders. A ruling against the *Watchdog* programme shows that the Commission also requires there to be evidence of malpractice before secret filming is attempted.

The Independent Television Commission says that secret recording is acceptable only when essential to establish a story of important public interest. Clearly, secret recording can become essential only if there is previous evidence of wrongdoing to make it so.

Under the ITC code, secret filming requires the consent of the broadcasting company's most senior programme executive.

The Press Complaints Commission code says that subterfuge can be justified only in the public interest and only when material cannot be obtained by other means.

What secret recording does best is demonstrate that something has happened or been said or a law has been broken. It is less successful in demonstrating a pattern. In the United States, part of the Food Lion shops' case against ABC TV (see below) was that the poor food-handling shown in the programme was not typical.

It is very difficult for secret recording to show that something did not happen. This was part of the controversy over a *Rantzen Report* programme in 1996 concerning the British Home and Hospital for Incurables. The programme sought to show that a patient was not taken out to the home's fête. The home replied that he *was* taken out: the secret-filmers were away changing their film at the time.

When journalists take jobs in order to show what is happening inside some enterprise, they are, strictly speaking, obtaining money by false pretences. The Crown Prosecution Service, however, decided not to prosecute a *World in Action* journalist who took a job in an abattoir to film the meat-handling there. *World in Action* returned the money earned.

Food Lion in the United States won $5.5 million punitive damages for fraud when TV journalists did their undercover study of food-handling in its shops. The North Carolina jury did not seem to like Yankee journalists from a wealthy TV station moving in on a well-regarded local company. But British civil cases, apart from libel, are normally decided by judges, who do not award punitive damages.

A SMUGGLER UNMASKED

An undercover operation was the only way an art smuggler could be unmasked in the inquiry described in Peter Watson's book *Sotheby's: Inside Story* (Bloomsbury, 1997). Watson describes in detail the scam which caused an art dealer in Milan to reveal himself on Channel 4 as a smuggler ready to export an old painting illegally from Italy.

The Channel 4 enterprise involved two women adopting fake identities and a third going to bid at an art sale. Watson's story shows that, if you set up a charade, you have to think of every detail that can contribute to the illusion or prevent suspicions being aroused. You don't want the enterprise to fail for a trivial reason.

Watson needed a London address to which the painting could be delivered. He borrowed a friend's flat but the friend would not accept the painting herself. He had to find another woman to pretend to be the flat-owner and accept the painting in her place. The phone was disconnected lest an incoming call should give the game away. What if the delivery man wanted to make a telephone call? The stand-in flat-owner had a mobile phone just in case. She also had to know the full address and where to find pen and pencil, and the lavatory, in case he wanted any of these

Only cool and quick-thinking people can take part in this sort of enterprise, because not everything nor every turn in a conversation can

Figure 9.1
The Sotheby affair: investigator Peter Watson outside the premises of the fine art auctioneers (picture Channel 4)

be foreseen. Watson's scam survived one false alarm and one serious slip of the tongue.

The first step in the unmasking of the smuggler was for Watson to acquire a good but inexpensive old master in Naples, well away from Milan and other art markets, without betraying the fact he was a journalist. In March 1996 he acquired a picture by Giuseppe Nogari, of an old woman holding a cup, for £9,545, less than half the asking price. The next step was to take it to Sotheby's office in Milan and see if the old masters expert there would offer to smuggle it to London.

Peter Watson couldn't take it himself as he was well known in the art world. It had to be taken by someone who had Italian connections but, for the benefit of the Channel 4 audience, spoke English. Watson also decided that the someone should have an address in Australia, so there would be no suspicion of a London connection. They chose an Australian camerawoman of Italian extraction called Victoria Parnall. The story was that she had inherited paintings from her grandmother in Italy.

She got to see the expert, a Dutchman, in late March. She had a tape-recorder in her handbag. In her brooch was a tiny camera linked to a tape machine, about the size of a cigarette packet, in her pocket. She knew where to sit in order to film the expert's face.

At the first meeting, it appeared the Nogari was not quite valuable enough to be worth smuggling. Peter Watson decided they should make it appear that this was just the beginning. There were more paintings, by a carefully selected group of artists, to come.

Victoria, on her next visit, asked the expert how much difference it would make to sell these paintings in London. The expert pointed out that there was a snag about selling pictures in Italy. They might get notified, that is, recorded by the government, and then people wouldn't buy them. But was there some way . . .?

Yes, said the expert. If Victoria had an address in London, they could smuggle the Nogari out. She agreed to leave the picture with him. He would send her, in Australia, a release note for her to sign, saying she took the picture away with her. When he got the note back, he would put the picture on a truck. But first he was going on holiday.

Victoria warned her cousins in Sydney that they might hear from Milan. Meanwhile Peter Watson found a friend to whose flat the painting could be delivered in London.

Victoria rang the expert in Milan after his holiday and pretended she was speaking from Sydney. He said he had taken to London a photograph of the Nogari which had been allotted a space in the catalogue for the next Sotheby's sale.

The release note reached Sydney on April 30, 1996. The picture needed to be in London by May 27 if possible, a week before the catalogue was published for the next sale. Unfortunately, Victoria's

Australian cousins sent the note to her by airmail, instead of by a courier service. It didn't reach her in London till May 7. If it were returned to Sydney, it would be May 14 before it got back to Milan and started the picture on its journey to Britain.

The Watson team despatched the note instead to the brother of their Italian researcher. He lived in Milan and delivered the package by hand. To suggest it came from Australia, it included a Reuter message from Melbourne about the Australian art market.

Victoria rang Milan two days later. All was well. The fee would be £200 cash on delivery: the couriers would ring the London flat.

On the 24th, a Friday, the flat was fixed up for secret filming. Eventually the truck with the picture arrived. The Milan expert rang the flat-owner at work to make sure the picture had turned up. She was to call his contact at Sotheby's and take the picture there.

Would it be in time for the sale catalogue? The contact had left for the weekend but all was well. Victoria rang the Milan expert on the Monday. He said Sotheby's already had the photograph of the picture, so it would be in the catalogue anyway.

At the auction, recorded by a cameraman with a camera in his tie and a monitor in his jacket to check his aim, a woman acting for the TV team bought the picture back. The *Old Woman with a Cup* went home to Italy once again.

UNDER COVER IN THE MIDLANDS

Martin Banks of the *Evening Mail*, Birmingham, describes some of his investigations in which cover had to be used to pursue a story.

Hostel horrors

The paper received complaints about some of Birmingham's hostels for the homeless. So, posing as a single, homeless man, I went looking for help at a hostel in the city centre. I had several days' growth of hair and hadn't washed for three days. I wore the scruffiest clothes I could find.

I spent several nights at three hostels and was shocked by the conditions and some of the things that went on. At one hostel, wallpaper was hanging from the wall, there was no hot or cold running water and I found human hair in the food. I also saw elderly residents being manhandled and verbally abused by members of staff. At another hostel, the use of drugs was commonplace. The *Mail* passed our file to the City Council.

Obtaining a firearm

The *Mail* wanted to discover how local gunmen obtained firearms. I started out by trawling seedy-looking back-street pubs and eventually got talking to a man who said he knew someone who could get guns, at a price.

After I spent a few weeks winning his confidence, he arranged for me to meet two men on the outskirts of Birmingham. I was met by a man who blindfolded me and walked me across the pub car park to a waiting car.

I was driven for about 45 minutes, with no conversation, to an isolated spot where the blindfold was removed and the contact unwrapped a blanket to reveal a sawn-off shotgun. It was mine, he said, for £95 but he warned: 'It's been used on a job.'

I declined the deal, saying it was not what I was looking for. I passed all the information later to the police.

Illegal working

Posing as a jobless man desperate for work, I answered an advertisement for labourers to do farm work. I was recruited by a gangmaster, one of the men who hire cheap labour for fruit farms. At 5.30 one morning I set out with a dozen others, crammed in a tiny van, for a farm in the Vale of Evesham. The work was backbreaking and tedious, and I was paid £1.30 an hour. When it rained, I didn't get a waterproof: they said I hadn't worked hard enough.

I spoke to people who told me they were from Eastern Europe and had no work permits. Others said they were working and claiming dole.

A gangmaster arrived at the site and started questioning me. I thought my cover was blown. Luckily, I managed to talk my way out of what could have been a difficult situation.

With the eco-warriors

A group of eco-warriors set up a tree camp on the site of the proposed Birmingham Northern Relief Road We wanted to know what made apparently normal people set up such a camp in the middle of winter.

I chatted with some of them in a pub, introducing myself as a sympathizer, and they agreed I could join the camp. It was important I should look the part so, before joining them, I rolled in the mud. I looked as if I had been in the camp for weeks.

I stayed a week, watching as they built tree houses and dug tunnels. I saw the holes they dug for toilets, the sleepless nights on cold floors and the way they struggled to feed themselves. It was heartening, however, to see a stream of well-wishers bring food, clothes and other items to help them in their campaign.

Most on the camp had taken part in the Manchester Airport protest: these were 'professional' eco-warriors. Others were there for the experience.

Puppies for sale

We got complaints from readers that puppies were being packed in cages and driven to the West Midlands for sale. I answered an advertisement and arranged to see a woman who was selling pups in a Birmingham pub car park. She had a van packed with pups and she said I could buy any for up to £250 each. She had travelled from South Wales.

We later spoke to several people who had bought them from her. All the animals had fallen ill a short time later.

A photographer and I travelled to her home which turned out to be a rambling farm. She became abusive and tried to attack us. We informed the RSPCA about her activities, and her local trading standards people later took action.

See also Chapter 15, Crime.

10 Writing it: problems and pitfalls

ANALYSIS OF A COURT CASE

Jo-Ann Goodwin's analysis which appeared in the *Daily Mail* of March 13, 1999, of the case against Michael Stone is an illustration of clear investigative writing. Stone was sentenced to life imprisonment in October 1998 for the murders of Lin Russell and her six-year-old daughter Megan, and the attempted murder of Megan's nine-year-old sister Josie. Many people must have wondered whether, on the evidence offered, he would have been found guilty in a less publicized and emotionally charged case.

First, Goodwin reminds readers of the attack with a hammer on the Russell family in a Kent lane. A year later, after a *Crimewatch* programme on BBC TV, a psychiatrist told the police that their E-fit picture of the man they sought looked like Stone, his former patient. Stone, however, denied the murders.

Goodwin looks in turn at each plank of the prosecution case against him. First, sightings of a man, or men, in the area around the time of the murders. Witnesses saw up to three men, of differing shapes, sizes and hair colour or headgear. The car they saw was beige or red or brown or rust. But Stone's car was a white Toyota.

Next, Goodwin shows that Stone did not match the forensic evidence found at the scene of the murder. This consisted of four hairs, some red fibres, a bloodstained fingerprint, and a shoelace used to tie up one of the girls. The hairs and fingerprint were not Stone's. The red fibres did not come from him or any of his family.

The prosecution argued that Stone used laces as tourniquets when taking drugs. Goodwin, however, explains how addicts use laces. They need one hand to inject a drug into the other arm. So they need to hold the lace/tourniquet with their teeth, where it is likely to acquire traces of saliva containing DNA. The lace from the murder scene was tested for traces of Stone's DNA. None was found.

Next Goodwin looks at the evidence given by an associate of Stone called Lawrence Calder, and Calder's girlfriend Sheree Blatt. Calder said Stone had turned up at his house covered in blood; but, in the witness box, he was not clear on what day this happened. Blatt remembered only a few spots of blood on Stone's T-shirt.

Then there was evidence from three prisoners about what Stone had said to them while held in prison. One came forward only after hearing that *The Sun* was offering money. A second prisoner, a few days after giving evidence, told *The Mirror*: 'None of what I said was true.'

The third said Stone spoke to him through a cracked drainpipe between their cells. This prisoner admitted that charges which he faced of arson, robbery and grievous bodily harm had been dropped. A week after the trial, the *Folkestone Herald* reported a fracas outside this third prisoner's home in which relatives berated him about his evidence.

To complete the picture, Goodwin mentions evidence inadmissible at Stone's trial. He was violent and mentally disturbed with a long criminal history.

Publication of this article brought Goodwin telephone calls with new information, casting further doubt on the prosecution case.

SELECT FACTS FAIRLY: LET THEM SPEAK FOR THEMSELVES

The guidelines for writing investigative articles are similar to those for other newspaper features, only more so. Not only should the text be simply and clearly written so it can be easily understood by its targeted readers whatever the subject. The facts should be allowed to speak for themselves, without loose and exaggerated expressions of opinion which could be hard to defend in court. The choice of facts to use needs to be fair. Important ones which you think might weigh against your case should not be left out. Investigative stories usually sound convincing at first reading. You want yours to remain convincing when challenged, so it is as well to cover points from which a challenge could be launched.

You need to show your work is well founded. Attribute, if possible, to someone or some document the facts you adduce. (You cannot, of course, do so if a source's identity needs to be protected.)

Make sure that your facts are accurate. If even a minor fact is wrong, this can diminish the value of your investigation. If the facts are complex, as they often are, it could pay to let your informants see what you have made of them, to clear up inaccuracies and misunderstandings.

Don't include some gratuitous comment, which adds nothing to the reader's understanding but can land you in unnecessary trouble. The *Liverpool Free Press* died because of a casual remark which wasn't even defamatory but resulted in its distributors being threatened with libel suits.

Your article should not be fogged with side tracks and side issues. These can wait for another day. Unrest at Portsmouth University raised a range of issues and claims. David Charter who wrote about it for the local evening paper, *The News*, put the side issues aside and concentrated on the main one: had public money been mis-spent?

The best advice for an investigative story then is to write what is relevant and what you're sure of, with some descriptive setting of the scene. Michael Bilton's *Sunday Times* article about the treatment of women at Harrogate police station, for instance, started with an account of what happened when the chief constable retired (see page 177). Then went into the story chronologically.

DON'T BEAT ABOUT THE BUSH

Investigative stories should not beat about the bush. Some, unfortunately, do. Machinations within Labour parties around Strathclyde attracted thousands of words in 1997 which left newspaper readers little the wiser. Hedge funds similarly attracted thousands of words in 1998, with little or no explanation of how they operate. Beating about the bush is a sign that the inquiries on which an article was based were inadequate to achieve a clear picture.

Television has an advantage by being forced into simplicity because it has room for fewer words. Some editions of Roger Cook's *The Cook Report* have a simple format. First he says who he accuses and of what. Then he gives his evidence. Then he tries, often unsuccessfully, to confront the guilty men.

The problem with the factual approach is that editors may not find it sufficiently eye-catching. However, any attempt to make the published story more eye-catching requires great care in case the end result is not founded on hard, provable fact.

Really skilful investigative reporters sense exactly how far they can go in pushing their point. They might have liked to go further but they know they will be on shakier ground.

There was an intriguing contrast between the magazine *Building Homes*' report on the heat resistance of chimney liners (see page 159) and *The Express*'s follow-up of the story three months later.

With a strapline 'Housebuilders and homeowners face safety risk', David Birkbeck began his report in *Building Homes*:

Real-fire chimneys in new homes built with a leading manufacturer's concrete flue liner risk failure in the event of a chimney fire.

The Express, under the headline 'Minister calls for probe into "killer" chimney on new homes', began:

More than 100,000 new homes built over the last two years could be fitted with potentially lethal chimney flues, it has been claimed.

The Express's report is more sensational, going beyond mere risk of failure in a chimney fire. But it is also less confident. *The Express* has felt it must dilute *Building Homes*' test results to the status of a mere claim or allegation.

THE CASE FOR BEGINNING AT THE BEGINNING

Bruce Page, former editor of Insight at *The Sunday Times*, argues that, if a story is complex it should be told as a narrative: you should begin the story at the beginning. This is easier to understand than the inverted-pyramid form of most news stories. He also believes that, if a story is easy to understand, it has a good chance of winning if challenged in court.

He points out that the old *Sunday Times* dictum 'We name the guilty men' has a legal justification. Generalized defamatory statements which could refer to several people, all of whom could sue, are dangerous.

One criticism of investigative writing might be that it is not memorable. But it can have a literary touch. Here is investigator Nick Davies in *Dark Heart* (Chatto, 1997) describing an incident in Leeds:

From down the hill to their left came a shriek like a witch in flames, and a car swung into the bottom of Hyde Park Road and roared up the hill towards them, shiny and black and very, very fast.

LIBEL: WHAT CAN HAPPEN

Investigative stories alleging folly or wrongdoing all have the potential to provoke a suit for libel. A statement is defamatory if it tends to lower someone in the estimation of right-thinking members of society. That is what investigative stories do. (Even if an article doesn't lower people's reputation but causes them damage, they can sue for malicious falsehood.)

The law of libel was an advance on the previous method of settling such matters, which was by fighting a duel. But this law evolved in the 18th century when newspapers were scurrilous. So it adopted the doctrine that the papers were in the wrong unless they could prove they were right. Eric Barendt and three other professors argued in *Libel and the Media* (Oxford, 1997) that this is unfair, since it is the people bringing libel suits who have the facts at their fingertips and are the better equipped to prove their point. The professors made a survey of opinion and decided that the law of libel unduly discouraged the media from publishing.

It is worth noting that, although the onus of proof lies on the publisher, someone bringing a libel suit normally has to give evidence and submit to cross-examination if the case goes to trial.

Investigative stories do get published despite the difficulties of winning libel cases in court and the heavy costs of losing them. The Court of Appeal in July 1998 introduced a public-interest defence in addition to the defence of justification (that is, the allegations can be shown to be true) on which investigative reporters usually have to rely. The new defence covers statements in which the public has an interest, provided they do not come from rivals or axe-grinders, have been checked as far as possible and have been put to the person defamed for rebuttal.

Thirty years ago, the appointment of James Evans as lawyer to *The Sunday Times* was an important step forward in this area. He wasn't simply a part-time lawyer asked for opinions on this article or that. He was a member of the *Sunday Times* team, interested in finding ways to get things published. Most famously, he argued it was possible to publish the moral case for better compensation for thalidomide-stricken families, even though the legal question of liability was *sub judice* and therefore off limits. His view was taken up in the Contempt of Court Act of 1981 which allows for discussion in good faith of public affairs.

He stresses that what mattered when he was with *The Sunday Times* was a change in its approach. In the 1950s it had been a deferential paper which didn't like to get involved in controversy. In the 1960s it was not worried about controversy, provided it was advised it had a better than evens prospect of winning if it was sued. He liked that. 'It was more of a challenge professionally to say, "This is the way to do it" rather than, "Don't do that or you will get a writ."'

Concerning libel, James Evans gave me this view in a letter:

'It is wise to assume that all statements of fact or opinion will be challenged. This applies particularly where the only likely defence to a libel action will be justification; but it applies equally where fair comment is likely to be relied on, since fair comment has no chance as a defence unless the substratum of fact on which the comment is based can be substantiated.

'The substantiation of facts for the purpose of either defence is about legal proof, not about truth, which, sadly, is not always the same thing.

'It is in the area of proof that the early involvement of legal advice can be helpful, particularly in relation to the admissibility and credibility of particular material and its likely availability in a form that can be put before a court.'

It is important to have your facts straight before you publish. You cannot rely on finding an extra fact at the last minute (as *The Guardian* did in the Jonathan Aitken case) which will win the case for you.

The discovery process before a court case, however, is useful in providing extra ammunition. When Reginald Maudling sued *World in Action*, it obtained in the discovery stage a letter damaging to him.

Note that documents disclosed through discovery are confidential. You cannot publish anything from them unless it crops up in the trial. This was one reason why *The Sunday Times* had a struggle to publish its work on thalidomide. Many of the documents it held had been disclosed by thalidomide's manufacturers when the affected families sued for compensation.

It is also worth noting that being able to win on the major points in your article is not the whole battle. In writing it, you need to be careful not to defame some secondary figure. Paul Halloran's and Mark Hollingsworth's book *Thatcher's Gold* had to be withdrawn for three weeks not because of any complaint from Mark Thatcher but because a businesswoman in Kuwait took out an injunction. Half a line, which she said was defamatory, was deleted. 'It was a nightmare at the time,' says Hollingsworth.

> You need to be aware, too, that, without ever taking the case to court, your opponent can lean on the distributors of your paper, book or magazine, who may decide it is too much hassle to handle. Under the 1996 Defamation Act, distributors have a defence if they exercise 'reasonable care', for example by handling publications of good repute.

THE SET-UP THAT BACKFIRED

World in Action made a programme about two policemen who were trying to blackmail a criminal in London into helping them lure other criminals into attempting an armed robbery. The policemen provided the criminal with a gun and a stocking mask. They would be waiting with a squad to net everybody, they said. The man blackmailed feared he might get shot, which would destroy evidence of the set-up.

World in Action got the whole plot on film. It also recorded telephone calls, in one of which a policeman said: 'Don't worry. We've done this before.'

The programme was transmitted and the two policemen were arrested. They denied charges arising from the *World in Action* programme. Throughout the bizarre trial which followed, the judge kept referring to the man who was blackmailed as the defendant. He was black. He shouted at the judge who sent him to prison for contempt of court.

The jury failed to agree on a verdict. Two jurors were struck out because they had allegedly gone to a pub and been overheard discussing the case. At the retrial there was a hung jury again.

The two police officers then sued *World in Action* for libel. Says Ray Fitzwalter, *World in Action*'s editor at the time:

'We still had a watertight case. And we had become aware that there were nine cases with parallel circumstances.

'Then we discovered that the sergeant [one of the two officers] had appeared as sole witness at an appeal before the Lord Chief Justice. The appeal ended with the Lord Chief Justice saying he was a liar and that no word that dropped from his lips could be believed.

'We put all this into our pleadings. The Police Federation moved in private chambers to get it struck out, on a technicality.

'At that point, the case went to sleep.'

Ray Fitzwalter says that, to win in court, you need extra material in reserve. 'If you can only just keep up with the pressure, you get into difficulties. You need to be able to trot out something more. We take careful note of anyone who rings up after a programme.'

'The other side,' he points out, 'may try to drive out one of your witnesses. If you have documents, the other side will try to deny them on technicalities. "You have a photocopy? You need the original."

'They will use endless means to discredit what you have got. To be able to keep producing a bit more is the position to be in.'

It is worth noting that what seems good and favourable evidence may be ruled inadmissible by the trial judge. When five police officers submitted they had been libelled by a *Guardian* report about an inquiry into North London police (see page 179), the judge excluded evidence of events that took place after the report was published. These subsequent events included the fact that the chief source of allegations, a convicted drugs dealer, had been cleared on appeal and had accepted damages from the Metropolitan Police. They also included the fact that, in all, more than £500,000 had been paid to defendants who claimed they had been falsely prosecuted. (*The Guardian* report did not name the five police officers as in any way responsible for malpractice.)

CONTRACT AND CONFIDENTIALITY

Libel is by no means the only law which can cause problems. ABC TV in the United States was sued for fraud over an undercover investigation (see pages 47 and 86).

Charles Raw, when he investigated the share dealings of the financiers Slater Walker, came up against the law of contract. He was in correspondence with the firm while working for *The Observer* and writing a book. But *The Observer* didn't publish his work and *The Sunday Times* took it over. Slater Walker then submitted that it had a contract with *The Observer* which couldn't be transferred to *The Sunday Times*. The case went to the Court of Appeal where *The Sunday Times* won permission to publish.

Investigative reporters are likelier to run into the law of confidentiality, which can combine awkwardly with contempt of court as in Bill Goodwin's case. This case also shows it is important, if you receive confidential information or a confidential document, not to approach the company concerned unless you can hide the source of your information or until you have it also from another source. The story is told in *McNae's Essential Law for Journalists* (Butterworth).

Bill Goodwin was a trainee reporter on *The Engineer* magazine at the time (1989). Someone rang him with information about an engineering company called Tetra Ltd. It had drawn up a business plan in order to obtain a bank loan and a copy of this plan had gone missing.

Goodwin phoned Tetra to check his information. Under the law of confidentiality, Tetra got an injunction preventing *The Engineer* from publishing anything from the business plan. It also wanted to know the source of Goodwin's information. So it obtained an order requiring Goodwin and *The Engineer* to hand over notes. Goodwin refused and was fined £5,000 for contempt of court. The European Court of Human Rights decided in 1996 that the order and the fine contravened his right to free expression under the European human rights convention.

> The law of confidentiality applies where someone has a contract or implied contract with an employer, to keep the employer's secrets. It also applies to documents disclosed in the discovery stage of a lawsuit, and it can be invoked by people seeking to prevent publication of personal data such as medical records.

In the case over the book *Spycatcher* (see page 33), the government used this law to try to stop author Peter Wright spilling the beans about his work in MI5. In the end, the government lost because so many beans had been spilled there was no longer any point in shutting the can. Similarly the Court of Appeal in 1982 refused to stop the *Watford Observer* from making use of a document from Robert Maxwell's Sun Printers. The document (about the firm losing money and seeking to cut staff) had already been widely circulated. In addition, the court held that disclosure of the document's contents was in the public interest.

JOURNALISTS' SOURCES

The public interest can also be cited by journalists seeking to keep their sources secret. The High Court in 1996 refused to jail Daniella Garavelli for refusing to disclose the source of allegations about Northumbria's crime figures. In the Bill Goodwin case, the European Human Rights Commission argued that forcing journalists to reveal sources would impair their ability to inform the public: compulsion should be used only in exceptional circumstances.

Acts of Parliament, however, empower Department of Trade inspectors, the Serious Fraud Office and (when investigating espionage or seeking to prevent terrorism) the police to require information. The police need a judge's order to secure journalistic material under the Police and Criminal Evidence Act. Confidential material is excluded.

Defence Advisory (DA) Notices cover military plans and operations, weapons, ciphers, security and intelligence services and some installations. These notices are advisory, not compulsory, but they indicate subjects which could bring trouble under the **Official Secrets Acts**. The Act of 1989, which is complex, covers six groups of official secrets: security and intelligence, defence, international relations, crime, phone-tapping and interception of communications, and secrets entrusted to other states or international organizations. It allows no defence on grounds of public interest or previous publication of a secret but the prosecution must show that disclosure of the secret was damaging.

Ten years after the 1989 Act, no one has yet come before a jury.

PRIVACY AND MEDIA CODES

There is no law of privacy in Britain beyond the laws protecting confidentiality and personal data and forbidding harassment. The privacy article in the European Convention of Human Rights is on the way to becoming part of British law; but Home Secretary Jack Straw has suggested that people with a grievance about privacy should take it to the Press Complaints Commission, rather than the courts.

The **Data Protection Act**, tightened up by the **Criminal Justice and Public Order Act of 1994**, could prove a minefield for journalists. Check that your employers are registered with the Data Protection Registrar. If not, and you don't want to register yourself, the only 100 per cent safe and trouble-free course is to avoid storing personal data on computer unless it has been published and is therefore a matter of public record.

It is an offence to sell computerized personal data. It is also an offence to seek and obtain such data from someone not authorized to supply it to you. People can claim access to data you have about them, but not if this would disclose the source.

The main safeguards for privacy against intrusion by journalists are the various media codes. That of the **Press Complaints Commission** contains provisions forbidding harassment, subterfuge, listening devices, and intrusions into privacy, hospitals, schools or the lives of children unless journalists can show they are acting in the public interest.

It gives as examples of the public interest: exposing crime, protecting public health and safety, and preventing the public being misled. The **Broadcasting Standards Commission** code adds disclosing significant incompetence in public office.

The BSC code expects broadcasters to seek consent to broadcast words and images not recorded in the public domain or in the domain of someone who has given permission to the broadcaster. Consent is also needed from people in sensitive places such as a police station or hospital, even if a general permission to broadcast has been given. The location of someone's home should not normally be disclosed.

Broadcasters, says the BSC, should normally seek agreement if they want to record a telephone call for broadcasting. Outside the news context, doorstepping (an uninvited approach to someone in a public place) may be legitimate where there has been repeated refusal to grant an interview. Repeated doorstepping can be an unwarranted infringement of privacy.

The BSC also says that victims or the immediate family of victims should be informed if a broadcast will retell an old story of crime or trauma.

The **Independent Television Commission** code covers similar ground. It says that no programme should encourage crime or political violence. Drug-taking should not appear problem-free or glamorous.

For a fuller discussion of these matters, see *McNae's Essential Law for Journalists* (Butterworth).

It may appear that journalists are hemmed in by the law and the codes. But at any rate the law on sedition, widely used against independent-minded journalists round the Commonwealth, is a dead letter in Britain. And a great number of investigative reports do get published, with important and worthwhile results.

INVESTIGATION AND ITS CONSEQUENCES

A single article or television programme rarely brings about change. Dr Phil Hammond's articles in *Private Eye* in 1992 about failed operations on children's hearts in Bristol had no immediate result (see page 154).

What is required is a response from other newspapers and a sustained campaign. *The Sunday Times'* investigation was only part of Harold Evans's effort to win a better deal for those who suffered in the thalidomide tragedy. He also argued the moral case and underpinned this by sending a reporter, Marjorie Wallace, to see all the families and publishing her reports.

In 1998 the arms-for-Sierra-Leone and cash-for-government-access investigations, which both started in *The Observer*, flew like wildfire through the media.

Around the same time, a journalist discovered by chance that Foreign Secretary Robin Cook was engaged in an affair. That story, too, ran and ran. Perhaps the sheer numbers of political journalists ensure the impact of a political inquiry.

Other investigative work can prove a lonely job. Few cheered on the dour effort of journalists to win justice for the unjustly convicted Birmingham Six and Bridgewater Four. Local newspapers, perhaps understandably, can be unenthusiastic about the arrival of investigative journalists on their patch. They resent the suggestion that well-respected local people and police might be wrongheaded.

The results of investigative reporting have been mixed. Phillip Knightley points out that winning more money for the victims of thalidomide left heartrending problems. A concerted investigative effort by many newspapers and broadcasters failed to win justice for John Stalker, whose suspension from Manchester police brought his inquiries into Northern Irish shootings to an end. Nor were the media able to prove the connection between events in Northern Ireland and Stalker's suspension.

Roger Cook, however, says that, even if an investigation merely gives a hearing to people whose case was previously unheard, then something has been gained.

Investigative reporting has been more successful in unseating errant politicians than rogue businessmen. It has forced a chief constable and a university vice-chancellor from office. It has promoted changes in the law. It has brought about the prosecution of many crooks. It has got wrongly convicted people released from prison. Angela and Tim Devlin pointed out in *The Times* in February 1998 that, if someone is wrongly convicted and needs inquiries to be made, the media may be their only feasible recourse. Hiring solicitors is expensive.

THE 11-PLUS FAILURE WHO GOT A FIRST

One night Bob Satchwell, then on the *Lancashire Evening Post*, was told that pupils in a village north of Preston would have to take their 11-plus test again. Nine had passed but there was room for only three at grammar school in Lancaster. Six pupils bright enough to qualify for grammar school faced being sent – in those pre-comprehensive days – to a secondary modern school.

Satchwell was a district reporter and still raw in journalism. He was still teaching himself shorthand and he hadn't passed the proficiency test. He had joined the *Post* in 1970, a year before.

He found out who the nine pupils were and interviewed their parents in his own time. He volunteered to cover Garstang magistrates' court, so he could meet a solicitor who chaired the parents' committee. The publicity led to more grammar-school places being found.

Ten years later, a woman wrote to him:

Dear Mr Satchwell,

I have just graduated from university with first-class honours. If it hadn't been for you, I would have gone to secondary modern from where very few get to university. My first-class degree is partly yours.

Bob Satchwell comments: 'There is no story of which I am more proud. That is what journalism is about.'

11 Two classic investigations

Two stories that demonstrate in detail how investigative journalists work are those of Jonathan Aitken, the charismatic Tory minister in John Major's government who fell from grace, and Kim Philby, the spy who fled to Moscow in 1963.

JONATHAN OF ARABIA

The Liar by Luke Harding, David Leigh and David Pallister (Penguin, 1997) gives a lucid account of how *The Guardian* and Granada TV's *World in Action* pursued the story of the mysterious weekend spent in Paris in 1993 by Jonathan Aitken, Minister for Defence Procurement in John Major's government. It shows the need for persistence, the importance of the historical background, and the possible importance of apparently trivial information.

The disgrace of Aitken, great-nephew of the newspaper tycoon Lord Beaverbrook, began with Mohammed Al Fayed, owner of Harrods and of the Paris Ritz Hotel where Aitken spent the weekend of September 17–19, 1993. Al Fayed spotted Aitken in the bar with a Saudi Arabian businessman called Said Ayas who, it turned out, had paid Aitken's bill (8,010 francs). Ministers are not supposed to have their hotel bills paid by Saudi businessmen.

Al Fayed, no friend of the Major government, told Peter Preston, editor of *The Guardian*.

CONFRONTATION BY CORRESPONDENCE

David Pallister of *The Guardian* rang Aitken about the Paris weekend but got nowhere. Not easily put off, Pallister put his questions in a letter. Aitken replied saying it was a family visit on which he had met his daughter Victoria's godparents and other friends. Pallister discovered that Victoria's godfather was Said Ayas.

Peter Preston then took a step for which he was called the 'whore from hell' in the House of Commons. To avoid betraying Al Fayed as his source, he had a fax sent to the Ritz asking for a copy of Aitken's bill. The fax purported to come from Aitken and had a House of Commons letterhead.

Having got the Ritz bill, Preston started an exchange of letters with Aitken. The upshot was that Aitken said part of the bill had been paid in error by a nephew of Said Ayas, whom he reimbursed. The rest had been paid by his wife, Mrs Lolicia Aitken, after she returned from taking their daughter Victoria to school in Switzerland. His wife, Aitken suggested, was the woman who made a payment at the hotel on Sunday afternoon September 19. (Actually, she wasn't. It was Manon Vidal, assistant to Said Ayas and to his boss, the Saudi king's son Prince Mohammed.)

FINDING THE HISTORY

David Leigh, at the time a producer for *World in Action*, was intrigued by what had been turned up. He decided to look at Aitken's history and his Saudi links.

Four useful people had contacted or been contacted by *The Guardian*. One, a taxi driver, had a letter signed 'Jonathan Aitken'. It concerned a Saudi prince and his dispute with chauffeurs and cleaners. Companies House records showed Aitken to have been a director of a company looking after the Saudi prince's London mansion. He hadn't declared this in the register of MPs' interests.

Nor had he declared a directorship of a company formed by a Lebanese, Fouad Makhzoumi, who, according to a second informant, was involved in an arms deal.

The third informant was Robin Kirk, an osteopath. He had run a Berkshire health farm called Inglewood until Aitken (who didn't declare his directorship of this in the register of MPs' interests) dismissed him. The farm, popular with rich Arabs, had been bought secretly by Said Ayas and two other Saudis.

After months of effort, Leigh got Kirk to agree to be filmed for his *Jonathan of Arabia* programme. It needed live witnesses.

Leigh found the fourth informant, Jo Lambert, selling villas in the Canary Islands. Jo, who also agreed to filming, had been Inglewood's matron until she was dismissed on what she said was a trumped-up charge of pilfering. Both she and Kirk had been shocked at what appeared to them to be suggestions from Aitken that they might bring in girls to the health farm, possibly from Swindon. She and Kirk also mentioned a mysterious Prince Mohammed.

TRAWLING FOR INFORMATION

Leigh next approached the many chauffeurs who had worked for rich Saudis. Most would say nothing. One produced a phone number. This took Leigh to Valerie Scott, Aitken's former secretary, who knew a lot about Said Ayas and about Prince Mohammed whose great wealth was alleged to come from commissions on trade and arms deals with Saudi Arabia. In 1979, according to Leigh and his colleagues in their book *The Liar*, Aitken became managing director of Al Bilad (The Nation), the prince's London company.

Valerie Scott recalled that Aitken bought the prince a plane. (Leigh's assistant, Quentin McDermott, went to Florida and filmed the man who sold the plane to Aitken.)

Scott, who was running a nursery when Leigh went to see her, declined to appear on screen. Her words were spoken by an actress.

THE RIGHT BALANCE

David Leigh was afraid the film's criticism of Saudi royal behaviour would appear racist and anti-Arab. To show Arabs made similar criticisms, he brought in Said Aburish, a Palestinian author. Aburish alleged that Saudi royals levied commissions on all Western export deals. A Saudi exile, Mohammed al-Masri, accused a Saudi prince of making high charges for the services of a monopoly he controlled in Saudi Arabia.

Independent Television Commission rules then required Leigh to give Aitken a chance to answer the allegations against him. For programme-makers, this can present the difficulty that their target will spend a long time 'considering' whether to appear in an interview, and will use this time to challenge the programme's contents and threaten legal action.

Aitken, however, ignored Leigh's letter. This, under ITC rules, allowed *World in Action* to approach and film Aitken, provided it was in a public place. McDermott approached Aitken outside his home. He asked him why he wouldn't talk about his Saudi business interests.

Aitken now complained he was being denied a right of reply. His solicitor offered that Aitken would appear, provided it was for seven minutes, live and at the end of the programme. *World in Action* turned him down.

'THE CANCER OF BENT JOURNALISM'

On April 9, 1995, *The Guardian* published the story which *World in Action* was about to broadcast. Aitken flew back from Switzerland and held a press conference. He had issued a writ for defamation, he said. He would fight to cut out the cancer of bent and twisted journalism with the sword of truth.

World in Action had only three hours to amend its programme to include passages from the press conference. In the nick of time, *Jonathan of Arabia* was ready for broadcasting.

The furore over the story attracted the attention of a freelance journalist called Ed Chapelle and sent him in search of Paula Strudwick (an ex-prostitute specializing in whippings) who had told him she had an affair with Aitken in 1981. A secretly videotaped meeting between Strudwick and Aitken's former *Evening Standard* colleague Dr Christine Pickard, who first introduced her to Aitken,

Figure 11.1
Jonathan of Arabia: Cabinet minister Aitken (right) with his daughter Victoria on April 10, 1995, the day *The Guardian* and *World in Action* published their allegations about him and his Middle Eastern friends (picture Martin Argles, *The Guardian*)

helped persuade the *Sunday Mirror* that Strudwick's story was true. The *Sunday Mirror* also recorded telephone calls between Aitken and Strudwick, and bought her story for £30,000. Aitken resigned from the government before the *Sunday Mirror* published.

Meanwhile, Said Ayas approached Valerie Scott, a likely witness in the forthcoming libel case, and offered her a job.

With the case looming, Leigh, McDermott and three *Guardian* reporters sought more witnesses and sifted through a flood of phone calls and letters. McDermott went to New Zealand to interview a former air hostess whom Aitken and a panel of Arabs had hired for Prince Mohammed's plane.

The Guardian faced a possible bill for £2 million for legal costs if it lost the libel case. Its new editor, Alan Rusbridger, offered Aitken a deal which wouldn't give him an apology but would restore his reputation. Aitken didn't accept it.

SEARCHING THE RECORDS

The libel case turned on Aitken's Paris weekend and who paid for it. Aitken's senior counsel, Charles Gray, thought his story about the weekend so complex he couldn't have made it up. Aitken stood by it through hours of cross-examination. But he had no evidence to prove his wife Lolicia was ever in Paris to pay his hotel bill.

Three days before the case opened, Owen Bowcott of *The Guardian* set out for Switzerland on a final inquiry. The hotel in Villars where Lolicia stayed during her husband's Paris weekend had gone bust. But did it have records which would throw light on her stay?

Three times rebuffed in seeking to see the records, Bowcott persevered. He finally got permission, from an accountant in Lausanne. Among the papers and printouts in a basement storeroom, he found one confirming Lolicia Aitken's arrival at the hotel on Friday September 17 and also showing that she got a single occupancy discount for the Saturday night (after she had taken her daughter Victoria to a nearby school). He found what she had for breakfast, and that she paid by American Express.

This rather ordinary information was important for two reasons. First, Aitken had phoned the hotel at 10.15 am on the Sunday, which, if Lolicia took the call, would have made it hard for her to get to Paris in time to pay his bill. But Aitken said the call was taken by Lolicia's mother. However, the mother could hardly have stayed Saturday night with Lolicia if the room had only a single occupant.

More important, Lolicia Aitken had failed to disclose the American Express card in the discovery of documents before the court case. (Each side in a libel action can ask the other to let it see relevant documents.)

On June 3, *The Guardian*'s solicitor, Geraldine Proudler, wrote to Aitken's solicitor, asking for the American Express records. When they had not turned up by June 9, she sent American Express a subpoena. It took Amex three more days to find the crucial entries. One was for hiring a car from 'Ankunftshalle', Switzerland. Ankunftshalle means arrival hall. It looked as if the car was hired at an airport. Did Lolicia Aitken travel to and from Switzerland by air and if so when?

Swissair couldn't help, so Geraldine Proudler subpoenaed British Airways. BA replied on June 11 that it would take 33 man-days to search the records. Proudler volunteered two juniors to do the search under the eye of a BA investigator, Wendy Harris. But Harris would not be available for five days and the trial was moving on.

On Monday June 16 the searchers scrolling through rolls of BA records on microfiche at Heathrow struck lucky. Lolicia Aitken had flown from Geneva to London on Monday September 20. She had never broken her journey in Paris at all.

Meanwhile a solicitor for Granada had instigated a search of car-hire records. They told a similar story. Mrs Aitken had hired a car in her maiden name and left it in Geneva at 6.25 pm on Sunday September 19, when, according to Aitken, she was in Paris.

So Aitken had lost. In January 1999 he was the first former Cabinet minister ever to stand in the dock at the Old Bailey. He pleaded Guilty to a charge of perjury and a charge of attempting to pervert the course of justice.

KIM PHILBY, MASTERSPY

A logical thread of questions led *Sunday Times* journalists from their first information about the mysterious Kim Philby to their discoveries about the people he betrayed.

Newspapers knew little about Philby when he suddenly disappeared from Beirut where he was working as a journalist in 1963 and reappeared in Moscow. After Philby's disappearance, Edward Heath, then Lord Privy Seal, admitted what Harold Macmillan had found no evidence for eight years earlier: that Philby, an apparently minor diplomat at the time, had warned the more famous diplomats-cum-spies Burgess and Maclean to flee. Their journey to Moscow created a sensation in 1951.

Harold Evans writes in *Good Times, Bad Times* (Weidenfeld and Nicolson, 1983) that he set off the *Sunday Times* investigation into Philby as a result of a remark by Jeremy Isaacs, at the time head of current affairs at Thames TV. Isaacs was intrigued that Burgess, Maclean and Philby were all at Cambridge in the 1930s. Evans remarked to Bruce Page, whom he had just appointed to head the Insight team, that they would perhaps find the man who recruited the three spies.

Philby, *The Sunday Times* quickly decided, had been in the Secret Intelligence Service, MI6, not the diplomatic service. (He had, in fact, joined MI6 in 1941.) So what was wrong with MI6 that it let Burgess and Maclean escape and harboured Philby whose heart was in Moscow? What did he do for MI6? At the inquiry's peak, 18 reporters were working on it.

In *Who's Who*, Bruce Page found MI6 contemporaries of Philby whose entries included the words 'attached Foreign Office' or whose careers had missing years. The attached FOs weren't in the Foreign Office list of diplomats. So they were probably MI6.

Cyril Connolly, *Sunday Times* reviewer, contributed the names of sources for his book about Burgess and Maclean. Reporters also read books about wartime intelligence.

They tried telephoning people with connections to Philby; but the question 'What did Philby do?' tended to end the interview. If the reporters showed they had information, bits of it were denied other bits corroborated. It helped if an informant suggested other informants. Hugh Trevor-Roper, another *Sunday Times* reviewer, who had been in intelligence in the war, recalled talking with Philby about historical analysis. Suddenly Philby had declared with great force his admiration for a book by Karl Marx.

THE TRAIL FROM CAMBRIDGE

The investigation really got going when David Leitch started exploring the Cambridge of the 1930s when Philby was there. He discovered that Philby had been a vehement Marxist (but had been discreet enough never to commit his views to print).

In 1933 Philby motorcycled to Vienna where his landlord's daughter Litzi Friedman swept him into the political struggle. Socialists were striving to defend themselves against the heavily armed Right-wing Heimwehr (home guard). Bruce Page learned that Philby had smuggled Socialists and Communists out of the city. Philby helped the escape of a group of workers, borrowing three old suits for them from Eric Gedye of *The Times*. He also married Litzi Friedman, to get her out of the country.

The defeat of democratic Socialism in Vienna probably convinced Philby that he should back Communism. But, when he returned to Britain, he joined a pro-German organization and reported the Spanish Civil War from Franco's side for *The Times*. Franco personally pinned the Red Cross of Military Merit to Philby's chest, after he survived a shell from a Russian gun which killed three journalist companions and nearly brought his career as a Russian spy to an early end.

Page guessed this Spanish expedition was a pretence behind which Philby hid his work for the Russians. A former Foreign Office man pointed out to *The Sunday Times* that Heath's 1963 statement had included a sentence about Philby working for the Soviet authorities before 1946.

115

CLASH WITH THE GOVERNMENT

So what was he up to all those years, before and after 1946? Leitch and Page went to ask Lord Chalfont, a minister at the Foreign Office who had been defence correspondent at *The Times*. Chalfont told them to stop their inquiries or they would be helping the enemy.

The possibility that the *Sunday Times* inquiries would do damage concerned Denis Hamilton, editor-in-chief of Times Newspapers. Harold Evans agreed to let the Foreign Office see a draft of the *Sunday Times* article before publication, to make sure no one was put at risk. He met more opposition from Sir Denis Greenhill, the Foreign Office's link man with MI6. Greenhill feared that Philby would appear glamorous like Ian Fleming's fictional MI6 agent James Bond. He also feared what the Americans would think of British intelligence in the light of the Philby story.

Evans didn't know why the Foreign Office was so twitchy. The *Sunday Times* inquiries were only beginning to throw light on Philby's doings. They showed he had gone to Istanbul, Turkey, in 1947 as 'temporary' first secretary, a cover for intelligence work. While in Turkey, he was active on the Soviet border. Later, in Beirut, he displayed a photograph of Ararat, the Soviet–Turkish border mountain, taken from the Soviet side.

By chance, the author and former *Guardian* journalist Michael Frayn recommended to Harold Evans a Foreign Office man called John Sackur who wanted to be a journalist. Sackur said he had written a report on the damage Philby had done but would not say what it was. What he did say was that Philby was a 'copper-bottomed bastard'.

(Phillip Knightley argues in the *British Journalism Review* [Vol. 9, No. 2, 1998] that Sackur was planted on *The Sunday Times* by a ginger group of MI5 and MI6 men who wanted its Philby inquiry to go ahead. They were seeking to unmask Soviet agents whom they believed to have been in the intelligence services: the story of Philby's treachery would be a sign their suspicions were justified. Sackur admitted to Frank Giles, Harold Evans's deputy, that he was a 'friend', that is, a member of MI6. Knightley some time later met Sackur at a party given by the ginger group.)

THE AMERICAN ANGLE

It was Knightley who, in the *Sunday Times* investigation, first showed clearly why Philby was important. With the help of the publisher of a tame but reportedly censored book called *British Agent*, Knightley traced Leslie Nicholson who had written it under a pseudonym. Nicholson was ill and down on his luck. Knightley took him out to lunch and eventually asked him about Philby. Over his second brandy, Nicholson said that Philby had been made head of a new anti-Soviet section of the Secret Intelligence Service in 1944.

So Philby in 1944 was MI6's anti-Soviet intelligence chief. In 1947 he was mysteriously employed on the Soviet–Turkish frontier. From 1950 he was temporary first secretary in Washington. What was he up to there?

Knightley went to see Lyman B. Kirkpatrick who had been assistant director of the American intelligence agency, the CIA, in the 1950s. Kirkpatrick said that Philby had been the British liaison officer with the CIA and FBI.

THE ALBANIAN DISASTER

What mischief might this liaison work have made possible? Kirkpatrick suggested a look at Albania. A similar hint came from a former MI6 man in Rome who told David Leitch that Philby 'lost us a lot of lives in Eastern Europe'. Thirdly, the MP Tom Driberg told *The Sunday Times* that the Foreign Office had asked for a paragraph about Albania to be deleted from a book he wrote. The paragraph was based on a remark by Burgess about an Albanian 'débâcle'.

Pursuing these hints, the *Sunday Times* reporters learned of a secret, American-sponsored effort starting in 1950 to unseat the Communist regime in the unsettled country of Albania on the Adriatic Sea. Yugoslavia had broken with the Soviet Union, and so Albania was cut off from the Soviet bloc. But the Albanian exiles sent back to overthrow Communism in their homeland were doomed, for Kim Philby learned all about them as liaison officer in Washington.

The Sunday Times discovered the details by seeking survivors. Some escaped from Albania into Greece and were admitted to Britain where the Ministry of Labour found them work with the Forestry Commission. A researcher for Insight discovered them. They said that a small army, including the royal guard of the former Albanian king, had been trained and inflitrated into Albania. At least 300 died. 'They always knew we were coming,' said one of the forestry workers.

In London, David Leitch looked up Philby in the phone book and came across his eldest son who agreed to go to Moscow to take his father's picture. (When *The Sunday Times* published its article, the photograph dominated the front page.)

In the meanwhile, official hostility to the *Sunday Times* project continued. There were insinuations that Bruce Page, in charge of the inquiry, was a Communist. Greenhill suggested that *The Sunday Times* should drop Philby and write about the KGB instead. An envelope arrived at the *Sunday Times* office containing a drawing of the KGB's structure.

A D-notice also arrived warning *The Sunday Times* against publishing anything about British intelligence. Harold Evans decided to ignore it. He sought the views of Lord Radcliffe who had chaired several security inquiries. Radcliffe offered no objection to publication.

The Observer forced the issue. It published an account by Eleanor, Philby's wife, of life with a spy. *The Sunday Times* immediately published its first Philby piece.

This produced more information. A former diplomat, John Reed, asked if *The Sunday Times* was going to mention an incident in Istanbul. Knightley went to see Reed in deepest Shropshire.

Reed said that in 1945 he had interviewed Volkov, the Soviet secret service chief in Istanbul, who wanted to defect. Volkov spoke of Soviet agents in London, including an officer in counter-intelligence. Reed reported this to London. For 20 days, nothing happened. Then Philby, head of the anti-Soviet section of MI6, arrived in Istanbul on an apparently fruitless journey. He was evasive about the reasons why he had not come sooner. Reed's efforts to get back in touch with Volkov failed. Philby left.

Later, said Reed, a Russian aircraft made an unscheduled and irregular landing at Istanbul's airport. A car raced out to the plane and a heavily bandaged figure was lifted into it.

Summing up the Philby investigation, Harold Evans points out that the earlier uproar in the press about Britain's defecting diplomats, Burgess and Maclean, was ineffective. It took *The Sunday Times*'s lengthy inquiry into Philby to make the government sit up.

The Philby inquiry was costly for *The Sunday Times*. It found a new way of easing the burden by producing a successful book. *Philby, the Spy who Betrayed a Generation*, by Bruce Page, David Leitch and Phillip Knightley, was published by Deutsch in 1968. It is based on interviews with a wide range of people who knew Philby, Burgess and Maclean.

12 Looking into companies

If you are investigating companies, you will find a good deal of information on public record. It is a question of reading through files, registers, accounts, reports and prospectuses.

THE FREELANCE DIRECTOR-GENERAL

A friend with BBC connections got in touch with Chris Blackhurst, then of *The Independent on Sunday*, in February 1993. He said that Sir John Birt, the BBC's director-general, was paid as a freelance. Blackhurst didn't believe it.

However, he went to Companies House, across the road from *The Independent*'s offices at that time. Filed there, he found John Birt Productions Ltd. Under the Companies Acts a small company of this kind does not need to file full accounts or even turnover, only assets. But Birt's accountant had filed full details down to clothes and travel expenses. The income shown was a little higher than Birt's BBC salary: it included something from his wife's art gallery.

Chris Blackhurst went to see an accountant, Barrie Kernon, who confirmed that the only advantage in being paid as a freelance lay in tax. Expense allowances for the self-employed are more generous and they may pay less national insurance.

Blackhurst rang the BBC. He told me:

'They tried to fob me off. They were very pompous. "It's ridiculous," they said. "We can't possibly talk to you. It's a private matter."

'On Saturday February 27 at 8 am I knocked on the door of Birt's house in Wandsworth. He came to the door in a track suit. "Can I ask you some questions?" I said.

' "I don't talk to journalists at my house," he replied, and began to close the door.

' "You are the director-general of the BBC. What do you mean, you don't talk to journalists?"

' "I'm not going to slam this door. I'm going to close it." '

Chris Blackhurst decided it was not appropriate to put his foot in the door and went to his office:

'We were completely stuck. We had a story full of ifs and coulds. I phoned Marmaduke Hussey, chairman of the BBC. Lady Susan Hussey answered. Her husband was on a business trip to the Far East.

'I phoned Birt at home. His American wife Jane answered. He was unavailable. I should ring the BBC press office.

'I did. They said that if I stopped phoning John Birt and Marmaduke Hussey at home they would prepare a statement. The fax machine started whirring. It said that freelance arrangements were commonplace in the TV world. John Birt had worked as a freelance for 20 years.

'I took the ifs and coulds out of my article.'

What this shows, says Blackhurst, is that you can never beat having a document. It makes denials more difficult. Without the Companies House file, he would have got nothing. 'The staff at Companies House are always very helpful. It's amazing how much information there is there,' says Blackhurst.

WHAT IS ON PUBLIC RECORD?

Information on companies is on public record at Companies House, in share registers, in prospectuses, in annual reports and accounts. This is helpful in investigating and checking the truth of allegations about them.

Businesses may be run by a sole trader or a partnership or (like C&A) by an unlimited liability company. None of these three is obliged to publish information.

The Companies Act, however, obliges other companies to publish information. Such companies come in several varieties. There are public companies, some with shares quoted on the Stock Exchange, others not. Public companies must call themselves public limited company or plc. There are private companies owned entirely by those involved in running them. There are companies limited by guarantee, which are non-profitmaking.

Companies (apart from unlimited liability companies) must file with Companies House:

1 Their articles of association.
2 Their memorandum of association. This includes the name and business of the company.
3 The address of the registered office and the name of the company secretary.
4 The names and home addresses of directors. (*The Sunday Times* looked up the address of the head of MI6, registered at Companies House as director of a private company.)
5 The names of other companies of which the directors are directors. (It is not unusual for them to be directors of several companies. You can discover further companies related to the one you are interested in by going to the registered office and seeing what else is registered there.)
6 A list of mortgages, hire-purchase arrangements and debentures (a form of loan), and notices when these are paid off. (Shares or property or even a commercial agreement may be mortgaged in exchange for loans.)
7 The company's share structure.
8 Notices allotting shares.
9 A list of shareholders.

10 The directors' annual report and accounts. (Small companies do not need to file a profit-and-loss account or a directors' report.)
11 Any purchase by a company of its own shares.
12 Resolutions passed at company meetings. (By skilful wording of a resolution, Robert Maxwell once hung on to the management of a key company he no longer owned.)
13 Appointments and resignations of auditors.
14 A prospectus if the company is making an offer to the public of shares or debentures.

The object of these requirements is to stop people taking money out of the company. Disclosure is the counterpart of limited liability which limits to their shareholding the responsibility of shareholders for the company's debts. Disclosure seeks to ensure that the company's creditors can see that money due to them is not being spirited away. Directors must not treat the company's money as their own.

It is possible to go to a branch of Companies House and, for a fee of £3.50, see what is filed there about a particular company. (A list of shareholders costs an additional £3.50.) Except in Belfast, the files will be in microfiche form and you will be able to use a microfiche reader. It is worth checking whether there is a reader in a local library, in case you want to look again at your microfiches.

To phone up and get a file by fax costs £7.50. There is also an on-line service to which media offices can subscribe.

Companies House addresses are: 64 Chichester Street, Belfast (tel.: 01232-234488); Birmingham Central Library (0121-233-9047); Crown Way, Cardiff (0292-038-0801); 37 Castle Terrace, Edinburgh (0131-535-5800); 7 West George Street, Glasgow (0141-221-5513); 25 Queen Street, Leeds (0113-233-8338); 55 City Road, London EC1 (0207-253-9393); 75 Mosley Street, Manchester (0161-236-7500).

Companies House also lists people disqualified to be directors. After a tip-off, Jonathan Smith of *The News*, Portsmouth, checked the list and found that a particular businessman was indeed a disqualified director. The entry gave the date of a court hearing. Smith was able to go to the court for more information and then look up a report of the case in the local newspaper. These inquiries contributed to a story about the disappearance of £100,000 collected for charities. Police investigated the allegations and made arrests.

THE DIRECTORS' REPORT AND ACCOUNTS

Much mystery surrounds the accounts of public companies especially among journalists, who normally claim to be bad at figures even if they are dab hands at expense sheets.

The general concept of recording what a public company has earned and spent is not especially difficult. It is also clear that a company may have problems if its accounts show a loss or that it has greatly increased its borrowing of money. A successful business can go bust if the cost of its borrowings is too high.

Companies publish a directors' report, a profit-and-loss account, a cashflow statement, and a balance sheet showing what they own and how it is financed.

Small companies need not produce a profit-and-loss account or a directors' report. (Paul Lashmar for *World in Action* in 1992 studied a property organization which was split into small companies, thus cutting down the information it needed to file.)

Medium-sized companies can produce a profit-and-loss account with fewer details than are normally required from bigger companies.

Essential Finance for Journalists (edited by Brian O'Kane: Oak Tree Press, 1993) cautions journalists against jumping to conclusions from a quick reading of company accounts. There could be several reasons for a drop in sales, from new competition to a strike. The company could be wealthier than its balance sheet implies because it has not revalued its property for years, and it is still using machines which have been written out of the accounts.

The significance of a company's profit figure depends on how it was calculated. Christopher Hird points out in *Challenging the Figures* (Pluto Press, 1983) that the company profit is only part of the company's surplus. The surplus, at its simplest, is the difference between what the company has earned and what it has spent over the year.

Even the surplus is not a hard and fast figure. It can be decreased by writing off debts which may yet be collected. It can be increased by revaluing stocks or property or by including income from some source other than trading and investment. It can also be increased by treating expenditure on research and development as a capital asset to be paid for over years, rather than a cost to be immediately deducted. This approach lost popularity after it helped push Rolls-Royce into failure in 1972.

A company's surplus is used to cover rents, interest payments, depreciation (to finance repairs and replacements) and directors' salaries. What is left is profit. The profit figure is, to some degree, a matter for negotiation between the management, its accountants and the company auditors. A small private company is likely to 'plough money back into the business' rather than show a large profit and pay extra tax. A public company, fearing or expecting takeover, will try to show a bigger profit, thus enhancing its share price. This will either discourage the takeover or make sure the price of the takeover is high.

A company ought to prepare its accounts on similar principles year by year; so the best way to judge how it is doing is to compare this year's accounts with previous years. *Essential Finance for Journalists* recommends keeping a lookout for inconsistencies and omissions.

Once again, the real story could be in a footnote which the auditors perhaps insisted should be included. Also worth a glance are what are called exceptional and extraordinary items. (Exceptional items are allowable against tax; extraordinary items are not.) Whether exceptional or extraordinary, these are costs, such as big redundancy payments or losses on foreign exchange, which are not expected to recur next year.

With the accounts will be the auditors' report. This normally says the accounts are true and fair and comply with the Companies Acts. It may complain that the auditors did not see all the data. If it says that the accounts have been prepared 'on a going-concern basis', this is a hint that the firm may not be going much longer.

The annual report from the directors should include:

1 Details of the company's business and turnover during the year, including a geographical breakdown.
2 Details of any issue of shares or purchase by the company of its own shares.

3 A list of holders of over 5 per cent of the company's shares.
4 Details of directors' pay, shares and share options, loans to directors, and contracts in which directors have an interest. The details of directors' pay will be the salary of the chairman and the highest-paid director (if other than the chairman), and a guide to other salaries.
5 Average number of UK employees and their salaries.
6 Changes in fixed assets including revaluation of property.
7 Political and charitable donations.

HOW AN EXCEPTIONAL ITEM BECAME AN INTANGIBLE ASSET

A search, as an example for this book, of the Companies House files of Chelsea Football Club Ltd and its parent company, Chelsea Village plc, showed that transfer fees used to be included in the profit-and-loss account as exceptional items. Then the players became 'intangible fixed assets' and the transfer fees were written off over the period of their contracts.

One director joined the Chelsea Village board and left again within months. A former director lent £2.5 million to the club which he was able to convert into seven million shares in Chelsea Village. Altogether he held about a quarter of the company, partly as a nominee for other people. The following year, however, he had disappeared from the major shareholders listed in the directors' report. However, the files also mentioned that he had become owner of the company holding the freehold of the Stamford Bridge ground.

The accounts showed millions being spent on developing Stamford Bridge. Revaluations of property were contributing around £2 million to the accounts each year. Chelsea raised money by offering £75 million worth of debentures in 1997, at a fixed interest rate.

This gives an idea of some of the information which Companies House files contain.

WHERE TO FIND REPORTS AND ACCOUNTS

Companies commonly send their reports and accounts to local as well as national media. They can also probably be consulted at the company or in a library.

Essential Finance for Journalists recommends careful reading of the statement on cashflow. Growing companies may lack cash to cover their growing expenses and may have spent more than they can afford on new equipment.

The accounts of a group's member or subsidiary companies require particularly careful reading. This is because groups of companies have obvious leeway in deciding, for example, what to charge for central services, loans or rent, and what price one subsidiary should charge another for goods and services.

FILED AT THE STOCK EXCHANGE

For public quoted companies, the Stock Exchange has additional rules requiring disclosure of information. The aim of these is to ensure that all shareholders are treated fairly and alike, and there is no favouritism or insider dealing (that is, buying or selling shares because of information not available to all shareholders).

A public quoted company must tell the Stock Exchange if someone buys or sells more than 3 per cent of its shares. Thereafter, it must report purchases of more than 1 per cent by the same buyer. It must also tell the exchange if a director deals in shares. These notifications can be viewed by the public.

A company must tell the Exchange of any development or forthcoming announcement which may substantially affect the price of its shares and securities. If a development is merely impending, the company can tell its advisers, trade unions, government departments and its counterparts in any transaction. They must not deal in the company's shares until the development is made public.

Tom Bower in his book *Tiny Rowland* writes about a Rowland manoeuvre to hide the development of a mine in Zimbabwe. It was owned by a South African subsidiary of Rowland's company, Lonrho, and Rowland wanted to buy out minority shareholders in the subsidiary without their realizing the mine's value.

Companies must keep an up-to-date register of shareholders and shareholdings. They must keep a register of share dealings by directors and their families. Quoted companies must keep a register of shareholders, or groups of shareholders, with more than 5 per cent of the shares. They can also keep a register of the real owners of shares held in the name of nominees. Companies have the power to ask who these real owners are. But they cannot do this if the nominees are foreign.

These company registers are open to inspection.

PROSPECTUSES

When a company sells shares or debentures to the public, it must issue a prospectus, telling people in detail what they are buying. It must file the prospectus with Companies House. A journalist looking into a company's activities could find useful information by looking up the prospectus.

A company must also issue a prospectus to shareholders and to the Stock Exchange if it makes a rights issue: that is, raises money by asking its shareholders to buy more shares.

Prospectuses or similar documents are also issued by companies seeking to take over other companies, and possibly by the companies they seek to take over.

Reporters of an inquiring turn of mind read such documents carefully, especially the footnotes, which could contain information the companies must mention but would rather not.

All this does not necessarily bring everything out into the open. Robert Maxwell shrouded his main family trusts in secrecy by basing them in Liechtenstein. At a crucial moment in his business manoeuvres, it was unclear who could speak for the trusts. Actually, *he* could. He was also a master at exploiting the difference between private and public companies, even when they had the same directors and held their stock-in-trade in the same place.

GO AND SEE

Take opportunities to visit companies and listen to what is said. Even the best journalists need a hint from an insider if they are to produce an unusual story. Visits also produce documents worth reading and filing.

Libraries hold reference books about companies, such as the *Stock Exchange Yearbook*, the *Directory of Directors*, *Kelly's Business Directory*, *Macmillan's Unquoted Companies*, *Britain's Top Privately Owned Companies* (published by Jordans) and Dun and Bradstreet's *Who Owns Whom*.

Dun and Bradstreet publishes regional business registers; for example, there are two covering Scotland.

Some companies have associated charities. What is on file about these at the Charity Commission (57 Haymarket, London SW1Y 4QX; tel. 0207-210-4433/4641 press; fax 0207-210-4403) could include new facts about solicitors and other people connected with the company.

Teachers at a university may have studied companies in your area. National companies are studied by leading stockbrokers. If you are inquiring into a company in detail, it is worth talking to competitors, customers and suppliers. They see the company from different angles.

For foreign companies, your public library may have registers from a publisher called Kompass. American companies file information with the Securities and Exchange Commission in Washington. The New York Stock Exchange also requires a lot of information. Some interesting companies file with the Vancouver Stock Exchange. You can find information about overseas stock exchanges in the *Stock Exchange Yearbook*.

OTHER BUSINESS ORGANIZATIONS

Not all organizations active in business are companies or partnerships. Some building societies and insurers are in mutual ownership, that is, owned in effect by their customers. There are co-operative societies, women's institutes and playgroups. Housing associations are important providers of homes.

You can inspect accounts of these organizations, preferably by appointment, at the Registry of Friendly Societies, 30 Kingsway, London WC2B 6ES (tel. 0207-663-5360 press; fax 0207-663-5062). Some organizations are registered as companies and their details are on file at Companies House.

Information (including names of committee members) and accounts of 2,200 housing associations can also be inspected at the Housing Corporation, 149 Tottenham Court Road, London W1P 0BN (tel. 0207-393-2096/95/93 press; fax 0207-393-2099).

Trade unions produce accounts for the Certification Office for Trade Unions and Employers Associations, 180 Borough High Street, London SE1 1LW (tel. 0207-210-3719; fax 0207-210-3612).

You may also get accounts of these organizations simply by approaching them.

Michael Gillard of *The Express* says there is no great trick about researching businessmen and companies other than doing basic things well and being assiduous. Find out who someone is, track their history back through the companies they've been connected with. Find out about their past business associates.

Read balance sheets and apply common sense. Go and find experts and put to them what troubles you. Ask: 'Am I right to say this doesn't make sense?' If you study something closely, if you endeavour to understand what it's all about and it still doesn't make sense, this isn't because you don't understand it. It's because it doesn't make sense.

THE POLLY PECK AFFAIR

The Observer decided in 1983 to look into Polly Peck, the company of the Turkish Cypriot businessman Asil Nadir. Its accounts didn't make sense. They claimed huge profits from oranges and lemons.

Michael Gillard, then of *The Observer*, says:

'Melvyn Marckus and I discussed it and I went out to Northern Cyprus and Turkey, visited the sites of factories and spoke to people there. We came to the conclusion the Polly Peck accounts were a figment of the imagination. It was all done with mirrors.

'What we couldn't work out was what was happening. We knew one reason that it didn't make sense was the devaluation of the Turkish lire which was depreciating fast. Nadir took no account of that in the accounts.'

Nadir used to say: 'I am buying at an advantageous rate. I pay locally at an advantageous rate. My costs are far less than in Morocco while all the money I get is in hard currency.'

But every time he brought money into his cardboard box factory in Cyprus, it was losing value. What didn't become clear till much later was that losses were being buried. The balance sheet showed assets of £900 million but they were worth nothing like that after currency loss.

Nadir sued Gillard and *The Observer*. Eventually they won when the court ruled in 1985 that Nadir must give access to the books. They argued that the article had to be seen as a whole. Nadir couldn't pick and choose from the article and so limit what he needed to disclose under the rules of discovery.

Despite the exposé, says Michael Gillard, 'people still believed his stories. It's living proof of the impotence of the press. Five years later Polly Peck collapsed.'

COMPANIES AND THE GOVERNMENT

Many firms see relations with public authorities as vital to their interests. The theory is that contracts are won in fair competition; but, to be on the safe side, it's nice to have an inside track to the winning post. Peter Marsh of the *Financial Times* discovered this was why businessmen contributed to the Conservative Party. They welcomed the chance to pick up information from ministers at Conservative industrial councils. Similarly it is hard not to suspect that more than a common enthusiasm for Europe lay behind the love-in between business leaders and the new Labour government in 1997.

Some British businesses have sought an inside track by hiring MPs as consultants and hoping they will provide information and contacts and ask useful questions. Paul Halloran's and Mark Hollingsworth's book *A Bit on the Side* (Simon and Schuster, 1994) showed that most Conservative members of the 1992–97 parliament had paid links with outside organizations.

THE SALE THAT NEVER TOOK PLACE

Former England coach Terry Venables signed an agreement in 1996 to buy 51 per cent of Portsmouth football club for £1. He became chairman of the club which he aimed to develop. But he never received the shares he was acquiring from club owner Martin Gregory. They had been pledged to Barclays Bank when it made a loan in 1995 to Gregory's garage firm.

This and related football investigations were on the front page of *The News*, Portsmouth, three days running in October 1998.

Venables' deal to buy 51 per cent was already public knowledge. A chance phone conversation gave Jonathan Smith of *The News* the story of Venables' failure to acquire the shares. Smith then needed to verify it.

Records at Companies House showed that, in January 1995, assets belonging to Blue Star Garages, a Gregory company, were mortgaged to Barclays as security against loans. The Portsmouth FC record at Companies House showed that between 1995 and 1997 the bulk of the club's shares were registered to Barclays as nominee.

To see the club's share register, Smith had to take lawyers with him to point out that it should be open for public scrutiny under the Companies Acts. The register disclosed that in May 1995, shares owned by Blue Star Garages and another Gregory company were transferred to Barclays. The public records thus confirmed what Smith had been told, that the shares promised to Terry Venables were in Barclays' hands.

The News also managed to see a solicitor's letter asking Barclays for the shares promised to Venables, and a letter from Barclays refusing to release them unless £1.5 million was paid. The shares were finally released by Barclays, but not transferred to Venables, in October 1997.

Terry Venables resigned as chairman of Portsmouth in January 1998.

Jonathan Smith says *The News* incurred substantial legal fees in the course of this investigation. Apart from the visit to the club, lawyers checked his reports every time he rewrote them.

NOT ON PUBLIC RECORD

Panorama's programme on Robert Maxwell (see page 141) and Chris Blackhurst's story of the freelance director-general (see page 120) both stemmed from material on public record. Some company stories, however, depend on confidential documents. Journalists have got hold of them from an inside source.

For journalists, documents not on public record present added complications. The company concerned can ask for them back or seek an injunction, under the law of confidentiality, to stop their use. It is important, therefore, not to betray the fact that you have them. (The House of Lords in 1984 obliged *The Guardian* to surrender a photostat of a Ministry of Defence document which it had received. As a result, a clerk called Sarah Tisdall was identified as sender of the photostat and was jailed for six months under the Official Secrets Act.)

Investigative journalist Paul Halloran points out: 'Companies don't want people prying into what they see as commercially sensitive. They would like to know where we get documents.' It is vital to keep such sources secret.

David Leppard of Insight at *The Sunday Times* says that one of his best stories concerned the Gulf War. Newspapers were publishing little apart from the war at the time, so an Insight investigation needed to relate to it. But what should it investigate? He fastened on information that British companies had been secretly selling arms-making machinery to Iraq. He rang Matrix Churchill, the Iraqi-owned company whose top managers were about to be prosecuted in a case that was to prove highly embarrassing for the then government.

Leppard recalls:

'The managing director answered the phone. I just rang at the right time. He said: "I have a document you need to see."

'We were able to reveal that Alan Clark [then Minister for Trade] had given Matrix a nod and a wink [about how best to secure approval for machine tool exports]. We had a memo about him meeting three businessmen [from the Machine Tool Technologies Association].'

(Clark said the *Sunday Times* article, which accused him of helping break an arms embargo, was defamatory. But, in the Matrix Churchill trial in November 1992, he admitted that, by implication, he had given the machine-tool manufacturers the message that, in seeking permission from the Department of Trade to export their machine tools, they should say nothing about possible military uses. With this admission, the trial collapsed.)

CORRUPT CONTRACTING

A man went to the *News of the World* with a story of corruption in a contracting company. An experienced reporter, Trevor Kempson, spent weeks getting every dot, comma and detail of the allegations and securing enough proof to stand them up.

Then he and an assistant editor, Bob Satchwell, went to confront a company employee. After waiting for hours for the man to return home, they knocked at his door at night on a Bank Holiday Monday. When he came to the door, the air was filled with the sound of children screaming. 'Do you think we can come in to talk about contracts?' they said.

They were smartly dressed and carried briefcases. The man didn't ask who they were. He didn't berate them for calling at so obviously inappropriate a time. He simply assumed, Satchwell believes, that they were going to offer him another dodgy deal.

After interviewing the employee, they went to the company office to see the managing director who they knew would have been warned of their likely arrival. The MD asked them to return in the afternoon. When they did so, he took them into the boardroom which their contact had told them contained a hidden tape-recorder. Bob Satchwell also had a recorder running. It picked up waves from the hidden recorder, and they agreed to switch both recorders off. But reporter Trevor Kempson also had a recorder with him and it continued to run. 'The managing director told us things by denying them,' says Satchwell, 'including things we hadn't put to him.'

They had been alerted that there was a tape-recorder in the boardroom and they had found it. This lent weight to the allegations that had been made. Satchwell comments: 'Small bits add up. If you can get one thing proved, it lends credibility to others. You don't always need every comma of proof. Sometimes isolated facts or incidents make the whole thing add up.'

INVESTIGATING SUCCESS

Peter Marsh of the *Financial Times* points out that investigative reporting is not necessarily a matter of inquiring into mistakes and wrongdoing. He has come to specialize in how companies operate and what affects their success. How did a small engineering works acquire the competitive edge to win a contract from a major motor manufacturer when other factories could have done the job?

He has talked not just to managers but to competitors and suppliers. He uncovered a web of industrial tourism: managers visiting other factories to see how things are done. This sort of inquiry is harder than it sounds. Managers tend to be reluctant to discuss the factors in their commercial success in case they give clues to competitors.

Marsh says that half-hour interviews with people who have what you want are no good for an investigative story. It's towards the end of three hours, when you have got to know each other, that the interesting facts emerge.

DOES THIS TIP HAVE AN ICEBERG?

John Stonborough is a poacher turned gamekeeper. For ten years he was an investigative journalist for radio and television, doing exposés every week for *4 What It's Worth*, a Channel 4 consumer programme of the time.

Then, in 1988, he did a story about cars stalling while using Formula Shell petrol. Shell's reaction, he says, was all wrong. First, it underreacted, denying there was a problem. Then it overreacted. When he and a researcher went to visit, they were greeted by senior Shell people who all said there was nothing wrong, though the size of the welcoming party gave a different message. He could, they said, choose who he wanted to interview. 'I picked a boffin who did an awful interview, falling into every single trap I set for him,' says Stonborough.

There was, in fact, a problem, particularly with some Vauxhall cars, but it was not a big problem. Shell should have admitted its mistake and made a gesture to the motorists affected.

John Stonborough now advises companies a   ations on
how to handle investigative journalists. He adv   orld-Wide
Fund for Nature when it discovered that a helico   supplied in
good faith for wildlife protection had been used as a gunship.

He advises clients to own up if they are plainly in the wrong. But he
pursues journalists if he thinks they have broken television rules. 'The
great danger,' he says, 'is this slightly spurious moral high ground of
the public's right to know.'

In his opinion, there are not all that many major issues to investigate.
So minor issues may get the major treatment.

Stonborough is particularly critical of 'tip of the iceberg' stories. In
these, the reporter finds three or four people with a complaint and
argues that they are just the tip of a hidden iceberg of other
complainants. The reporter then finds an expert who supports the
complaints. But other experts may think differently and there may be
no hidden iceberg of justified complaints at all.

13 The Maxwell investigations

Robert Maxwell loomed giant-sized both as a man and as a subject for investigative journalism. Everything about Maxwell, one-time owner of the *Daily Mirror*, was intimidatingly large.

The BBC risked £90 million in broadcasting *The Max Factor*, the Panorama investigation of him, two months before his death in 1991. This makes the £2 million risked by *The Guardian* in the Aitken libel case seem like pocket money.

Maxwell's campaign against Tom Bower, who published an unauthorized biography in 1988, was surreal in its intensity and absurdity. Maxwell was obsessed with the idea that Bower's computer was a mine of information about him. He inspired a hare-brained scheme for parking a scanner at the bottom of Bower's garden to read what the computer contained. An ex-policeman working for the Control Risks agency went on reconnaissance. On his advice, Peter Jay, then Maxwell's chief of staff, declared the scanner scheme not practical.

MAXWELL AND *THE SUNDAY TIMES*

One of the first journalists to cross Maxwell was Godfrey Hodgson, who in 1969 was editor of *The Sunday Times*' Insight investigations team and set out to profile him as a man in the news.

Hodgson recalls: 'Most people found him a charming rascal. He was never charming to me. He simply saw me as a danger. He had just about made it into the long grass when here was this chap asking rude questions. He couldn't believe it wasn't part of some conspiracy.'

Maxwell at the time was struggling with the consequences of a scheme that went wrong – his publishing of encyclopaedias.

Maxwell came originally from Ruthenia, the eastern tip of prewar Czechoslovakia, and won the Military Cross in the wartime British Army. After the war, he spotted a business opportunity in scientists' appetite for information. He seized it first with the Springer company in Germany and then through his own publisher of scientific journals, Pergamon Press.

In 1965, he bought the encyclopaedia publisher George Newnes and, in 1967, its competitor, Caxton. In partnership with the British Printing Corporation, he formed the International Learning Systems Corporation (ILSC) to sell encyclopaedias worldwide. He announced it would make at least £500,000 profit a year. However, Tom Bower shows in his book *Maxwell the Outsider* that it was hard to check how many encyclopaedias were sold and to ensure that customers would pay.

Godfrey Hodgson says that Maxwell set about building the market value of his Pergamon company through schemes which involved inflating its profits. One scheme was to revalue the 'flat stock' of encyclopaedias (copies not yet bound into volumes). He raised the value of this stock by £500,000 and claimed this as profit under what he said was 'the Spanish prospecting company rule'. He had discovered a 19th century court decision which he said allowed him to revalue work in progress.

His aim in inflating the profits was to sell Pergamon to an American conglomerate at a handsome price. He had three such conglomerates in mind and chose a computer company, Leasco. To justify the price which Leasco was to pay for the shares, Maxwell needed to show that Pergamon, including the encyclopaedia company ILSC, had made a profit of £2 million in 1968. He did. But, apart from the revalued encyclopaedia pages, the profits included £800,000 of sales to a private Maxwell family company called MSI Inc. Since MSI had the right to sell back what it had bought, these were not necessarily sales at all.

Tom Bower shows in *Maxwell the Outsider* that Maxwell also later dressed up ILSC's figures with £356,000 from Pergamon.

At first, Maxwell got his manoeuvres past the accountants, the auditors, the bankers and Leasco. Then an auditor, John Briggs, told Maxwell that he had been visited by Colin Simpson of *The Sunday Times* Insight team who questioned the auditing.

Godfrey Hodgson, Insight's editor, recalls:

'Over a very few days, several people I knew in publishing told me: "This man Maxwell can't be making anywhere near the profits he says he's making." I called Maxwell and said I would like to talk to him.

'Within hours Maxwell had telephoned Harold Evans [then editor of the Sunday Times*], Denis Hamilton [editor-in-chief] and Roy Thomson [the owner], making wild charges against me.'*

This convinced Hodgson that Maxwell was up to something. Hodgson says he told Maxwell that he hadn't known whether he (Maxwell) had done anything wrong till he saw him in action. Then he knew.

Hodgson continues: 'He claimed to have sold encyclopaedias he hadn't sold. He was on the point of selling Pergamon for a great deal of money on the basis of accounts he knew to be fraudulent.'

Godfrey Hodgson alerted Rodney Leach of Rothschilds who were acting for Leasco. He was once in Leach's office when 'suddenly Maxwell was to be heard shouting and swearing in the corridor. I had to hide while Maxwell told lies about me.'

During an acrimonious meeting at *The Sunday Times*, Godfrey Hodgson told Maxwell he reminded him of a restaurant chef whose mayonnaise he once sent back as possibly out of a Heinz bottle. The chef rushed out of the kitchen shouting: 'Who's the bastard who's calling me a liar?'

'As soon as Maxwell started shouting at me,' says Hodgson, 'I knew he was a fraud.'

Despite the acrimony, Maxwell agreed to co-operate in a profile. Harold Evans told him he could see but not change the text. Godfrey Hodgson went with Bruce Page to interview Maxwell about the encyclopaedia sales and ILSC's accounts. 'The meeting began,' recalls

Hodgson, 'with Maxwell offering me a copy of the Great Soviet Encyclopaedia and ended with him threatening to hang me from the dome of St Paul's.'

Sunday Times journalists spoke to 30 people or more, including many executives of ILSC and other Maxwell companies. They spoke to old business associates of Maxwell. When Leasco withdrew its bid for Pergamon, Insight was well placed to tell the stories of ILSC and the Maxwell family company MSI which helped boost Pergamon's profits. Maxwell called the article 'highly inaccurate and grossly defamatory'.

In October 1969, *The Sunday Times* printed the first part of its Maxwell profile, and helped to ensure Maxwell was voted out of the chairmanship of Pergamon. Having read it earlier in advance (as Harold Evans had promised) Maxwell delivered a writ to try to stop it appearing. He trawled from country to country, trying to discover who had told *The Sunday Times* what.

On October 5, the article appeared. Two more parts of the profile followed, plus an article headed 'The structure of a Pergamon profit'.

This was Maxwell's low point. His comeback was about to begin.

Leasco, in advance of offering to buy Pergamon shares, had foolishly acquired millions of them in the market at inflated prices. But who sold them to Leasco? Robert Jones of *The Times* checked Pergamon's share register. Nearly 200,000 had been sold by Bahamas Trustee and Executor, a Maxwell family trust. Maxwell in fact picked up £1 million through sales of Pergamon shares from family trusts.

Moreover, some deft Maxwell footwork prevented the Maxwell-free Pergamon from taking control of Pergamon Press Incorporated, its American sales arm. As a result, Pergamon was starved of cash, and began to look to Maxwell to save it.

He confirmed his recovery by getting *The Sunday Times* to give him, in exchange for withdrawing his writs, a chance to reply to what it had published. Hodgson and Page were both away on holiday at the time.

In his reply, Maxwell sought to justify himself by reinterpreting, in his favour, an accountants' report. A favourite Maxwell tactic was to re-establish himself by attacking his attackers, seizing on any small favourable point in a report or court judgement and forgetting the rest.

Hodgson recalls: 'He used to say "So and so was forced to apologize on bended knees." So and so had done no such thing.'

Department of Trade inspectors pronounced Maxwell 'not in our opinion a person who can be relied on to exercise proper stewardship of a publicly quoted company'.

Nevertheless in 1974 Maxwell got Pergamon back, buying Leasco's shares for only 12p each. He went on to acquire the British Printing Corporation (which he eventually renamed the Maxwell Communications Corporation) in 1981 and the *Daily Mirror* in 1984.

MAXWELL AND *PANORAMA*

In 1988 Maxwell again overreached himself by buying the Macmillan publishing company of New York. Maxwell Communications Corporation shares went down in value from 395p to 165p. A recession made it hard to get the price back up again. He had debt to repay. He tried to sell assets in order to reduce the debt but there were too few buyers. The price of the shares became even more important when he began mortgaging his shareholding to obtain loans.

In the autumn of 1990, Mark Killick of *Panorama* ran across what was going on. He got a press handout from MCC, announcing the sale for £60 million of an Italian subsidiary, and phoned a man mentioned on the handout. There wasn't any sale, he was told. The supposed buyers also said they weren't buying.

A search at Companies House disclosed that Maxwell had mortgaged shares on September 5 in exchange for a loan from the Bank of Nova Scotia.

Even more important, *Panorama* discovered a series of announcements sent to the Stock Exchange. The first on August 23 said that Maxwell, his family and associated companies had acquired 15,650,000 shares in Maxwell Communications. Another on September 5 showed the acquisition was not taking place immediately but on or before November 30 at 185p per share. A third announcement in December said the shares had been the subject of a 'put option' by a third party. A put option gives the buyer of shares a right to sell them at a given price by a given date.

MAXWELL
COMMUNICATIONS

PRESS INFORMATION

Contact: Mr Kevin Maxwell (MCC) - 071 822 2000
Mr John Moulton (Schroder Venture Advisers) 0732 450025

Release Date: IMMEDIATE 7 October 1990

Maxwell Communication Corporation plc, (MCC) announces the sale to funds
advised by Schroder Venture Advisers of 100% of MCC Italia - consisting of
Panini Children's Album Collection Publishers - for a consideration of
approximately £60 million. Completion is planned during November 1990.

Ends

0033d

World Communications
Maxwell Communications Corporation plc PO Box 285 33 Holborn London EC1N 2NE
Telephone 071 822 3646 Telex 896715 Facsimile 071 353 0360
Registered Office: Headington Hill Hall Oxford OX3 0BW. Registered in England 298465

Figure 13.1
A sale that never was. In the autumn of 1990 publishing tycoon Robert Maxwell was eager to
reduce debts by selling assets. He was also keen to show he was doing so. Maxwell
Communications Corporation issued this press release on October 7 announcing a sale raising £60
million. However, when Mark Killick of *Panorama* enquired, he was told no sale had taken place

What all this means is that someone bought the 15,650,000 shares in August subject to an agreement that they could be sold to Maxwell on November 30 at 185p each. The December announcement shows they were in fact sold to Maxwell on that date.

This was important not just because Maxwell was gambling that the share price would indeed reach 185p by November 30. MCC was to publish its accounts in October, and Stock Exchange rules did not allow Maxwell to deal in MCC shares in the two previous months. However, he had in effect encouraged someone to buy shares just before the close period and hold them till November. Buying 15 million shares would lift, or at least support, the price of all Maxwell Communications shares.

On the face of it, Maxwell was engaged in a share support operation. An employee admitted to Killick, in confidence, that this was so.

Mark Killick of *Panorama* stresses that all this was discovered from public paperwork available from Maxwell Communications, Companies House and the Stock Exchange. 'Nothing I've been involved with has depended on secret sources,' he says.

Killick had another string to his bow. *Panorama* knew that a Spot the Ball competition in the then Maxwell-owned *Daily Mirror* had been rigged to save the £1 million prize. Maxwell had met the then editor and a competitions manager and decided there would be no ball in the picture. *Panorama* had confirmation from the former editor; but Maxwell could have challenged what the former editor said. Killick needed confirmation from the competitions manager, who still worked for the Mirror group. Killick persuaded him that the programme deserved to be aired. Killick had to take the risk that the competitions manager would tell Maxwell what was afoot.

Panorama had its programme checked by the leading accountants KPMG. The final decision to transmit lay with John Birt, then the BBC's deputy director-general. 'We knew we were putting the White City site on the line,' says Mark Killick. 'We had to get it right.' Maxwell was suing for £90 million, the value of the BBC's White City building.

There was a staff meeting. Birt said to the QC called in to give advice: 'Will we win? Do you believe the story's right?'

'I think it's a true bill,' said the QC. Birt gave the go-ahead.

Daily Mail, Thursday, February 4, 1999   DailMail

COVER-

T HE INDICTMENT is simple but appalling. Seven years after the £2 billion frauds of the Maxwell empire were exposed, no one has been convicted of any crime.

Worse, only a tiny handful among the army of so-called members of the Establishment — highly paid bankers, lawyers, accountants and managers — have been reprimanded.

Not one of the hundreds of well-educated, supposedly moral professionals, given huge sums by Robert Maxwell to oil his path through Britain's laws so he could perpetuate his frauds, has noticeably suffered for their mistakes — or for their failure to report his crimes.

In a succession of recklessly self-destructive decisions, Britain's law enforcement and regulatory agencies — and now the Labour Government — have enshrined a culture of inactivity which avoids shaming those responsible for tolerating Maxwell's dishonesty.

context, the belated admission by Coopers & Lybrand, auditors of empire, that it 'lost what

It is seven years since the £2billion Maxwell frauds were exposed and still no one – repeat no one – has been found guilty of any wrongdoing.

Figure 13.2
Aftermath of the Maxwell affair: investigative journalist Tom Bower's devastating indictment of Robert Maxwell's associates, in the *Daily Mail* seven years later

MAXWELL VERSUS BOWER

Investigative journalists can expect their subjects to hit back. But, apart from those who turn to violence, none hit back harder than Robert Maxwell. 'Don't rely on a sniper if a howitzer might perform the task,' is how Tom Bower sums it up.

He tells the story in the introduction to the paperback edition of his unauthorized biography, *Maxwell the Outsider* (Mandarin, 1991), and in that to the sequel, *Maxwell the Final Verdict* (HarperCollins, 1995).

February 4, 1999

GUILTY: The men and women who failed to blow the whistle

ACCUSED: Agriculture Minister Lord Donoughue. Nominated Labour life peer by Neil Kinnock.
ROLE: Hired on £436 a year to manage Ma film London and Bishopgate Inve which move pounds o shares private know scan Max self £9 H b o

ACCUSED: Minister Helen Liddell. summ

ACC

Tom Bower, who says Maxwell had qualities he admired, was for many years a BBC producer. He met Maxwell in 1973 when, with Max Hastings (later editor of the *Evening Standard*), he was making a television documentary about him. The night before transmission, the soundtrack was stolen; but the film editor had another copy.

In retrospect, *Maxwell the Outsider*, a book for which Tom Bower interviewed over 350 people, reads like an objective, unslanted account of Maxwell's career. But Maxwell didn't see it that way. His first writ, of 12, arrived three weeks before publication in 1988. Even before that he had sent a writ concerning an article in *The Listener*. Another writ preceded serialization in *The Sunday Times*. A judge refused an injunction to stop publication.

Peter Jay, Maxwell's office manager, asked Bower's interviewees to submit reports. Those quoted were asked if they were correctly quoted.

Bower's book was intended to launch a new publishing company, Aurum Press. The script of the book eluded raiders who broke into the publisher's office. When it became known that *The Sunday Times* would serialize the book, Maxwell telephoned the editor, Andrew Neil, and the owner, Rupert Murdoch. When Andrew Lloyd Webber's Really Useful Group took over Aurum, Maxwell rang Lloyd Webber in his box at the New York premiere of *Phantom of the Opera*. Lloyd Webber refused to stop the book.

Maxwell newspapers attacked Tom Bower. He in turn sued Maxwell.

Bower's book became a bestseller but Maxwell turned his artillery on those who sold it. He wrote to every bookshop in Britain, and served writs on any who kept the book on display. In the end, only Hatchards in Piccadilly, London, continued to sell it.

Maxwell succeeded three times in stopping the book appearing in paperback, once by buying the publisher (whose managing director revoked the paperback-publishing rights just before the takeover). Maxwell prevented publication in New York and Germany. He sued after publication in France but lost and had to pay Tom Bower 10,000 francs in damages.

At this point, Maxwell became obsessed with the possible contents of Bower's computer. He asked a barrister, Stephen Nathan, whether Bower could be prosecuted under the Data Protection Act or whether the police might seize the computer on instructions from the Director of Public Prosecutions. For this, said Nathan, he would have to convince the DPP that the computer had dangerous contents.

Maxwell instructed another lawyer, Lord Mishcon, to seek seizure of the computer under what is called an Anton Piller order. A Piller order would allow the computer to be seized but could be made only for the investigation of fraud or dishonesty. Since there was no suggestion that Bower was fraudulent or dishonest, a Piller order could not be obtained. Hence the abortive scheme to read the computer with a scanner at the bottom of the garden.

Tom Bower writes that the campaign against his book helped discourage most newspapers from exposing Maxwell in his lifetime. He blames not only the libel laws for Maxwell's long survival but also the reluctance of newspaper chiefs to challenge a powerbroker, the failure of the Department of Trade inspectors to accuse Maxwell of crime in his fraud on Leasco, and the failure of police officers, civil servants and accountants to discover what he was doing.

14 Social and consumer affairs

POVERTY IN LEEDS

John was a skilled man, a carpenter and cabinet-maker, and he had the tools to prove it – hammers of different weights, chisels of different breadths, screwdrivers of different sizes, wood saws, jigsaws, fret saws, hacksaws, keyhole saws. But he was unemployed. By the time he was thirty-four, he had been made redundant five times.

When he was a single man, this didn't worry him too much. He simply took his box of tools and found himself bits and bobs of work from friends and neighbours. But now he had a wife and two small children to support so he signed on for State benefit.

He and his family found it hard to get by on the money they were given but, when he tried to do a little carpentry work on the side to make ends meet, he was warned very sternly that, if he was caught doing that, he would lose benefit.

So slowly, over a period of time, to cover the costs of keeping his family, he sold each and every one of his tools.

(from Nick Davies: *Dark Heart*, Chatto & Windus, 1997)

Nick Davies, an investigative journalist at *The Guardian*, has done for the poor of 1990s Leeds what Guy de Maupassant, in his short stories, did for the middle-class of 19th century France. In language even terser than Maupassant's Davies describes in *Dark Heart* their lives of quiet desperation, their doomed struggles against lack of money. Often in Davies's true stories as in Maupassant's fiction, some weakness or chance misfortune turns struggle into disaster.

Davies says that, in deciding where to pursue his inquiry into hidden, socially excluded Britain, he sought the advice of the chairman of Leeds' social services committee with whom he had worked before. The chairman suggested he should not study a notoriously poor estate. Taking his advice, Davies went to Hyde Park, near the university and the city centre, which had a mixed society of old and young, black and white, poor and middle class, council and private homes. He arrived shortly before a dramatic, headline-hitting moment. A war in Hyde Park's council housing, between delinquent youths on the one hand and the police and some tenants on the other, culminated in a riot in which the local pub was burned down.

Davies spent weeks knocking on doors round Hyde Park talking to everyone he could, sometimes picking up leads from the local press.

There was a woman who had been happy in her Hyde Park council house but was beaten up and forced out for trying to stand up to the young thieves who made life there a misery. He spoke to the misery-makers, lads at a loose end, full of hatred for students and the police. Yet they had ambitions, to be a fireman, to go parachuting, to have a steady job and family life.

Then there was the disabled woman who got into debt and lost her lifeline, her telephone connection; and there was the desperate mother who made a pathetic attempt at arson and was sent to prison. And there was Ruth, the desperate, violent transvestite.

Nick Davies makes the point that all this was happening not in some notorious blackspot but in an area which, during the 1980s, had lost the foundation of its economy: jobs in factories that had shut down or scaled down on Kirkstall Road. Hyde Park, he believes, had public problems and private misery because so many of its people were unemployed and poor.

CONSUMER COMPLAINTS: *WATCHDOG*

Investigative reporters often have difficulty deciding whether they have a story which justifies inquiry. Journalists looking into consumer complaints can be inundated with such stories. The BBC's popular

Watchdog series receives so many complaints from dissatisfied shoppers and holidaymakers that people able to complain by e-mail have an advantage. E-mail commands immediate attention while the complaint is still fresh.

The number of complaints makes it possible for *Watchdog* to detect patterns: the loss of Peugeot spare wheels, a leaking Hyundai sunroof, reissue of used mobile phones. In early 1999 it discovered that some French right-hand-drive cars were being sold with windscreen wipers designed for left-hand-drive. As a result, water on the screen was swept towards the driver and a top right section of the screen was not swept.

With so much help from the public, *Watchdog* has been early in spotting serious problems including the effects of mobile phones on the brain and the side-effects of the anti-malaria drug Lariam. It got 67,000 Fiesta cars withdrawn for the fitting of new brakes.

My daughter-in-law's wedding dress didn't fit when delivered to her, though the sample dress she had tried on in the shop had fitted well. That was annoying but it didn't make a publishable story. By coincidence, *Watchdog* found a pattern of similar complaints. In November 1998 it featured several ill-fitting wedding and bridesmaids' dresses from a particular firm.

It is important for journalists handling complaints to file them, preferably on computer, so it is possible to see whether a new complaint chimes in with others received earlier. *Watchdog* writes down complaints received by phone so they can be added to the database.

The obvious problem is that of deciding whether a complaint is justified. I recall while at *The Northern Echo* handling a reader's letter criticizing hover-mowers. The mower manufacturer rejected the criticism. I couldn't get to see the offending mower in action, so there was no way of resolving the dispute.

Complaints about holidays can present special problems, since they are spent many miles away and people vary in what they like and what they regard as acceptable. But video-cameras have made life easier. *Watchdog* finds that people who complain about their holidays bring back the evidence on videotape.

The programme takes up individual complaints only after whoever is complaining has put the complaint to whoever supplied the goods or service and failed to get satisfaction. This means that the basic facts of the dispute are set out in letters and replies. *Watchdog* likes to have 90 per cent of the facts straight before approaching the supplier again. After *Watchdog* worked on a complaint about a car alarm, it discovered that the car had been in a crash which could have affected the alarm system. The item was pulled out of the programme.

The Broadcasting Standards Commission once criticized *Watchdog* for making a general criticism of Parcelforce on the basis of five valid complaints from customers.

'You have to be spot on,' says Helen O'Rahilly, *Watchdog*'s editor. 'Otherwise they come down on you like a ton of bricks. If we were doing things badly, we would be sued out of existence.'

ARE YOU PAYING TOO MUCH?

One focus for consumer journalism is the level of prices for products and services.

Journalists have begun to question whether supermarkets give such good value as we have come to assume. Welsh farmers have complained that, while they were receiving poor prices for animals, meat in the supermarkets was little cheaper than before. A television programme compared supermarket prices in a Lincolnshire town with those charged by local butchers and greengrocers.

If you attempt this sort of comparison, it is important to make sure you are comparing like with like. The potatoes must be of the same variety, the meat the same cut. If you show a trader's goods to be more expensive than other traders' but he can show them to be of higher quality, he is likely to complain about your reporting. If you decide to compare prices for a basket of goods, you will have to work hard to ensure the goods are comparable. Choose goods for the basket which are commonly bought locally, rather than simply those you would buy yourself: journalists are probably more fashion conscious in their purchases than other people. The fact that you can buy some French delicacy cheaper in France does not mean you are being overcharged in Britain.

Manufacturers (except those making medicines sold without prescription) cannot legally instruct shops to charge a particular price for their goods. However, a series of investigations by Paul Nuki, consumer affairs editor of *The Sunday Times*, has shown that many of them keep trying.

Electrical and electronic goods are commonly more expensive in Britain than on the Continent or in the United States. Nuki says, however, that it is difficult to demonstrate that manufacturers are instructing retailers to charge higher prices in Britain than elsewhere. It is difficult to find such instructions set out in documents or memos.

Nuki's typical approach is to set up a company to sell, say, cars or electrical goods, invite manufacturers to supply the new company and record on tape and film his meetings with manufacturers' representatives. Typically, the representatives are only too happy to have new sales outlets until he slips into the conversation the question: 'Do you mind if, at our own expense, we sell your goods at a discount?'

At that point, those who are dictating prices to retailers do not want to supply the new company any more. It is illegal to withhold supplies from a discounter; but an electronic firm's manager explained to Nuki how it can be done. 'People would say "I am sorry we are out of stock" or "There have been delays from the factory" or "We don't have any more available of this particular product."'

For the car prices inquiry, Nuki and fellow *Sunday Times* journalist Andrew Alderson invented a consortium called Motor Mart which aimed to sell cars from big sites including one near the French entrance to the Channel Tunnel. The cars would include right-hand-drive models for Britain.

Nuki and Alderson made presentations in Paris and Amsterdam to executives from six car manufacturers, claiming the new sites would revolutionize the sale of cars in Europe and improve purchasers' opportunities to compare different makes. Executives from one company spent an hour asking questions about the Motor Mart venture; so it had to be well thought out.

The *Sunday Times* men recorded the conversations. One executive they spoke to said: 'Because the level of price in Britain is very, very much higher than the market in Europe, I think all the manufacturers are very satisfied with this situation.'

An executive from another company admitted: 'If you install a right-hand-drive centre in France selling cars, it would be a problem.'

(According to *The Guardian*, stockbrokers Salomons have calculated that inflated British prices generate a quarter or more of the profits of two major European car manufacturers.)

Nuki says that, for this sort of inquiry, it isn't worth going to the length of registering a company. Such a company would be obviously new if anyone checked. Instead, he invents a company based in some uncheckable part of the world such as the Cayman Islands. He gets well-printed business cards and headed notepaper. He and his colleagues meet people in expensive hotels and take along a glamorous secretary or assistant. 'It's a lot of front basically,' he says.

> During another inquiry, representatives of electrical-goods makers were invited to the Hyde Park Hotel in London and asked to supply what might have been the customer of their dreams: Electraserve, a well-financed retail chain intending to open 15 stores in its first year and offer first-class service to customers. The representative of only one firm out of eight was enthusiastic about Electraserve selling goods at below the standard British prices. These can be double the prices for the same goods in the United States.

Nuki has also investigated the poor living conditions and low pay, only 17p to 20p an hour, of workers at a Romanian firm making furniture for sale in Britain and elsewhere. This inquiry followed from a *Sunday Times* article on low wages. 'Why don't you look at IKEA [the Swedish furniture company]?' asked a reader. It took *The Sunday Times* two weeks to establish what suppliers IKEA bought furniture from and to select Romania as the focus for this inquiry.

Spurred by Christian Aid and other agencies, customers in British shops are growing concerned about the working conditions of the people who make the goods on display. There is a dilemma here. If shops cease to buy such goods, people now earning a poor living might have no living at all.

Reporters for *The Sunday Times* have worked or lived in several British homes for elderly people, exposing the discourtesies, unkindnesses and humiliations of life there. Nuki says he got stringers throughout the country to read social-services reports on homes so he could select those for study.

He also asked *Sunday Times* readers to phone, e-mail or write to him in confidence with their complaints or observations about such homes. Over 700 responded, one of the biggest responses he has ever had. The letters were very moving. Unfortunately they didn't amount to proof that residents of homes had been abused. Hard evidence of abuse is rare.

Paul Nuki says he enjoys consumer investigations because this is one of the few areas where a journalist can be of direct service to readers.

INQUIRING INTO THE HEALTH SERVICE: CHILD CASUALTIES IN BRISTOL

Dr Phil Hammond, now presenter of BBC TV's *Trust Me (I'm a Doctor)* but then a casualty doctor in Taunton, met Ian Hislop, editor of *Private Eye*, at a BBC Radio Christmas party in 1991. He asked Hislop if he would like a medical correspondent. Hammond was attending the party because he and a fellow doctor, Tony Gardner, had formed a medical comedy double act, *Struck off and Die*, which broadcast two radio series.

Hammond began writing for *Private Eye* under a pseudonym and collecting information about Bristol West, constituency of the then Health Secretary, William Waldegrave. In particular, he and Gardner were interested in the working conditions of junior doctors.

In his book *Trust Me (I'm a Doctor)* written with Michael Mosley (Metro, 1999), Hammond relates that he then learned about a high casualty rate in the children's heart surgery unit of the United Bristol Healthcare Trust. (He discovered later that doctors in South Wales had been referring difficult cases to London, rather than to Bristol. 'Difficult cases die in Bristol,' one doctor had said.)

Local journalists failed to crack the story but, as a doctor, Phil Hammond was able to do so. He wrote his first *Private Eye* report on it in May 1992, pointing out that for a certain operation carried out successfully on 160 babies in Liverpool, Bristol had a 20 to 30 per cent mortality rate. In a second article he made a similar point about Bristol's performance of a second operation.

Bristol children's heart surgery unit had been built up from scratch by James Wisheart, a heart surgeon who joined Bristol Royal Infirmary in 1974. Wisheart was hardworking and well respected. He repeatedly asked the hospital trust to appoint a specialist children's heart surgeon to do the operations, but none was appointed so Wisheart continued operating. An anaesthetist, Steve Bolsin, however, was concerned about the mortality rate and began his own audit of the unit's results.

Hammond's articles brought letters to Private Eye *from patients and parents but no reaction from the Health Service.*

Three years later in 1995, BBC West broadcast the story, as a result of a fortuitous meeting between a journalist and a hospital doctor. Only in 1996 when Channel 4's *Dispatches* series covered the story did it achieve widespread national attention. The General Medical Council, the medical profession's disciplinary body, began inquiries after members read an article by Lord Rees-Mogg, in *The Times*.

The trouble, Phil Hammond explains, was that no one had defined competence in relation to the work of surgeons. Wisheart's defenders argue that he took on the sickest patients, which was bound to affect his success rate. They also argue he was fall guy for a wider problem.

The situation took the General Medical Council weeks to sort out. In the end the GMC's Professional Conduct Committee found that Wisheart and a second surgeon had continued to perform certain operations without establishing why they were getting poor results.

The Bristol hospital trust appointed the specialist child surgeon it failed to appoint earlier. His results have been posted on the Internet. They are better than the national average.

However, the two Bristol surgeons investigated by the GMC are not the only ones who have been carrying out operations which they would more wisely have left to someone else somewhere else. Phil Hammond argues that, in general, operations are best done by surgeons who do that particular operation repeatedly.

Media coverage of the shortcomings of the Health Service usually focuses on lack of money. Hammond shows there is much more to it. He paints an alarming picture of a sketchy medical training which left him needing to learn from better-trained nurses when he began to practise. He mentions an operation for rectal cancer pioneered by a Basingstoke surgeon, Bill Heald. Heald's operations showed cancer recurrence rates only a seventh of the national average. He has revolutionized rectal cancer care, outside the United Kingdom. Inside the UK, writes Hammond, Heald's work has been largely ignored. Hammond blames the British tradition of producing general surgeons, rather than specialists whose training includes new skills like the Heald operation.

Hammond's book gives inquiring journalists a good deal to inquire into: Do babies with cleft palates get them properly repaired? What results are shown by the treatment of cancers in your area? What chances do local people have of escaping death or serious disablement after a stroke?

Hammond thinks it has become easier for journalists to inquire into failings in the Health Service since the Labour government ended competition between hospitals for work. But Hammond himself drew a blank when he inquired about a liver transplant unit said to have poorer results than the other six such units. Only the Health Secretary, he was told, could release the information.

A snag for inquiring journalists remains the plea of patient confidentiality – 'I can't answer your question. It's a confidential matter.' Journalists need the help of patients and their relatives if they are to find things out. And newspapers tend to want health stories to be human stories, not just research findings.

BUILDERS THEY WISHED THEY'D NEVER HAD

The *Evening Mail*, Birmingham, decided to find out about the builders whom Birmingham people wished they'd never had. Martin McGlown spent two months compiling information so that the

Figure 14.1

A reader service: the *Evening Mail*, Birmingham, campaigning against shoddy and swindling builders, investigates a roofer who started jobs, then left them unfinished

campaign could run for the first week or two. After that, readers were likely to ring in with further stories. (Unfortunately, few of these calls provided usable stories.)

He looked at cuttings in the library and spoke to trading standards officers who told him about victims of shoddy workmanship. He got in touch with a long list of local organizations.

The next task was to persuade enough people to let their stories be used with their names and pictures. 'Getting people to stand up and be counted is difficult,' says McGlown.

He started the campaign on the *Mail*'s front page in April, 1998, with stories from people who had building workers coming to the door and offering to lower the kerb to make a run-in for a car. The workers claimed to be from the council and quoted low prices. After agreeing to have work done, the householders discovered that the work was not just poor, it had been done without the council's permission and they would have to pay again for it to be done properly.

In the next two days the *Mail* turned its attention to a roofer. Two householders complained of leaking roofs and others had other complaints. Martin McGlown had difficulty catching up with the man. 'Anywhere he was supposed to be, he wasn't. I camped outside his shop for three days.'

The roofer was prosecuted for trading standards offences and magistrates ordered him to pay about £2,000 in fines and costs.

A month after the roofer stories, the *Mail* aired the complaints of householders on a new estate. Then came complaints against another builder, an emergency service and another roofer who disappeared leaving roofs part-finished. McGlown traced the disappearing roofer with the help of readers' phone calls.

The campaign had its critics. 'You get criticized for slagging off rogue builders,' says Martin McGlown, 'because it doesn't help good ones.' So in July the *Mail* featured an initiative by members of the Federation of Master Builders who finished free of charge a pensioner's patio left incomplete after a dispute over payment for materials.

NEW HOUSES

Defects in new houses are a common subject for investigative reporting. On BBC2 in February 1999, Paul Kenyon with the help of two experts working under cover found houses under construction which did not meet National House-Building Council guidelines. They had rubbish in the wall cavities; or they had doorways inaccurately positioned, so that the lintels carrying the brickwork above them had insufficient support.

The programme *Raising the Roof* accused the NHBC, which inspects and certifies new houses, of failing to ensure they are fault-free. A more fundamental question worth exploring is whether the traditional British method of house construction is conducive to producing fault-free homes meeting the buyers' wishes. Houses are built on open sites in all weathers, making accurate work difficult. Many buyers have little opportunity to influence the design and layout of their new homes.

CAN CHIMNEYS STAND THE HEAT?

A company called Dunbrik marketed a concrete liner for chimney flues which by 1998 had captured 75 per cent of the national market. Competitors cried foul, however, and the magazine *Building Homes* went to the expense of asking a commercial laboratory to test the liners for heat-resistance. In the test, liners began to crack at 550 degrees Celsius, half the 1,100 degrees recommended in both British Standards and the building regulations. The testers also decided that the liners were not made of the special heatproof concrete which the regulations recommended. Dunbrik has vigorously defended its liners but has replaced the product under investigation.

Why the heat-resistance matters is that temperatures above 1,000 degrees Celsius can be reached if soot builds up in a chimney and it catches fire. David Birkbeck, editor of *Building Homes*, points out that chimney fires are rare nowadays. Most buyers of new homes probably use the chimneys as outlets from gas fires. But some want a real, soot-creating fire. Others install wood stoves with narrow flues which could be blocked by fragments of a failed chimney liner.

In February 1999 the government announced it was conducting a safety review of flue liners. If this confirms *Building Homes'* findings, insurers could be asked to replace tens of thousands of chimneys. At the least, the safety review should clear up confusion about what standards a chimney flue should reach and what it should be made of.

So a magazine interested in inquiries to help the public has drawn attention to a problem which official bodies did not successfully clear up. Its editor, David Birkbeck, is keen that, when *Building Homes* receives complaints from the public, these are investigated, not simply published with a lengthy reply from the firm concerned.

WHO TO CONSULT?

A wide variety of officials and committees handle consumer complaints. There may also be local consumer groups as well as such national bodies as the National Consumer Council (tel. 0207-730-3469), Scottish Consumer Council (0141-226-5261) and Consumers Association (0207-830-6373/6064/6062 press).

Trading standards officers deal with dangerous goods in the shops and enforce the Trades Description Act which ensures that people get what they think they are buying

Community health councils and district health authorities handle complaints about health services (if these are not resolved by conciliation). There is also a Health Services Ombudsman (0207-217-4077). Serious medical complaints go to professional bodies – the General Medical Council (0207-580-7642), the General Dental Council (0207-486-2171), the General Optical Council (0207-580-3898).

Gas, water, electricity and railways have regional users committees (see phone book).

The Office of Telecommunications (0207-634-8751 press) handles complaints about telephones.

There are ombudsmen for banking (0207-404-9944), building societies (0207-931-0044), estate agents (01722-333306), funerals (0207-430-1112), housing association tenants (0207-437-1422), insurance (0207-928-7600), investment (0207-796-3065), legal services

(0161-236-9532), pensions (0207-834-9144). The pensions ombudsman deals only with occupational pensions, and complainants must approach the Occupational Pensions Advisory Service (0207-233-8080) first. Personal pensions are dealt with by the Personal Investment Authority ombudsman (0207-216-0016).

The government is planning to introduce one ombudsman scheme for all financial services.

15 Crime

TAKE CARE!

In inquiring into some kinds of criminal activity, investigative reporters tread on dangerous ground. People involved with drugs, for example, can be violent and unpredictable. The more daring the exploit – *The Cook Report*, for instance, once bought plutonium from the Russian mafia – the greater the care required. It is important that reporters think through what they are doing and try to anticipate possible trouble.

They need close liaison with the news editor or TV producer responsible for their work. They need to know as much as possible about the situation they are entering and about the attitudes and sensitivities of the people in that situation. They need to be calming and reassuring towards these people and not provoke them. Donal McIntyre, who investigated drug dealing in Nottingham for *World in Action*, says: 'You have to be methodical, vigilant, never take too many risks.'

Crime reporters seek information about crimes mainly from contacts in the police and, if possible, witnesses. A few reporters, however, inquire into the people committing crimes, sometimes with the help of contacts in the underworld, sometimes at the suggestion of police officers keen for the leads which the reporters may pick up.

THE SOLUTION OF A MURDER

Wensley Clarkson's investigation into the murder of fellow journalist Jonathan Moyle was unusual. Clarkson, formerly of the *Sunday Mirror*, tells how he solved the murder in *The Valkyrie Operation* (Blake, 1998).

Moyle, formerly in the Royal Air Force, had become editor of *Defence Helicopter World*. He went to an air show in Chile to seek proof that a Chilean manufacturer, Carlos Cardoen, had plans for converting civilian helicopters into gunships for Iraq. Moyle was found dead strung up in a cupboard in his hotel room.

The Chilean police said Moyle's death was suicide even though there was a needle-mark in his shin. The British authorities, for whom Moyle seems to have provided intelligence on the side, were happy to go along with the suicide verdict. A Chilean judge and Moyle's father weren't. Moyle had been in good spirits and looking forward to his forthcoming wedding.

Clarkson spoke to everyone he could find who knew Moyle and had been with him in Chile. He eventually found a man to whom Cardoen's public relations officer had confessed that he had commissioned the murder. Moyle, it seemed, had kept asking questions about the helicopters. The PR man (who had since died) was afraid someone would in the end talk to Moyle.

The irony of the story is that the Iraqis invaded Kuwait before the helicopter conversion kits were ready.

The Valkyrie Operation shows a journalist achieving what official agencies failed to achieve: the probable explanation of a murder.

Emily O'Reilly in her book *Veronica Guerin* (Vintage, 1998) questions whether journalists should get involved in investigating criminals. It can be particularly dangerous if, like Guerin, you have a high profile as a crime fighter. She was shot dead at traffic lights on a Dublin dual carriageway. (See Figure 2.2, page 16.)

Yet a criminal activity that affects readers and viewers is a legitimate subject for reporting. Chris White of *The Parliament Magazine* believes that his exposure of an international fraud in Canadian company shares saved hundreds of people from losing their savings (see pages 167–8).

DEALING WITH THE UNDERWORLD

Mazher Mahmood, investigations editor of the *News of the World*, maintains his contacts are criminals rather than the police He says people have several times taken out contracts on his life, and his parents' home was attacked after he exposed credit-card fraudsters. 'They macheted everything, splitting the TV in two,' he says.

For him, the high profile goes with the job. If people didn't know about him, he wouldn't get the tips.

Crime-investigation stories are sometimes criticized because they concern the small fry: drug dealers, not drug wholesalers nor the bankers who put up the money. Mazher Mahmood replies that getting into a drug-dealing web and reaching the top man would require months of investigation and undercover work.

He believes he has taken kilogrammes of drugs off the streets, simply by exposing dealers. He also claims that, through his crime-fighting investigations, the police have convicted 93 criminals. He regards catching criminals as his paper's contribution to the public welfare.

Mahmood's speciality is the masquerade. He presents himself to wrongdoers as the sort of person they will want to do business with. He may play, for example, the high-roller with a luxurious villa. 'If the story is big enough, we will spend money.'

To John Alford (of the TV show *London's Burning*), Mahmood presented himself as a sheikh who wanted a celebrity guest for the opening of his new night club. (Alford, at Snaresbrook Crown Court in May 1999, was jailed for 9 months for supplying Mahmood with cocaine.)

For the *News of the World* and before that *The Sunday Times*, Mahmood has exposed arms dealers, doctors who sold blank prescriptions, a cosmetic-containers plant employing illegal immigrants for £1.50 an hour and factory owners in India employing children to make carpets for Harrods. He is proudest of getting a couple jailed for abusing children in a council home. A girl of 13 wrote to him: 'Thank you for saving my life.'

Mahmood receives around 50 telephone calls with tips each week, including some from prostitutes in the middle of the night. Only perhaps one tip a week makes a story. Others are about neighbours wrongly claiming the dole, or husbands who have run off. Every case he pursues must be nailed down with videotapes, audiotapes, affidavits: 'We have to check and double check. The level of evidence required outweighs anything anyone else does. Then we have to write it so that it's lively and attracts the readers.'

RELATIONS WITH THE POLICE

It can now be difficult, in England and Wales at any rate, for journalists to pass on their evidence to the police before publishing a story. In 1997, a judge fined the *News of the World* £50,000 for contempt of court because it published its account of a Mahmood counterfeiting investigation after it informed the police. The judge ruled that, once the police were informed, criminal proceedings had begun.

Complaints from *Daily Mail* readers led Jo-Ann Goodwin to investigate drug-dealing at Minehead in Somerset. After the *Mail* published her article, those named in it had left by the time the police arrived. The police, says Goodwin, tend not to like what they regard as interference. They asked her to go back to Minehead to help their inquiries and threatened to prosecute her for possessing a class A substance, amphetamine paste.

However, the police are sometimes happy for journalists to mount an investigation (see the section on Burglary, page 173). In the 1980s, *The Cook Report* helped the police combat extortion by paramilitary organizations in Northern Ireland.

Roger Cook says that, on behalf of a bogus security company which funded the Ulster Defence Association, a man named Eddie Sayers used to leave calling cards at building sites. His message was that, if contractors did not pay him, their staff or sites would suffer.

Cook pretended to be a property developer planning to extend Craigavon town centre. He went to the length of registering a company and seeking outline planning permission. Then he got in touch with Sayers who came to a meeting with a gun in his waistband. Sayers asked for 1 per cent of the value of the contract up front, though he offered a discount after Cook had approached him.

Cook recalls: 'I had to make sure I didn't ask him any leading questions but I had to encourage him to say what I wanted to hear.'

Largely on *The Cook Report*'s evidence, Sayers was convicted of attempted extortion while carrying a gun. The judge thanked *The Cook Report* for a 'very brave piece of work, the finest possible example of public service broadcasting'.

In Italy a detective in Florence once suggested to art specialist Peter Watson that he should try to recover stolen paintings. In 1983 Watson posed as a wealthy art dealer and got on the trail of a restorer in Northern Italy whose trick was to take away old pictures hung high in churches where it was hard to examine them. He would bring them back, apparently restored. What the restorer actually returned were copies. The originals went to New York, a priest with the Vatican's mission at the United Nations acting as courier. Watson's investigation recovered six old-master paintings. Four people including the priest were arrested.

THE $40 MILLION FRAUDSTER

Chris White, when writing freelance articles for *The European*, had a useful relationship with the police in Brussels. It began after Scotland Yard sought *The European*'s help in nailing Angus Hans Labunski, who was netting a million dollars a year by submitting invoices for services he had not provided. Labunski, who came originally from near Gdansk, is believed to have carried out frauds worth $40 million over 20 years.

White says that Labunski pretended to publish books called *International Yellow Pages*, *International Telex Fax Directory* and *International Hotel Trade Directory*. Using a database of two million companies worldwide, he asked people to put an entry in his directories or to correct entries he supplied. When they wrote back, he sent their companies invoices which could be for thousands of dollars, saying that Mr So-and-So (the name on the reply) had placed an order. Companies large and small paid up. If they did not, Labunski threatened them with court action or damaged their credit ratings. People in some small companies and charities were panic-stricken.

When police raided what they thought was Labunski's address in London, they found only a telephone, rigged to another telephone elsewhere. Labunski sent invoices to Britain from the United States and Belgium, to Belgium from Britain.

The police, however, gave Chris White a Brussels address which seemed promising. He stood outside it for a fortnight, finally spotting a man who turned out to be Labunski. He told Labunski: 'I am not here to hound you. If you have nothing to hide, it would be very sensible for us to sit down and talk. These allegations are being made. What is your answer?'

Labunski agreed to talk and White spent a lot of time with him and his accountant, drinking till two in the morning. It was, says White, a liver-damaging job. But, by joining in these drinking sessions, Labunski made a big mistake. He talked about his past and his opinions, opening the way to further inquiries. After White published the Labunski story in *The European*, Labunski was arrested and got five years. His accountant was given a suspended sentence.

Oddly enough, the British police who inspired the inquiry showed no interest in this outcome. They were content to leave Labunski to the Belgians.

White's next tip concerned a milk scam. The milk was going from Belgium to Poland via Austria, then returning into the European Union, picking up subsidy payments on the way. The investigation, however, came to an end when the man under suspicion died on a plane.

However, as a result of White's investigations in Brussels, both politicians and the Belgian police were now working closely with him. Publicity could force villains to make a move. The police could then pick them up at the airport. Journalists can also record telephone conversations, which it is illegal for the police to do in Belgium. And they can snare villains by pretending to be people they are not, which is again difficult for the police. Co-operation between police and journalist in Belgium became mutually beneficial. 'I get a story,' says White. 'They get leads.'

The Belgian police put White on to what was called the boilerhouse fraud. The rank-and-file fraudsters were 30 young people with telephones in Prague. The mastermind was officially resident in the

Turks and Caicos Islands but actually lived in the Dominican Republic, another part of the Caribbean.

This man exploited the mystique attaching to new technology by forming high-tech companies in Canada which, he said, were going places. They were unlisted on any stock exchange but he and his team bought the shares until they looked to be valuable. Backed by a mouthwatering prospectus, the shares then seemed a good buy. They even paid a dividend. Punters bought them, only to discover they were worthless.

Chris White pretended to be a punter with £10,000 to invest. The fraudsters were very suspicious but he convinced them he was a genuine punter. He rang the mastermind in the Dominican Republic who put him on to another miscreant in California. He also rang Canada and Indonesia. His exposure of the fraud saved many people from hefty losses.

White says he had earlier found the police willing to work with him in London but working with a journalist was something new for the Belgian police. Belgian journalists began to establish their own links with police officers when they saw White's stories in *The European*. There is now, he says, a good tradition of investigative journalism growing up in Belgium.

ENTRAPMENT

One worry for crime-fighting journalists is that they will be accused of entrapment, that is, causing someone to break a law which they would not otherwise have broken. In point of fact, entrapment is not in itself an offence in Britain at present, though the Law Commission is suggesting it should be. Entrapment is a possible defence in a criminal case: an accused can argue that he or she was trapped into committing the offence alleged.

Generally, before attempting any sort of sting, journalists need evidence that the law is being broken or that some malpractice is taking place.

To avoid being accused of encouraging an offence, Jo-Ann Goodwin couldn't ask for drugs when she was investigating drug-dealing at

Minehead. She had to chat up young men and see if they offered her any. She calls this investigation her grimmest story. It took 'four days. It seemed like most of my life.'

Roger Cook of *The Cook Report*, however, says he does not mind being an agent provocateur, provided he does not provoke people to do things outside their normal character and practice.

WAYNE'S WORLD

The Cook Report once showed how illegal bodybuilding steroids made their way from an Indian manufacturer via Plymouth to British cities. It was able to do this because a dealer about whom *The Cook Report* had done an earlier programme offered the Cook team his business. Pretending to take it over, they found his sources of supply.

In November 1996 *World in Action* broadcast two programmes about drug-dealing in Nottingham. The first, *The Untouchables*, used secret film to show that bouncers at night club doors were dealing in drugs, unknown to the club managements and without the police being able to prosecute them. The second, *Wayne's World*, focused on Wayne Hardy who, the programme alleged, was bringing drugs into the city.

A year later, Hardy was arrested when police trailed cars involved in a drugs deal. In October 1998, Hardy was sent to prison for three and a half years after admitting involvement in a conspiracy to bring 25 kilogrammes of cannabis resin into the East Midlands.

The two programmes were made by a *World in Action* reporter, Donal McIntyre, who spent 11 months under cover in Nottingham working as a night club bouncer and winning Hardy's confidence by training with him in a gym.

McIntyre, who represented Ireland at World Championship level as a canoeist, had the build for the bouncer's job. 'You have the biggest shoulders,' said a *World in Action* producer, Pip Clothier. 'I recommend you go under cover.'

McIntyre's first experience of covert filming was with BBC TV's investigative series about sport, *On the Line*. The film showed greyhounds being blooded with live rabbits at a training track in Ireland.

Figure 15.1
World in Action investigator Donal McIntyre on duty outside a Nottingham nightspot. He spent 11 months as a bouncer to secretly film drug-dealing by fellow bouncers and expose a drugs supplier (picture Granada TV)

For the Nottingham films McIntyre needed a new identity. He became Tony, taking the name of a friend who had emigrated. It was an expensive enterprise for *World in Action*, costing £320,000 for two programmes, as opposed to a normal cost of £60,000 a programme.

Mazher Mahmood of the *News of the World* had pointed out to me that it is hard to make a case against a drug supplier without becoming a dealer yourself. McIntyre tackled this problem by pretending to be a dealer. He drove an expensive new four-wheel-drive car. He had new clothes, money to throw around, without any obvious source of income. He had a mysterious friend he called Billy the Kid who, he suggested, was eager to supply drugs to Nottingham, with him (McIntyre) as go-between.

McIntyre spent four months as a bouncer before he filmed anything. He had to talk to bouncers in their own language. Smoking, chewing gum, talking the lingo, he fitted easily into the scene. Some bouncers were high on speed and bodybuilding steroids and wanted trouble. McIntyre was the most ethical bouncer, trying to stop trouble before it started.

He says that if you go under cover you have to decide in advance the principles on which you will work. When you come to the moment for a decision, it's too late if you haven't already determined the basis on which you will decide. McIntyre's principles were:

1 Never make friends with anyone who isn't a criminal. Your friend might otherwise suffer retribution after you've gone. You have to be careful for the people you leave behind.
2 Do not break the law. You may buy drugs in certain limited circumstances but you must send them for analysis to check whether they are true narcotics. Give orders that they must be destroyed, or given to the police.
3 Do not compromise your sources.
4 Simply be a witness of what you see. It's not your job to convict anyone. You are not a police officer.
5 Remember that anything written or recorded is a matter of record and may become evidence in a court case. Never be flippant in any inquiry.

Apart from being comfortable with his principles, McIntyre also had to be comfortable with his recording equipment. 'I became technically adept. You have to be able to fix it if it goes wrong. You need radio mikes on the right frequency. You don't want to go out with a camera not working. I had two cameras going, one in a bag. You have to be methodical, vigilant, never take too many risks.'

McIntyre saw the task as more than simply exposing drug-dealing. He was giving viewers a chance to glimpse a segment of society normally unseen. In an ordinary city which isn't Liverpool, Manchester or London, he told viewers that this is what is happening.

The problem for the police, as Assistant Chief Constable Robert Searle explained in the *Wayne's World* programme, is that of catching suppliers in possession of the drugs they are supplying. They usually leave the handling to other people. McIntyre learns in the programme that, in drugs trading, the money and the drugs change hands in different cars.

Figure 15.2
Investigator Roger Cook stocks up with gold in order to trap a man who specialized in melting down stolen gold bars (picture Carlton TV)

In December 1997, police tailed three cars to Hardy's home. Cannabis resin brought from London was transferred from one car to another. Wayne Hardy and four others were arrested. In court, they admitted conspiracy to supply the cannabis.

BURGLARY

Media investigations into crime are not solely about nailing villains. *The Cook Report*'s burglary programme on ITV in April 1999 showed a receiver melting down a gold bar to remove its identification number. But the programme was mainly concerned with burglary as an anti-social activity which bears particularly hard on poor, lonely and elderly people. While Nick Davies's book *Dark Heart* (see page 149) interpreted burglary in Leeds as an expression of blighted lives, *The Cook Report* saw it as a response to a market for stolen goods so thriving that burglary is commoner in Britain than anywhere else in Western Europe.

The *Report* team set up a secondhand shop in Smethwick near Birmingham with the name Cash for It. Although the shop did not ask for stolen goods, it found £1,000 worth coming in every week. The goods were brought in by teenagers who wanted to enjoy a social life they could not otherwise afford.

To show how receivers can induce people to commit burglary, the *Report* team acquired a house in Cambridge and, posing as a receiver, put the word out that it would like goods that had been placed in this particular house. Several burglars broke in, a woman being by far the most thorough, scooping a wide range of goods into plastic bags before staggering out of the front door.

The programme also had comment from a senior policeman, a Cambridge criminologist and a reformed burglar who had become a church minister. It showed that the simplest scams can be the best.

MALE RAPE

Terry Kelleher had the help of the police in making a film for Channel 4 about male rape.

He says he reads a lot of newspapers and magazines and had come across a few stories concerning this little-known crime. Having just made a film with the City of London Police about a big robbery, he was able to secure the co-operation of the Association of Chief Police Officers. He collected information by devising a questionnaire for police forces throughout the country.

Through support groups, he also sent a questionnaire to victims. He engaged a counsellor to deal with victims sensitively.

His aim was to make a serious film giving new information of import to anyone interested in social services or criminality. He arranged a confidential helpline. To ensure the film could not be sold on piecemeal for sensational use, he stipulated to Channel 4 that, if re-shown, it must be re-shown complete: sections must not be taken out of context.

The film established that male rape does happen, that the police have a lot to learn about it and that it isn't a gay crime. Rather it is an exercise in power and control. A high proportion of assailants and victims would describe themselves as straight.

IT COULD BE YOU

What if you were 'recognized' by a closed circuit TV camera and jailed for a crime you didn't commit? Alan Church was convicted of a robbery on the evidence of a CCTV picture, even though an expert from University College, London, said that the man pictured could not be him. Church featured in a Channel 4 investigation in which Joe Layburn showed how hard it is to identify someone for certain from a grainy CCTV photograph.

16 Trail of the bent coppers

THE IRANIAN SCOTCH

One of the more hilarious investigative stories concerning the police is that of the Iranian Scotch. Investigator David Murphy tells it in *What News?* which he wrote with Bob Franklin (Routledge, 1991).

The police in Manchester had arrested students protesting against the Shah whom Ayatollah Khomenei was about to supplant. Andrew Jennings, working for a fringe paper called the *New Manchester Review*, got a tip that the Iranian consul, Dr Jahannema, had given a crate of whisky to senior police officers. It would be against regulations for them to accept it.

Jennings needed a firm story if he were to put it to the police. He asked the consul for an interview about the reaction of local Iranians to events in Teheran, and went to see him with David Murphy.

If Jennings had asked outright about the Scotch, the consul could simply have denied the gift, and that would have been the end of the story. Instead, Jennings pretended to talk of other things while trying to lead the conversation round to the whisky.

Dr Jahannema said he was anxious not to be quoted about events in Iran. He happened to mention he got on well with the police.

Jennings said he'd been down at Bootle Street police station and the lads had really appreciated the Christmas whisky. The consul didn't react. So Jennings tried again.

'What whisky?' asked the consul. He added he had given some to people at the student disturbance.

Jennings tried once more. This time it struck a chord with Dr Jahannema. They'd sent out about 200 bottles of whisky to leading citizens, he said, about five of them to the police.

'As soon as he said it,' says Murphy, 'we rang Manchester police.'

This produced a statement from Chief Constable James Anderton:

'It appears,' said the statement, 'that unknown to the Chief Constable a parcel allegedly containing intoxicating liquor from the Iranian consulate in Manchester may have been delivered to a Manchester police station before Christmas. The matter is now being investigated.

'Another parcel addressed to the Chief Constable and Mrs Anderton from the Consul General of Iran in Manchester and his wife was delivered at the same time to the Chief Constable. This gift was passed on to the Northern Police Convalescent Home at Harrogate since it is the Chief Constable's policy that personal gifts should not be retained.'

MALPRACTICE IN POLICE FORCES

Not all newspaper reports concerning the police have been so lighthearted.

Between 1969 and 1975, *The Times*, *The People*, *World in Action* and London Weekend TV demonstrated widespread illegal activities by London detectives (see pages 181–6).

James Morton in his book *Bent Coppers* (Warner, 1993) reports an incident in 1983 when police officers jumped out of a Transit van and waded into four youths in Holloway Road, North London. No officer would say which van crew was responsible until the *Police Review* denounced the assailants and suggested anyone giving information should be offered immunity.

The opportunities for police officers to do wrong have been reduced. The Police and Criminal Evidence Act introduced the recording of interviews.

The takeover of prosecutions by the Crown Prosecution Service means police can no longer receive backhanders in return for reducing charges.

However, *Panorama* in 1993 and again in 1998 showed the problems that remain. It told of payments or requested payments totalling nearly £30,000, for bail, information and the destruction of evidence. It told of £5,000 stolen from a suspect. It also reported that only one of the officers against whom it had collected evidence was prosecuted and jailed.

This demonstrates how hard it is to build a case strong enough to get a suspect officer dismissed or prosecuted. One participant in the 1998 *Panorama* said: 'You can have dodgy officers and they still work.'

Panorama returned to the subject in October 1998 with a programme about West Midlands detectives who complained at other officers' failure to hand in all the money and drugs seized on raids. They were cold-shouldered by colleagues but the Chief Constable set up an inquiry.

The Director of Public Prosecutions decided against prosecuting the officers about whom the detectives complained but, in disciplinary proceedings, three were dismissed (two of whom were appealing). The officer facing the most serious allegations including drug-dealing was declared unfit to face the disciplinary tribunal and, to the Chief Constable's disgust, retired with an index-linked pension and a £60,000 lump sum. However, the West Midlands now has a full-time anti-corruption squad.

SEXISM IN THE FORCE

A common cause of complaint against police forces concerns the treatment of women officers. In the autumn of 1996, journalists discovered that North Yorkshire police had agreed to pay £100,000 to settle an industrial tribunal case without a hearing. This was three times as much as the tribunal would normally have awarded. The woman officer concerned, Libby Ashurst, also received a pension of nearly £18,000 after seven years' service, as much as a chief inspector would receive after 30 years.

Michael Bilton told the story behind the award in the *Sunday Times magazine*. A woman administrator and two women officers had been unfairly treated by a detective chief inspector at Harrogate, where the CID had a macho culture. When Libby Ashurst gave evidence to an inquiry, she was ostracized by fellow officers, her locker was broken into and she received silent phone calls to her home in the middle of the night. A disciplinary tribunal, reported Bilton, found the detective chief inspector guilty of abusive conduct and fined him £1,300.

A further inquiry, set off by a letter from two detective inspectors, accused the then chief constable of lack of thoroughness in pursuing complaints. He retired with the matter unresolved.

MISCARRIAGES OF JUSTICE

Ray Fitzwalter, in charge of *World in Action* when it campaigned for the Birmingham Six, points out that no police officer was successfully prosecuted as a result of what was discovered about the way the Six were treated (see page 187).

'In a case like this,' he says, 'the authorities will use everything at their disposal to deny and suppress, or to avoid doing anything. Their position is: "You prove it. We needn't do anything."' Police officers must have broken the law (the Birmingham Six were injured while in custody). But no one was successfully prosecuted over the Birmingham Six, the Guildford Four or the Birmingham Serious Crime Squad cases.

Says Fitzwalter:

'Lord Justice May was appointed to look into miscarriages of justice. He started getting blackballed by other judges.

'A police superintendent left the force after a programme we made. Three doctors signed that he was sick. Yet we had filmed him completing the London Marathon. He'd been protecting a criminal who wasn't touched in 20 years of murder, arson and armed robbery and was arrested only when another authority, the Customs, got him on VAT fraud.'

James Morton, editor of *New Law Journal*, points out in his book *Bent Coppers* that the police are very vulnerable.

Suppose, he says, that officers, only a short time in their first job, see or hear an older colleague do or say something irregular. They can tell a senior officer and be thought disloyal; and the older colleague may well deny everything. They can say nothing and become parties to malpractice.

The police form a discrete society with bonds of mutual loyalty among its members. They work mainly out of sight of senior officers. To solve crime, they need the help of criminals.

Integrity gives no guaranteed protection. Morton tells the story of a sergeant pursuing a dealer in forged notes. A chief inspector set a trap for the sergeant in order to protect the dealer who was his informant.

THE LIBEL WEAPON

Allegations against police officers need careful handling. Duncan Campbell wrote in *The Guardian* in February, 1997, that it is not unusual for people facing long sentences to make allegations against the police. '*The Guardian* receives such claims virtually every day,' he wrote. 'Some may be bogus and self-seeking, some genuine but most are unprovable and never form the basis of a story.'

The police officers' union, the Police Federation, argues that the police are vulnerable to defamation and it frequently backs a suit for libel, even if newspapers do not name the police officer against whom an allegation has been made.

It argues that other officers will know who it is, even if the public doesn't: the legal test of identity is whether acquaintances will know it is him. So, particularly if the allegation is investigated and rejected, the newspaper could face a 'garage' action: so called because it commonly yields the few thousand pounds necessary for the officer to build himself a garage.

The problem for newspapers is that people who make allegations are likely to be regarded as in some degree disreputable; otherwise they would not have come up against the police in the first place. The Police Federation won well over £1 million in damages in around 100 actions before it finally lost one to *The Guardian* in 1997.

The Guardian case related to a report three years earlier. To a police statement about eight unnamed officers at Stoke Newington, North

London, being transferred to new duties, Duncan Campbell had attached an account of an inquiry into allegations against officers at the station. Five officers maintained in the High Court that he had thereby suggested they had been involved in dealing and planting drugs, and this had had a devastating effect on their lives.

Campbell denied making any aspersion against the five officers. He had merely wanted to alert people to the fact that an important inquiry was under way (he had interviewed the detective superintendent in charge of it) and that allegations by known drug dealers and users were being investigated. Two senior police officers and the head of the Police Complaints Authority gave evidence for *The Guardian* and the jury found for the newspaper.

After the Stoke Newington inquiry, the police there adopted a better tactic. They sought filmed evidence against drug dealers on a street known locally as the Front Line. In this way, they put the dealers out of business on that street.

Newspapers publish if they are sure of their ground. Dominic Kennedy and Stewart Tendler reported in *The Times* in November 1997 how two London detectives who retired sick after allegations were made against them had re-emerged as directors of a security firm. To back up their report, Kennedy and Tendler had a Commons committee hearing, feature articles about the firm from two newspapers, and an interview with one of the two men.

In one important respect, investigation of police mistakes or malpractice has become more difficult. Journalists are no longer allowed to visit people in prison, except in special circumstances such as Roger Cook's 1999 interview with a remorseful burglar after whose crime the victim died of a heart attack. Prisoners can speak to journalists on the phone. Police authorities overseeing the police, however, are subject to the Local Government (Access to Information) Act, which means you can see their documents except those giving personal details.

The police who's who is the *Police and Constabulary Almanac*. The bi-monthly publication *Statewatch* (tel. 0208-802-1882; fax 0208-880-1727) covers the police, prisons and security.

CORRUPTION IN THE MET

Garry Lloyd went to work as usual at *The Times* one day in 1969 and set off a reform of criminal investigation in London which still continues. He and his colleague Julian Mounter were to show that three named Metropolitan Police detectives were taking money from a criminal. It was, a lawyer commented, like catching the Archbishop of Canterbury in bed with a prostitute.

Lloyd had been a member of what *The Times* called the News Team. The then editor, William Rees-Mogg, set it up to tackle big stories as they broke.

In 1968 there was an upsurge in thefts of antiques. *The Times* had the idea of getting a burglar to show how easily he could burgle a country house, and so inform people how to make burglary more difficult. It advertised in the *Evening Standard*. A retired burglar called Eddie Brennan responded. Then *The Times* gave up its planned burglary in favour of a simple advisory article.

A year later Brennan turned up at *The Times*'s office with a frightened young friend called Michael Perry. Perry's flat had been raided by police engaged in Operation Coathanger, which aimed to solve a succession of raids on clothes shops. The police found whisky and charged Perry with dishonestly handling it. Detective Sergeant Gordon Harris, however, suggested he 'give the big bloke a drink'. Perry agreed to pay £25 to Detective Inspector Bernard Robson. He was pleased that, subsequently, Harris did not mention in court a previous conviction.

A few days later, Perry alleged, Robson pressed against his (Perry's) fingers a package which Robson said was gelignite. Robson suggested Perry would be arrested on an explosives charge unless he named receivers of stolen goods. Neither five years for an explosives offence nor a beating up for betraying receivers was attractive for Perry. He decided to see a solicitor but it was Saturday afternoon. Brennan, whom he happened to meet, took him to *The Times*.

'People came to *The Times* with all sorts of stories,' Lloyd recalls. 'We had very high standards of testing. I interrogated Perry at great length and took down a statement: "I am Michael Perry. I have previous convictions. And so on." It was signed and witnessed. He and several associates swore statements about bribing detectives.'

Apart from Robson and Harris of the Coathanger squad, Perry was also paying money to a local South London detective sergeant, John Symonds.

Confirming this was difficult. Meetings took place in pubs. Detectives were wary, although they had no idea journalists would be after them. Garry Lloyd says: 'I got the editor's permission to bug telephones. It was inconclusive. Perry would call a detective and get the squad room. Sometimes he had to ring from telephone boxes, which we couldn't record. It was a nightmare.'

Lloyd and Mounter decided to tape-record meetings between Perry and the detectives, which up to that time scarcely anyone had tried. They hired a recording engineer. A microphone was fixed under the dashboard of Perry's car and wired to a recorder in the boot, which was ideal. Perry got Harris into the car and they discussed the money needed to get Perry off the gelignite charge. But the detectives generally preferred their own cars.

On another occasion, Lloyd and Mounter used four recorders, of which three worked and recorded Robson talking about the gelignite incident. In the end, Lloyd and Mounter had tapes on which the detectives incriminated themselves. 'There are more villains in our game than yours,' said Symonds on one tape.

The Times published on Saturday November 29, 1969, and delivered its evidence to Scotland Yard the night before. The thinking was that the Yard would not at that time be able to find a judge to stop publication.

It didn't try to find one. Two detective chief superintendents set to work to prepare a report for Assistant Commissioner (Crime) Peter Brodie. Symonds knew by 2 am what was afoot.

He, Robson and Harris were not suspended. Nor were their homes and lockers searched. Instead, the Yard turned on Lloyd and Mounter. *The Times*, wishing to play by the book, provided two suites of offices where Lloyd and Mounter were separately interrogated for three weeks, eight hours a day.

The interrogators tried first to suggest that the two reporters were *agents provocateurs*. Garry Lloyd recalls: 'They were trying to suggest we were using *Times* money to offer inducements. In fact we were investigating serious allegations.'

They had been careful to see that any money which Perry gave the policemen was his own. Before each of his meetings with the police they searched him and took down the serial numbers of his money.

After the *agents provocateurs'* allegation, the interrogators sought to discredit the tape-recordings. They brought in specialists to do this. It was tantamount to accusing Lloyd and Mounter of conspiracy and perjury. However, a scientist from the National Physical Laboratory at Teddington later said the tapes were genuine.

Meanwhile, another drama was in progress on the police side. Jim Callaghan, then the Home Secretary, brought in Inspector of Constabulary Frank Williamson to supervise a Scotland Yard inquiry into *The Times*'s allegations. He got no change out of Assistant Commissioner Brodie who sought to defend both his detectives and the exclusive right of the Yard to inquire into itself. Williamson did, however, bring in some provincial policemen who found a new witness against Symonds.

However, the Yard's own inquiry nearly hit on another big scandal, the payments being made to members of the Obscene Publications ('Dirty') Squad by the Soho porn trade. Detective Chief Superintendent Fred Lambert, in charge of the Yard's inquiry, was hurriedly sidelined. Detective Chief Superintendent Bill Moody, head of the Dirty Squad, took his place and the Yard's inquiry into *The Times*'s allegations got nowhere. Scarcely any leads, apart from the one further incriminating Symonds, were successfully followed up.

Meanwhile, the phones of Lloyd and Mounter were bugged and they received menacing phone calls at night, saying such things as: 'We'll get you for this.' *The Times* got a tip that an attempt would be made to plant drugs on them.

When Robson and Harris went on trial, the evidence against them was essentially the tapes which Garry Lloyd and Julian Mounter had provided. Since the defence brought in the specialists to discredit the tapes, Lloyd and Mounter were effectively on trial also. 'The jury aren't buying it, lads,' Detective Chief Superintendent Moody told them as they waited to give evidence. 'It's not going well for you.'

Even if the jury accepted the tapes (and tapes had never been accepted in evidence before), Robson and Harris had another argument. Perry was a good source of information and they were giving *him* money, they argued, not he them. However, there was nothing to back up their story, and Robson couldn't show any useful information that Perry had given. Stanley Hyde of the National Physical Laboratory was forthright that the tapes were genuine and not edited. Robson and Harris were convicted.

When they vainly appealed, Lord Justice Edmond Davies praised the two journalists Lloyd and Mounter for a 'great public service . . . It was, it would appear, mainly their intrepidity and skill which laid bare a hideous cancer.'

For Garry Lloyd's promising career at *The Times*, however, it was a disaster. 'I didn't know,' he says, 'that it was going to tie up my life for years.'

He had reported from round the world. Now he had to stay in Britain while the case dragged on. It didn't end until 1972, and reopened years later for the trial of Symonds who had fled the country and returned. Lloyd took up a fellowship in the United States for a year. Then he joined the BBC.

But he hasn't a down on the police. One detective said to him in the court washroom: 'I just want to say you two have done a tremendous job.'

THE TOP COP AND THE CROOK

It was another newspaper, *The People*, which caught up with Metropolitan police officers in Soho. Three television journalists, Barry Cox, John Shirley and Martin Short, tell the story in *The Fall of Scotland Yard* (Penguin, 1977).

While the Robson/Harris trial was in progress, *The People* reported that the head of the Flying Squad, Commander Kenneth Drury, had been on holiday in Cyprus with Jimmy Humphreys, an unsuccessful former petty crook, who had made money out of strip clubs and moved into dirty bookshops.

For *The People*, the story had begun badly. Two years earlier, executives of the International Publishing Corporation, the paper's owners, had spotted a news report about the crash landing in Belgium of a plane carrying 700 blue films, wrapped in Christmas paper and bound for Britain. Laurie Manifold, an assistant editor at that time, sent two reporters to make inquiries in Soho. He also set up Maurice Fahmi, a freelance, in an expensive flat, posing as a wealthy Middle Eastern blue-film buyer. The plot was to accuse Stuart Crispie, agent for a Danish film company, of being involved in an illegal blue-film enterprise. With luck Crispie would bring his film company boss Big Jeff Phillips to a meeting at the London Hilton.

Unfortunately, the reporters in Soho had asked bookshop owner Jimmy Humphreys about Big Jeff. Humphreys had heard about an Arab film buyer (Fahmi) and was shrewd enough to link Fahmi to the reporters' visit.

He got his police contacts to check on Fahmi. They found that the expensive flat was rented by Odhams Press, publisher of *The People*. So when Crispie turned up at the Hilton he was accompanied by a photographer and by a solicitor who accused the *People* journalists of blackmail.

Hugh Cudlipp, chairman of IPC, didn't take this defeat lying down. A year later, Laurie Manifold and his reporters were back in Soho, with as much time and money as they needed. Pretending to buy books, they built up a picture of the porn trade.

On February 6, 1972, they gave 12 columns to exposing Big Jeff as Britain's first blue-film millionaire.

The previous year, an *Observer* journalist, Raymond Palmer, had profiled the Soho porn business and asked: 'How do they get away with it?' The answer, he reported, was that they paid the police. 'It's like insurance,' said one man, 'but more expensive.'

On February 27, *The People* came up with the chapter and verse. 'Police officers in London,' it said, 'are being systematically bribed by dealers in pornography.'

February 27 also brought the story of the Humphreys/Drury holiday. This came from an old criminal friend of Humphreys called Joseph Pyle. His house had been raided by police seeking Freddie Sewell, wanted for a police murder in Blackpool. They found no sign of Sewell but they charged Pyle with having a gun and ammunition. He denied the charge and was acquitted. He got his own back on the police by telling a *People* reporter about Drury's friendship with Humphreys. In passing, he mentioned the holiday in Cyprus.

The new head of Scotland Yard, Sir Robert Mark, sent in East End detectives to sort out the West End. Thirteen police officers, including Drury and Moody, were sent to prison for a total of 96 years.

THE BRIDGEWATER FOUR

Paul Foot fought a long and, in 1997, successful campaign in the *Daily Mirror* and *Private Eye* for the release of three petty criminals wrongly jailed 18 years before for the murder of a newspaper boy, Carl Bridgewater, at Yew Tree Farm in the Midlands. A fourth man, Pat Molloy, died in jail.

In *Murder at the Farm* (Sidgwick & Jackson, 1986) Foot says he was persistently approached by Ann Whelan, mother of the youngest accused, Michael Hickey. He took up the case because of Hickey's long protest on a jail rooftop.

The case generated a vast number of papers to be read: 1,500 pages of statements were produced at the trial, and the transcript of evidence ran to a further 1,500. A solicitor, Jim Nichol, got permission from the Director of Public Prosecutions to see 7,000 statements. Paul Foot also got Pat Molloy's legal papers.

The story behind the case was that Vincent Hickey, a relative of Michael, robbed Chapel Farm, Romsley. To escape being charged for this, he suggested he knew about Carl Bridgewater's murder, and implicated the others.

Pat Molloy after long questioning confessed to robbing the farm at the time the murder took place. But when police took him to Yew Tree Farm, he didn't recognize it. All four accused had alibis. According to Foot, the police pressured witnesses to try to break these. One witness, Dave Waller, secured £1,000 damages from the police.

At the trial, Molloy made a decision disastrous for the others. On legal advice, he let his confession stand, since he would be sentenced for robbery not murder.

Soon after the trial, Hubert Wilkes at the farm next door to Yew Tree was murdered by Hubert Spencer whom police had at one stage questioned about Carl Bridgewater.

Paul Foot interviewed everyone involved in the case. He met hostility from some. Several people refused to talk to him. But he persevered.

At one stage he made a film with Terry Kelleher for TV. Kelleher says: 'We uncovered new evidence and new witnesses. Most of the work was extremely unglamorous.'

Foot wrote in *The Journalist's Handbook* (October, 1997) that most of the press, especially the Midlands press, had been profoundly hostile to the campaigners who were trying to set this injustice right.

THE BIRMINGHAM SIX

The Birmingham Six were six Irishmen on the fringe of the Republican movement, five of whom were arrested at Heysham, near Morecambe, on their way to the funeral in Ireland of an IRA man who had blown himself up. They were convicted of Birmingham pub bombings which caused horrendous casualties.

Peter Chippindale of *The Guardian* who covered their trial suggested to a freelance, Chris Mullin, that they were wrongly convicted. Mullin had become interested in investigative journalism when, on a break in Asia from work as a sub-editor for the BBC World Service, he ran across the story of a CIA operation in Tibet. Concerning the Birmingham Six, he went to see Ray Fitzwalter, then running Granada TV's *World in Action*.

Fitzwalter says that he had already been approached by the men's families. 'We declined to get involved. There was no evidence. Mullin, however, persuaded me it was so suspicious that we ought to take it up. I took the decision to put together a team:

'For a long time we had nothing concrete. Mullin thought we could make a programme anyway. But without hard evidence you can't use loose allegations and circumstantial evidence. It took three months, which is a lot of time. Only then did we know we had something.

There were people in Sinn Fein prepared to say some things and acknowledge some degree of mistake.'

At this point, *World in Action* had police photographs as evidence that the men had been beaten up. Some prison officers who were prosecuted but did not appear in court had prepared statements in case they were needed for trial. From these *World in Action* knew the Six had arrived at Winson Green Prison in a police van and that rules for the delivery of prisoners to a prison had been broken.

Fitzwalter says: 'Some of the Six had confessed, but the confessions didn't marry up with the known facts about the bombing. The bombs weren't placed where the confessions said they were. Ours was a remorseless, factual, scientific effort plus some luck.' *World in Action* made six programmes in all.

Chris Mullin, now a junior minister in the government, recalls:

'Peter Chippindale [of The Guardian*] said he thought they got the wrong people. I tried to interest publishers and TV and I wrote a piece in* Tribune. *I tried many times over years to get* World in Action *interested.*

'At the end of 1984, Ray Fitzwalter agreed to take me on for some months for a preliminary investigation. The first programme was in October 1985.

'We went looking for police officers who might give a different version of events. We started in Morecambe since that was the location of violence against the Six. We looked especially for retired officers since they were more likely to talk to us. Morecambe is a small town, which made them easier to find. Eventually we set out to find everyone who was in Morecambe Police Station between 1 am and 5 pm on the relevant day, including receptionists and cleaners. One of the cleaners had an interesting story about blood on the walls.

'After that, we tried the West Midlands. We didn't get anywhere.

'Then we had a bit of luck. We looked for prison officers who had been at Winson Green. Off the back of a lorry fell a bundle of statements. Four or five described injuries to the men.'

The prosecution case depended in part on the confessions, in part on a test, the Griess test, which a scientist called Skuse interpreted as meaning that two of the Six had handled nitroglycerine.

Mullin says: 'We decided to get two scientists, independently of each other, to conduct forensic tests to see whether any innocent substances would produce a positive Griess test. This gave us our first breakthrough. You had to have a television company willing to pay the cost.'

The *World in Action* programme in October 1985 was based on these tests. They showed that cellulose on the cards the men had played with on their train journey to Heysham could have given a positive Griess test. (The prosecution countered that the independent tests had used different quantities of reagent from that used by Skuse. A researcher found a document in the defence papers showing the formula in the independent tests was the same as Skuse's.)

It was hard to persuade journalists to attend the preview of the first *World in Action* programme. It was received, says Chris Mullin, in almost total silence. However:

'Things started for the first time to go our way as a result of the publicity.

'In December 1986 I wrote a letter to the Birmingham Post *appealing for anyone who had been in the Queens Road police station to come forward. An ex-police officer called Tom Clarke came forward. He had been dismissed for stealing £5. He told a compelling and detailed story about dogs and shotguns being brought into cells. My second programme was with him.'*

In his book *Error of Judgment* (Poolbeg), Chris Mullin discloses that he obtained documents from Lancashire County Council's archive about negotiations with West Midlands police at the time of civil hearings over the Six's claim for damages for assault. In 1987, Granada also obtained a file from the Special Branch archive in the Criminal Record Office about an interview with a man who said he knew one of the people who bombed the pubs.

These county and police archives are not open to public view. Mullin and Granada got access because of their persistent interest in the case.

The first edition of Mullin's book was seriously reviewed by *The Guardian* and *The Times*, ignored by the *Daily Mail* and abused by *The Sunday Express*, he says. A later *Sun* headline read: 'Loony MP backs bomb gang':

'I have it framed on my wall,' says Chris Mullin. 'Another read: "Twenty things you don't know about Crackpot Chris". I didn't know some of them either.

'The Sunday Mercury [the Birmingham Sunday paper] reviewed the book in neutral terms on about page 40. The Birmingham Post *reviewed it and then tried not to refer to the subject again. Only when an assiduous journalist called Gerry Hunt went to the editor and asked if he was banned from writing about the subject did something appear.*

'Central TV took an interest from the outset. BBC TV in Birmingham imposed a total blackout saying: "We haven't got space to review all the new books that are published".'

After *World in Action*'s Tom Clarke programme the Home Office ordered an inquiry but it was made clear that Clarke was to be discredited. For a second inquiry, a chief constable was brought in. He commissioned a newly devised electrostatic test which showed that notes of the alleged confessions had been rewritten and added to, a year after the event. The Six were freed.

In parallel with his *World in Action* inquiries, Chris Mullin did detective work in Ireland over a period of two years. He set out to contact members of the IRA, to find out who really did the bombing. He started with those who had been arrested around Birmingham for IRA offences. One or two were still in prison. Some had been released. At first, they were very suspicious. He stressed that his purpose was to rescue the unfortunate Six. Some accepted that and some didn't. 'As the bandwagon rolled, people who had refused got in touch. Granada eventually got interested.'

Mullin calculated that the IRA had about 30 members in the West Midlands at the time of the bombing and he drew up a short list of those who were around at the time the bombs went off, eliminating those who had an alibi. One informant came forward after a public meeting. 'He saw I was interested in a man who disappeared shortly after the bombing. He gave me the man's parents' address in Dublin.'

Chris Mullin discovered someone who knew the code word the bombers had used. In the end, he secured an interview with a man who admitted planting the bombs. A second man also owned up.

'THE CHIEF MUST GO'

Stanley Parr, head of the Lancashire Constabulary in the 1970s, Britain's second largest at the time, liked to oblige his friends and acquaintances by intervening in police cases which concerned them. It could be letting a woman off a trivial £10 motoring fine. It could be rescuing a friend's son from a charge of causing grievous bodily harm.

The son of an acquaintance threatened a man with a shotgun. Parr phoned a police station late on Saturday night and said: 'Let him out.'

Parr had many friends and acquaintances, particularly in Blackpool where he had served most of his career.

A detective sergeant made a complaint against Chief Constable Parr which led to an inquiry by the Chief Constable of Hampshire, Sir Douglas Osmond. The county police committee was keen to play down Sir Douglas's report. It wasn't very important, the committee suggested.

These were the Poulson days when parts of local government had an aroma of corruption. Editor Barry Askew and two other journalists at the *Lancashire Evening Post* in Preston decided to find out what was happening. Unfortunately, no one would tell them. They tried the members of the police committee in vain.

Bob Satchwell, who was news editor, says: 'I got a guy who almost told me things. I saw him at an airport and I thought he was going to give the report to me. At the last minute, he didn't.'

The man left on holiday with the report. Bob Satchwell followed on the next plane. He arrived quite late, checked into a hotel and went for a walk round town. (He still declines to say where the plane took him, in case this betrays his contact.)

Satchwell says:

'I walked past a private club. Some instinct told me he was in there. I found a phone box, phoned the club and asked for this guy. "You had

better come in," he said. "You really want this thing, don't you? How did you find me?"

' *"Skill and cunning." '*

To avoid rousing suspicions, Satchwell presented himself as a travel journalist, doing a piece on holidays. But he spent 48 hours trying to convince his contact to let him have the report, or at any rate let him have a sight of it. In the end, Satchwell photographed the 150-page report page by page on his bathroom floor with a 35 mm camera.

He returned to the airport, remembering at the last moment not to let the films go through the X-ray machine.

In the report, people appeared as Mr X or Mr Z. But checks with the files showed who they were. Bob Satchwell and his colleagues were amazed at what they read. Apart from letting people off offences and pursuing unwise friendships with businessmen, Stanley Parr had made free use of police cars, at a time when petrol was short and the cars were limited to 38 miles a shift.

One car picked up fish from Fleetwood. Others were alleged to have taken people to parties. On Saturday morning, Parr used a car to go shopping round Blackpool.

It was important not to betray Satchwell's source. So the *Lancashire Evening Post* story named all three journalists in the byline, leaving it unclear which of them had obtained the report. As they retyped it, they destroyed the original film.

One way of tracing a leak is to see that every copy of a secret report differs slightly in layout or in minor spelling errors from the rest and can therefore be identified and ascribed to a particular recipient. The journalists altered their retyped version to ensure it did not betray whose copy it had been made from.

On February 25, 1977, the *Lancashire Evening Post* gave four broadsheet pages to the report, the front page headline reading: 'Why the Lancs police chief must go'.

'All hell broke loose,' says Bob Satchwell. The leaker of the report was described as a skunk.

Two detective chief inspectors were given the task of identifying the leaker:

'I would be in a pub and one of them would turn up,' says Satchwell. 'Every time they put a name to me I said: "Yes, it was him."

'It was very stressful. The typed-up report never left my side. I had it in a battered briefcase, or sometimes in a carrier bag. Even in a pub, I would be talking to someone about it and it would be on the floor. I wasn't prepared to put my source at risk. He was one of the most honourable men I ever met. He said: "I want to tell you. It's desperate this becomes known because what is contained in this report is dreadful and they're trying to find ways to cover it up." '

But the honourable informant didn't want to betray a confidence. 'He took some persuading. I had seen him a dozen times. I debated with him for hours and hours and hours,' says Satchwell.

The police committee tried to prosecute the *Post* under the Official Secrets Act. But a report by a chief constable was not, technically, an official secret. Stanley Parr said he had answers to everything. The Blackpool paper, the *West Lancashire Gazette*, said Parr hadn't been treated fairly.

The police committee held secret meetings, and the *Post* kept reporting them. 'They thought we were bugging the chamber,' says Satchwell.

Parr wrote to the committee asking to be allowed to retire. Bob Satchwell got a copy of the letter, 15 minutes before edition time. 'You have a new splash,' he told the sub-editors.

The publicity meant that Parr couldn't retire. The Osmond report was boiled down into charges heard before a tribunal with Patrick Bennett QC presiding. The *Post* disclosed what the charges were. Bennett found many of them proved and Parr was dismissed.

The *Post* won British Press Awards. It handed to the police and to MPs a 50-page dossier alleging corruption in local government. This led to inquiries by the head of Nottinghamshire CID and by Sir Peter Imbert, who was later to head the Metropolitan Police. However, Blackpool being a cash society without paperwork, cases were hard to prove. Only a couple of prosecutions followed, the chairman of the police committee being acquitted on a charge concerning planning permissions. The *Post* also had to settle, for £10,000, a libel action brought by two senior police officers mentioned in the Osmond Report. Despite its support of Parr, the *West Lancashire Gazette* was joined in the action.

The Parr affair and its aftermath helped bring two changes in the law. Parr had exploited the police's power to decide what charges an accused will face. This power has now passed to the Crown Prosecution Service. One case where the Lancashire police reduced a dangerous driving charge, rightly as it turned out, concerned a fatal traffic accident. A new offence of reckless driving was introduced.

17 Security and intelligence

THE NEW ANTI-TERRORIST FACE OF MI5

The British government has two intelligence services to provide it with secret information. In the Cold War, the Security Service MI5, working with the Special Branch of the police, sought to detect Soviet spies and to warn of the activities of people who might seek to subvert the British state. Today it concentrates on countering terrorism. The Secret Intelligence Service, MI6, seeks information about what is happening abroad.

One school of thought sees MI5 and MI6 as bastions of Britain: we have agents – other countries have spies. Secret information, however, is power and British governments love to have secret information. Journalists have been uneasy about the ways in which they suspect it has been used (to plant stories in newspapers, for example). They have also questioned whether, during the Cold War, some people were placed under unfair suspicion of subversive tendencies.

The end of the Cold War brought an important change. In its pamphlet about itself *MI5 The Security Service* (Stationery Office), MI5 says that Britain in the past faced a real threat from subversive organizations; but there are no current MI5 investigations into subversion. Instead, MI5 which has a staff of 1,900 largely concentrates on combating terrorism, along with some anti-espionage work. The pamphlet says it also has a new role against serious crime.

The pamphlet stresses that MI5 is politically impartial. Government departments still seek its advice on candidates for sensitive posts but this advice is based solely on MI5's records. A candidate or his relatives are presumably no longer subject to the sort of grilling described by investigative journalist David Leigh in his book *The Wilson Plot* (Heinemann, 1988).

THE BAD OLD DAYS

When Harold Wilson was prime minister, David Leigh recounts, the maverick MI5 agent Peter Wright took the opportunity of a possible ministerial appointment for a sick Labour MP to harry the MP about his past Communist connections. The MP, Bernard Floud, already in a disturbed state of mind, killed himself. After hearing of his death, a woman who unwittingly gave his name to MI5 threw herself under a tube train.

Leigh went to see a former Labour minister at the Treasury, Niall MacDermot, whose wife, Ludmila, of mixed Russian and Italian parentage, became an MI5 victim shortly after Floud.

Ludmila and her mother had been expelled from the Soviet Union to Italy in 1938. They struggled to survive. Then the war came and Ludmila joined an escape organization for Allied prisoners. When Rome was freed, she worked for a Soviet envoy, hoping to be able to rejoin her father in Russia. After the war she learned that he had died from torture. She became a UN interpreter in Geneva.

It was her work for the Soviet envoy in Rome that MI5 agents fastened on. Leigh writes that they interrogated Ludmila for a week, at the end of which they denounced her as a liar and a suspected Soviet agent. Her husband resigned from the government in disgust.

The main thesis of David Leigh's *The Wilson Plot* is that MI5 became suspicious of Harold Wilson when he negotiated with the Soviet Union as President of the Board of Trade in the 1940s, and that Wright and other MI5 men plotted against him when he was Prime Minister. MI5 in its pamphlet replies that an exhaustive investigation into this allegation concluded that no Wilson plot had existed. The pamphlet says that Wright admitted on *Panorama* in 1988 that his account in the book *Spycatcher* had been unreliable.

Wilson's resignation as Prime Minister, however, does seem to have been preceded by poor relations with MI5 and by press criticism which Leigh interprets as in part MI5-inspired.

BETTANEY AND REFORM

What both MI5 and investigative journalists agree on is the importance of the case of Michael Bettaney, a troubled MI5 agent who was jailed for 30 years in 1983 for offering information to the Soviet KGB. MI5 writes in its pamphlet, after mentioning Bettaney:

'Following a Security Commission inquiry, whose findings were critical of aspects of the Service, Sir Antony Duff was appointed as Director-General. He initiated the discussions which laid the foundations for the Service as it exists today.'

Bettaney's conviction caught the attention of two TV filmmakers, Claudia Milne and Geoffrey Seed. They were engaged on a film about the Special Branch when they found that younger MI5 people thought Bettaney had been poorly treated. He was heading for a nervous breakdown, got drunk and contacted the Russians. (He was released from prison in 1998.)

Milne says that she and Seed came across an article by Miranda Ingrams in *New Society* and asked Ingrams if she knew anything about Special Branch's relationship with MI5. Ingrams said they should talk to Cathy Massiter who had written a letter to *New Society* after the Ingrams article. Massiter was in the MI5 section dealing with domestic subversion. They discovered that she knew about surveillance of members of trade unions and of the Campaign for Nuclear Disarmament, Friends of the Earth, and the National Council for Civil Liberties.

It was ten months before Claudia Milne's and Geoffrey Seed's programme *MI5's Official Secrets* was broadcast. It breached the Official Secrets Act. The Ponting secrets trial (about the sinking of the Argentine warship Belgrano in the Falklands War) was in the offing. The Independent Broadcasting Authority had approved other programmes but those had been about history, not the contemporary situation.

Claudia Milne thinks *MI5's Official Secrets* could not have been made by a high-profile organization. She showed tapes to the IBA but wouldn't let it keep a copy.

The programme had to be made in complete secrecy as Cathy Massiter, who had helped them, was staying with friends and was vulnerable to arrest and imprisonment. 'Her motivation was moral,' says Milne. 'She never asked for a penny.'

OVERSIGHT OF THE SERVICES

The Sir Antony Duff reforms of MI5 in the 1980s were accompanied by the Security Service Act of 1989 which established a system of oversight of MI5's activities. The Act places MI5 under the authority of the Home Secretary (who must authorize any telephone-tapping or entry into private property). It provides for an independent tribunal and a commissioner to deal with complaints and sets out the tasks of MI5's director-general, including ensuring that it is impartial and that it discloses information only in accordance with its statutory functions. These functions are protecting national security, safeguarding the UK's economic well-being from overseas threats, and helping prevent and detect serious crime.

As MI5's pamphlet acknowledges, the crime role has an inherent snag. MI5 deals in secret information provided or gathered by secret informants and agents. The courts, in which criminals are prosecuted, require disclosure of information and informants. The pamphlet explains that, if there is a dispute whether information should be disclosed or not, the court will decide.

Apart from the Security Service Act provisions, MI5 is also subject to scrutiny by a Parliamentary committee which also scrutinizes the foreign intelligence service MI6.

There remains an inevitable problem with secret services: only their members can know fully what is going on inside them. It is hard for journalists to assess any secret information that may be offered. Such information is inevitably unattributable. It is also hard for anyone to counter secret information against them if they do not know what it is.

MI5 has changed but journalists still need to be vigilant.

MI6

Britain's foreign intelligence service, MI6, has like MI5 a shadowy presence in the worlds explored by investigative journalism. It is represented in just about any British embassy or high commission overseas.

It may well have played a major part in the short life of Jonathan Moyle, the magazine editor murdered in Chile because of his interest in the arming of helicopters for Iraq (see page 163). It also recruited as an agent Paul Henderson, the managing director of the machines-for-Iraq firm Matrix Churchill. It distanced itself from Henderson when things went wrong.

Financial Times journalists in 1991 asked the question: Which British bank has been most involved in financing arms sales? They came up with the story of a loss-making Midland Bank enterprise called Midland International Trade Services. The story referred to an arms sales unit staffed by former members of the intelligence services.

Two publications keep an eye on what MI5 and MI6 are doing. They are *Lobster* magazine, 214 Westbourne Avenue, Hull HU5 3JB (tel. 01482-447558; e-mail robin@lobster.karoo.co.uk) and *Statewatch*, PO Box 1516, London N16 0EW (tel. 0208-802-1882; fax 0208-880-1727).

University researchers about intelligence services include Professor Bernard Porter, Newcastle (0191-222-6694), and Professor Laurence Lustgarten, Southampton (023-8059-3414/3550).

MI5 and MI6 both now have unofficial press officers. Officially, the Foreign Office news department (0207-270-3100) handles queries for MI6 and the Home Office press office (0207-273-4610) for MI5. Both MI5 and MI6 have direct lines, known to some favoured journalists, but these are not much good unless you also have a name to ask for.

18 Investigating local government

CLUES THAT SPELL CORRUPTION

Several investigative journalists have had their curiosity roused initially by what they saw going on in local government. *The Independent* reported in 1992 that investigations were in progress in 19 out of 32 London authorities into allegations ranging from the sale of council flat keys to bribery of inspectors of street markets.

John Ware of *Panorama* started in journalism at the *Droitwich Guardian* where he discovered the wealthy local mayor had failed to declare to the planning committee his interest in a planning application made on his behalf. John Ware wrote the story. 'It was the splash. It created a huge fuss,' he says.

David Hencke of *The Guardian* says his interest was first stirred when he worked at Wellingborough for the *Northamptonshire Evening Telegraph*. The council there discussed six options for an inner ring road and kept them secret. However, a councillor gave him a copy of the options.

This incident also showed him that in matters of public policy there is often a private agenda as well as the public one. In theory there may be consultation. In fact, someone has already made the decision and is pushing it through.

Tony Collins of *Computer Weekly* began his journalism on a weekly in the Reigate area. He got interested in the council reports that were printed on pink paper and were therefore confidential. One of them concerned the redevelopment of Redhill town centre. He told me:

'I thought people should know about it. The developers and councillors asked me not to run stories. Then they went to the editor.

'We had a change of editor and the new one said: "Stop". So I left.'

Councils are subject to the Local Government (Access to Information) Act which gives the public access to council, committee and subcommittee meetings and a wide range of documents (see Appendix C). They include not just reports and minutes but also registers such as those of planning applications and residential homes and the land charges register which shows if a building is in a conservation area or has had a planning permission granted. Councils must publish lists showing where the various public documents can be seen.

It is also possible to inspect a council's accounts, at the time of the annual audit. *McNae's Essential Law for Journalists* points out that the *Express and Star*, Wolverhampton, has made good use of this. It once disclosed the existence of a Birmingham City car pool with chauffeur-driven cars. As with most trawls through documents, it helps to have some idea what you are looking for.

There is an important exception to the public's right to know. It is not allowed confidential information about people or forthcoming contracts: but, once a contract is made, disclosure can no longer prejudice its award.

The ownership of property is confidential. If you ask the council who owns No. 6 Acacia Avenue, it ought not to tell you. You might find out by going to the house. You could also look to see if the house has figured in a planning application. Applications name the applicant, who may not be the property owner. You could also find out, somewhat laboriously, from the local office of the Land Registry (see phone book).

Though there is far wider access to local than central government information, problems for journalists remain. Geoff Elliott, editor of

The News, Portsmouth, says that decisions sometimes get hidden in working parties that don't have to be open to the public. Richard Bettsworth, *The News*'s political editor, says Portsmouth council has been criticized for its handling of the millennium scheme for reviving the harbour area. Discussions have been held in private, on the plea that they concern tenders.

MONITORING THE COUNCILS

Councils, and their coverage by journalists, have changed over the past 30 years.

Councils are less liberally funded than in the 1960s and 1970s. New bodies such as training and enterprise councils have moved on to their patch. They themselves have formed new partnerships with business and voluntary organizations to promote the local economy or to make improvements using money from the government's Single Regeneration Budget. These partnerships differ from one another in how they handle press relations.

Sandwell Council in the West Midlands, for instance, which has several partnership projects, aims at total openness. The projects put in reports to the council. There is an overall Sandwell Regeneration Partnership which meets every six weeks and has representatives of business, colleges, voluntary organizations, the training and enterprise council, Business Link, the health authority and the employment service. These meetings are open to the press, even if reporters do not show up.

In the London borough of Redbridge, the Bridging the Gap scheme at Woodford has a management board whose meetings are open to the public. In Bristol, the Western Development Partnership, which seeks to promote economic development, deals with the press through a public relations consultant.

In the early 1960s, one of Harold Evans's changes at *The Northern Echo* of which he was then editor was to curtail the coverage of council and committee meetings and give more space to off-diary stories with pictures. Since then, many newspapers have curtailed their coverage, either because council meetings are no longer so interesting or because they have other priorities. Councils have responded by producing handouts (particularly popular with free sheets) and their own municipal newspapers.

Journalists interested in investigations, however, need to bear in mind that what is said at council meetings, like what is said in courts, provides raw material for their work. If council meetings are not reported, this source of facts is not available.

CONTACTS AND INFORMATION

Geoff Elliott says *The News* at Portsmouth is now not much concerned with the proceedings of councils and committees but with pursuing local municipal issues that affect people, such as Portsmouth's need for another secondary school.

David Bell, municipal editor at the *Evening Mail*, Birmingham, says council meetings are like the tundra belt – nothing happens there:

'Going back ten or 15 years, you couldn't get a seat at a council meeting. Now it's only me who goes.

'I go and show my face. Then I go and stand in a different room and have a coffee and stories walk up to me.'

There are still committees worth going to, he says, and he also gets permission to cover some private sessions.

Bell has investigated several stories concerning grants for renovating houses. One councillor got a grant for £52,000, one of the highest ever made. 'Then he complained about the job that had been done. A climate has built up where people feel that they will be allowed to get away with these things.'

Forty-five thousand pounds was granted for two houses, one owned by a councillor's wife, the other by his son. Normally it is not possible to sell a house for three years if it has been renovated with a grant. The ownership of these, however, was transferred to other relatives and they were sold immediately.

The normal penalty for a Birmingham councillor caught out in such a manoeuvre, says David Bell, is to be dropped as candidate at the next election.

> Another councillor bought land from the council for his back garden. There was a restrictive covenant saying he couldn't build on it; but he got planning permission to build a garage. He built a double garage that had a window and front door like a house.

David Bell says there are people who love giving information to newspapers and seeing the story there. His problem is to confirm stories when there can be no confirmation in public reports (since data relating to particular people is confidential). 'You have to be spot on. The background to a lot of stories is in internal audit reports. They try their best not to let me get my hands on them.'

Local government reporting, says Bell, is all about contacts. 'You have to get people to trust you, so they know what they tell you off the record isn't going to have their name associated with it.'

It is a rule of local government that someone paid by a council, such as a teacher, cannot be a member of it. However, someone paid by a council-funded organization can be a councillor. Wives of councillors can also have council jobs. 'It's a question where you draw the line between patronage and corruption,' says David Bell.

How does he stay on good terms with the Birmingham Council when he keeps investigating some councillors' questionable activities? He gives a fair wind to major enterprises the council is involved in:

'I couldn't do my job if I was kicking them all the time. I do a fair job. I report what goes on.

'We don't get many complaints from the council because we make sure we are right.

KEEPING A SOURCE SECRET

In the 1980s, the former Wessex Regional Health Authority embarked on a scheme to computerize 300 hospitals. If the work of hospitals could be computerized, it would make them run more smoothly. Each department would no longer be a separate business. Patients' details would be required only once, not by every department they deal with. If they went for an X-ray examination, the radiographers would know of previous examinations. Wards would have access through the computer to the results of tests. However, it is hard to computerize one hospital, let alone 300.

Tony Collins of *Computer Weekly* began reporting the Wessex scheme's progress in 1989. Two years later, it was abandoned. One of Collins' stories concerned the loss of a million pounds on one contract. This led to him being told about a person he needed to speak to, someone who had the facts and was concerned about them.

He rang this key source to ask for a meeting. It was refused. He rang again. It was refused again.

A few days later his source agreed to a meeting in a Southampton hotel, and listened to what he had to say but told him nothing. A week later the contact had had no comeback as a result of meeting him and was pleasantly surprised that nothing had appeared in print. Thus reassured, the contact gave Collins an outline of what had gone wrong with the computerization scheme. Collins learned that there were two audit reports in which the scheme's troubles were set out. He said he wanted to see them. He didn't get them.

Two weeks passed. Then he was asked to go to a café in a remote village which it took him a long time to find. One report was handed over, the other following a short time later.

The reports showed that £63 million of public money had been lost: £43 million through the abandonment of the scheme, £20 million on associated contracts.

The reports alleged that in the allocation of contracts there were serious conflicts of interest. A member of the regional health authority worked for a company which won the main contract even though its bid had initially been judged one of the less attractive. The chairman of the authority knew a director of a company bidding for another contract. A computer was bought for £3 million and never unpacked before being scrapped. These were a few of the audit reports' allegations.

THE KIRKBY SKI SLOPE AFFAIR

To spend its remaining money before it was absorbed in 1974 into Knowsley, Kirkby Council built a ski slope. A correspondent told the *Liverpool Free Press*, one of the most successful fringe papers of the 1970s, that the council had used volunteer schoolchildren to finish it and had paid 25p an hour for weekend working. It also turned out that the slope lacked planning permission, was built over Kirkby's main water pipe and faced on to a main road.

Brian Whitaker, one of three journalists then running the *Free Press* and now managing editor of *The Guardian*, tells the story in *News Ltd* (Minority Press, 1981).

A *Free Press* report about the ski slope attracted an anonymous letter. It said that the contractor, George Leatherbarrow, had charged for the earth he used but hadn't paid for it. He had advertised the site in the *Liverpool Echo* as a free tip. The letter also said he was to be seen lunching in a named pub with the council leader, Dave Tempest, and the architect, Eric Spencer Stevenson.

Steve Scott of the *Free Press* spoke to councillors but they knew nothing. He spent a fortnight in the public library going through council minutes. This showed that Leatherbarrow had received about £10 million worth of council contracts. The big national builders hardly got a look in.

Scott also found in the minutes the names of officials who had left Kirkby. He went to see one who sounded helpful but who feared he would never get another job in local government if it was known he had talked. This official said enough to confirm there was a story.

There were rumours of work done by Leatherbarrow for people involved in Kirkby Council. A tenants' organization led the *Free Press* to a former shop steward who gave the names of other Leatherbarrow workers. They in turn mentioned something called the Star Gang at Leatherbarrows, made up of privileged workers who did special jobs. Steve Scott kept turning up on the doorstep of one member of the gang who said a little more each time. The Star Gang members eventually disclosed that Leatherbarrow had built a house extension for the council architect Stevenson and a bigger extension for council leader Tempest.

Chris Oxley of the *Free Press* traced a former council sports centre manager who had been jailed for obtaining £2,000 by deception. In court, he had attributed his downfall to high living while he worked for the council. He had told the court about lavish entertainment by contractors.

He told the *Free Press* about a trip to London paid for by Leatherbarrow, in which Tempest and Stevenson took part. He also disclosed that Stevenson had a car known as Leatherbarrow's.

Leatherbarrow's ex-wife said the car was a maroon Alfa Romeo. She also said that Stevenson was best man at Leatherbarrow's second wedding. A copy of the marriage certificate from Birkenhead Register Office showed Stevenson as one of the witnesses.

The *Free Press* still wanted to prove that Leatherbarrow had paid for the trip to London. A call to the hotel where they were said to have stayed was unsuccessful. Chris Oxley phoned the travel agent, posing as Leatherbarrow's accountant, and asked for the price of the tickets. The agent confirmed that the bill went to Leatherbarrow.

Steve Scott rang Tempest who claimed to have paid for his house extension. But the journalists knew that materials had come from a council site. A Liverpool surveyor said that, if they were on the site, the council must have paid for them. They should not have been used in the extension.

One problem remained. Stevenson's current Alfa Romeo was cream, whereas Leatherbarrow's ex-wife had mentioned that the car provided by Leatherbarrow was maroon. The *Free Press* men took the story to *BBC Nationwide*, and a *Nationwide* producer pointed out that few garages service Alfas. He found the garage that had serviced a maroon Alfa, which Stevenson had been driving before the cream one.

The police began a long investigation. Leatherbarrow, Stevenson and Tempest were accused of conspiracy and later went to jail.

Brian Whitaker stresses that the *Free Press*'s inquiry was more time-consuming and less straightforward than it sounds. They spent time studying the tactics of other builders and vainly pursuing other rumours. It took four months, a big effort for a small paper.

SCANDAL AT THE TOWN HALL

Ray Fitzwalter's exposure of John Poulson, the architect who won contracts by bribery, showed how some councillors and public officials had profited from the inrush of money into public construction work in the 1960s and 1970s.

Alan Doig makes it clear in *Corruption and Misconduct in Contemporary British Politics* (Penguin, 1984) that Poulson was by no means the only businessman corruptly seeking to exploit the construction boom. (Five hundred town-centre redevelopment schemes were in progress in 1965.)

Those in public posts who took Poulson's money claimed they didn't think they were doing wrong.

Until 200 years ago, public servants were expected to make use of their office to secure an income. Parliament did not pass an Act to pay public officials until 1816. Press allegations about the rebuilding of Shaftesbury Avenue in London led to the Public Bodies Corrupt Practices Act of 1889 which forbids people in local government from accepting gifts. Further Corruption Acts were passed in 1906 and 1916. The Local Government Act of 1933 requires councillors to declare their business interests.

> John Poulson, the Pontefract architect, however, was good at psychology. He gave influential people what they wanted: help with building work on their home, a day at the races, a mortgage. In return, he got contracts from councils and other public undertakings. At Eston on Teesside, he got contracts for the civic hall, town hall, sports hall, swimming pools, Labour club and for housing.

He paid his contacts through the Newcastle public relations firm of Dan Smith who, disappointed in his hopes of advancement in the Labour Party, decided that, as he put it, 'I could combine my real desire to give public service with what they call a piece of the action.'

In the end, Poulson paid so much for contracts that he bankrupted himself and the whole story came out in court.

For years there had been nothing to draw him to a journalist's attention. The evidence of his importance was scattered in council minutes throughout the North-East and Yorkshire. There was no reason why someone who read the Eston minutes should also look at those of Felling (Tyneside), Pontefract (West Yorkshire) and the Sunderland Police Authority.

Ray Fitzwalter, when he stumbled on Poulson, was deputy news editor of the *Telegraph and Argus*, Bradford, and did investigations in his spare time. 'We did an enormous piece on illegal immigration. We also exposed a fraudulent businessman who was one of our biggest advertisers.'

Four corruption cases in Bradford court led to his meeting a contractor who was the chief prosecution witness in the four cases. The contractor insisted that they met at midnight. 'I am a small operator,' he said. 'This man Poulson operates on three levels, local, regional and national.'

He suggested inquiring into a company called Open Systems Building. Ray Fitzwalter looked it up at Companies House. The directors included the clerk to the West Riding County Council, a Coal Board divisional chairman and Reginald Maudling, then deputy leader of the Conservative Party. OSB was based at Poulson's Pontefract office. There was a document with an undecipherable signature bearing an address in Spitaltongues, Newcastle. It was Dan Smith's address. So at the very start of his inquiries Ray Fitzwalter had tied Poulson and Smith together.

A search through Bradford, Pontefract and West Riding minutes showed that Poulson had won one contract after another. Fitzwalter also sought out former Poulson employees. Some hated Poulson and were prepared to tell what they knew.

Because of the danger of a libel action, the *Telegraph and Argus*'s article was low-key; but it was spotted by Paul Foot who, with Fitzwalter's help, wrote three pages about the 'Slicker of Wakefield' for *Private Eye*. The rest of the media failed to react until the bankruptcy hearing two years later.

After leaving Bradford, Ray Fitzwalter pursued the Poulson story for *World in Action*. He and David Taylor also wrote *Web of Corruption*, published by Granada in 1981.

Both Fitzwalter and public administration expert Alan Doig were disappointed by the reaction of the British Establishment. It tended to see corruption as involving individuals rather than as highlighting problems in local government itself. The Redcliffe Maud inquiry into local government did not really ask why the press and other safeguards had failed to stop Poulson and other conspirators. (One reason for the failure, suggests Doig, was that local media were eager to protect their local monopolies by cultivating a non-controversial, bi-partisan image.)

A Royal Commission headed by Lord Salmon looked deeper. It pointed to poorly rewarded councillors and the dangers of one-party rule.

Councils were relieved to put Poulson behind them. The clerk to Newburn Urban Council on Tyneside commented: 'They [the police] have gone now and I hope they won't be pestering us again. Mr Poulson was our consultant architect for six or seven years. He designed our new swimming pool, library, shopping centre and some housing.'

Poulson-style scandals, however, emerged at Pontefract and in the North-East (again), and in Birmingham and South Wales. One building firm had 575 people on its gifts list. Another hired councillors as scouts and advocates of planning permission.

Inadequately supported allegations, however, can be costly. The Swansea Five (businessmen) received an out-of-court settlement of £100,000 after a *Man Alive* television programme in 1975.

POWER THAT CORRUPTS

A Dundee councillor watched one of *World in Action*'s Poulson programmes called *Business in Gozo*. Then he rang Ray Fitzwalter and said: 'You are the only people who can solve our problems.'

Dundee had seen big developments: housing estates, tower blocks, a new city centre, one of the most expensive hospitals in the country. One construction firm, Crudens, had picked up contracts worth £62 million. But some councillors were also businessmen. The Lord Provost had a plant-hire company which in 1969 reached a £1 million turnover. Was everything properly decided?

The police made inquiries in the 1960s. The town clerk made inquiries. *The Sunday Times* in 1973 made inquiries. Nobody cracked the Dundee riddle. So was it going to be a frustrating waste of time for *World in Action*?

> The nub of Ray Fitzwalter's inquiries was whether a small group of powerful councillors had attended planning meetings and whether they had declared their interest in planning applications. Other councillors said: 'We are just councillors. We get a big bundle of minutes at 6 pm when we haven't time to read them. They do things in committee. They are running rings round us.'

Some businessmen were frightened to speak out because they feared the consequences. One businessman had watched Dundee for years but had been unable to operate there. 'When we came, he realized someone was going to crack it,' says Ray Fitzwalter:

'Dundee had a Labour council in power for a long time. I had help from the Conservative party, the Liberal party, disaffected Labour, frightened businessmen. Even the police wanted to help us. The leader of the Conservatives came to meet me at a businessman's house with a bag over his head.

'Everybody was prepared to help but everybody was frightened. They feared arson.

'People had come to blows at council meetings. The Lord Provost fought with an opponent while wearing his ermine robes.

'What we did was comb the records. We went through 18 years of council minutes. I read them all and I read them again. They were very well kept minutes, showing who attended a meeting, who declared an interest. You could see patterns of behaviour and decision-making. All of these were in the public library.

'Second, we had records from Companies House. Third, a friend also got me some confidential papers. Fourth, there were the Scottish land records which are open to the public and are kept in Edinburgh. [These showed when land was bought and at what price.]'

As a bonus, someone had photographed relevant documents held in an office safe. This gave *World in Action* a fifth group of papers. Ray Fitzwalter drew chronologies of events from these five groups and put them side by side. There was a mysterious estate agent involved with a London developer. He seemed to have no role and yet he was receiving £10,000. Councillors were forming small private companies and taking on subcontracts.

It all led to a *World in Action* programme in 1975, which a local paper dismissed in four paragraphs beginning: 'Three Dundee councillors were in the TV spotlight last night . . .' A local MP said it was trial by television.

But the longest local criminal trial followed in 1980. James Stewart who had been the leader of the Labour group on the council got five years. He was found guilty of corruptly soliciting and receiving rewards concerning the construction of Dundee's Wellgate shopping complex, and also of asking for contracts for his electrical firm. Two others were cleared on appeal.

19 Sleaze

THE CASH-FOR-QUESTIONS TANGLE

On October 20, 1994, *The Guardian* accused two junior ministers in John Major's government of accepting payment for asking questions in the House of Commons. One of them, Tim Smith, immediately resigned from the government. The other, Neil Hamilton, and the lobbyist Ian Greer sued *The Guardian*. On September 30, 1996, they withdrew their action, paying £15,000 towards *The Guardian*'s costs.

But the issue has never been, and may never be, finally resolved. Mohammed Al Fayed, owner of Harrods, says that he paid Hamilton thousands of pounds in brown envelopes. Hamilton has always denied receiving it. In 1999 he was seeking to reopen the matter by persuading the Court of Appeal to let him bring a new libel suit, against Al Fayed.

None of the cash which Hamilton is alleged to have been paid by Al Fayed shows up in his bank accounts. Sir Gordon Downey, then Parliamentary Commissioner for Standards, who held an inquiry, concluded that the evidence for Hamilton having taken money was nevertheless compelling. But the Select Committee on Standards and Privileges did not endorse his conclusion. It pointed out that there was no way of proving whether Hamilton took the money or not.

Investigations and inquiries seek a clear-cut conclusion but they do not necessarily achieve one.

Figure 19.1
Front cover of *Sleaze* (Fourth Estate, 1997), the story of *The Guardian*'s investigation into cash payments by Mohammed Al Fayed to get questions asked in Parliament. Neil Hamilton, pictured, vainly sued *The Guardian* over its allegations against him

The investigative work behind *The Guardian*'s story and its defeat of the Greer/Hamilton lawsuit is described by authors David Leigh and Ed Vulliamy in their book *Sleaze* (Fourth Estate, 1997).

Ten years earlier, in 1985, Professor Philip Norton had alleged in the book *Parliamentary Questions* that the going rate for getting a question asked in Parliament was then £150. He quoted no specific instance.

HOW THE EDITOR OF *THE GUARDIAN* MET AL FAYED

The Guardian's work started by chance in 1993, as a result of its inquiries into secret gifts to the Conservative Party which led to a front-page lead alleging that the givers included members of the Saudi royal family. Controversy broke out and *The Guardian* later had to withdraw this allegation. However, the story brought a message to Hugo Young of *The Guardian* from a Liberal peer, Lord Lester. It was an offer of help from Mohammed Al Fayed, owner of Harrods store. Peter Preston, then *The Guardian*'s editor, went to Harrods to see him.

Al Fayed held forth about an array of Saudi princes. Preston asked how this related to any gifts to the Conservatives. Al Fayed replied that Tim Smith MP had asked him for money before the 1991 election but he had refused him.

This set the conversation in a new direction. In the 1980s, Al Fayed had been under attack from Tiny Rowland of Lonrho who wanted to own Harrods and disputed Al Fayed's takeover of the store. Al Fayed told Peter Preston that the lobbyist Ian Greer had offered him help and had introduced Tim Smith and Neil Hamilton to him. Al Fayed said they had asked questions in Parliament for him and had been paid to do so. Al Fayed also said that Hamilton and Mrs Hamilton had stayed a week at the Ritz Hotel in Paris (which Al Fayed owned) and had run up a bill for thousands of pounds.

Authors Leigh and Vulliamy explain the background to this discussion between Al Fayed and Preston: it was, they say, that Hamilton had been obliged to distance himself from Al Fayed after becoming a minister at the Department of Trade. The department was in a legal dispute with Al Fayed because of Al Fayed's endeavours to overturn the report of its inquiry into his takeover of Harrods. Leigh and Vulliamy surmise that Al Fayed was unlikely to take kindly to being brushed off by Hamilton.

Preston, after the meeting with Al Fayed, asked his investigative reporter David Hencke and another reporter John Mullin to find out about questions which Al Fayed said Smith and Hamilton had asked in Parliament and also whether any money had been declared in the Register of Members' Interests. The two reporters were also asked to find out about Greer's lobbying firm, Ian Greer Associates. During their inquiries they discovered that Greer in 1990 had admitted paying money to three MPs.

Guardian editor Peter Preston returned to see Al Fayed but found him less forthcoming than before. He showed Preston the Hamiltons' Ritz bill but was not prepared to let Preston take it away as documentary evidence.

Leigh and Vulliamy write that, challenged by the reporters Hencke and Mullin, Tim Smith and Neil Hamilton denied taking money; but Hamilton conceded he might have stayed a night at the Ritz. He also wrote a long letter to editor Preston, warning him off the investigation. Hencke and Mullin published in *The Guardian* an article 'The power and prestige of Ian Greer', detailing the important companies who were Greer's clients.

THE SUNDAY TIMES JOINS IN

The Sunday Times next took a hand. Al Fayed had repeated to its editor Andrew Neil his claim that he had paid MPs. Al Fayed made clear he did not want to be named and he did not want the MPs to be approached. *The Sunday Times* Insight team amassed print-outs of Parliamentary questions and found MPs taking an interest in all manner of commercial causes.

Jonathan Calvert of Insight fixed up a meeting with Ian Greer Associates, claiming to be a Welsh haulier who wanted the Severn Bridge tolls abolished. He asked if Ian Greer Associates could arrange for MPs to ask questions about it, and would the MPs have to be paid? 'We would never pay MPs,' said one of the associates.

Sylvia Jones and Clive Entwhistle of television's *The Cook Report* were on a similar tack. They sought Greer's aid in recruiting MPs to help 'legitimize' the UK business interests of a phoney Russian company. Having secretly recorded Greer's boasts, they then planned to test them by using the services of Greer's recommended list of MPs. But by this time *The Cook Report* was off the air. Before the next series began *The Guardian*, with which the programme had been working, ran the story anyway (see below).

Then Mark Skipworth, deputy editor of Insight at *The Sunday Times*, had a new idea. Why not ask MPs directly if they would accept £1,000 to table a written Parliamentary question? Ten Conservatives and ten Labour MPs were asked. Two Conservatives rose to the bait. *The Sunday Times* headline read: 'Revealed: MPs who accept £1,000 to ask a Parliamentary question'. The House of Commons' Committee of Privileges briefly suspended the two MPs concerned. It also reprimanded *The Sunday Times* for conduct it said was below the standard of legitimate investigative journalism.

PROMISE OF PROOF

Authors Leigh and Vulliamy relate that in September 1994 Mohammed Al Fayed asked Peter Preston, editor of *The Guardian*, to call again. Al Fayed had hoped the European Court of Human Rights would demolish the Department of Trade inquiry report criticizing his takeover of Harrods. The court was looking unlikely to do so. 'Now I am right behind you,' Al Fayed told Preston. He promised Preston documentary proof of his allegations against the MPs, Smith and Hamilton.

Al Fayed also spoke to Brian Hitchen, then editor of the *Sunday Express*, who warned John Major that Al Fayed had four ministers – Michael Howard, Jonathan Aitken, Tim Smith and Neil Hamilton – in his sights. Sir Robin Butler, the Cabinet Secretary, soon decided that Howard and Aitken had not taken cash for asking questions. Smith, who had declared fees from Al Fayed on his tax return, confessed to taking cash. Hamilton denied to Butler that he had taken cash and said that he had stayed, when at the Ritz, in Al Fayed's private accommodation. Meanwhile, evidence from Al Fayed was reaching *The Guardian*. It headed its story on October 20: 'Tory MPs were paid to plant questions says Harrods chief'.

Ian Greer Associates denied everything and served writs on *The Guardian*. Tim Smith resigned as a Northern Ireland minister. Hamilton decided to fight and sued *The Guardian*.

Questioned by Michael Heseltine, Secretary for Trade and Industry, Hamilton denied any financial relationship with Ian Greer. With this assurance, Prime Minister Major let him stay as Minister for Corporate Affairs. There were, however, other controversies concerning Hamilton apart from the allegations which *The Guardian* had made. Within a week of the *Guardian* article, Hamilton had left the government. Prime Minister John Major announced he was setting up the Committee on Standards in Public Life.

HAMILTON AND GREER SUE FOR LIBEL

Hamilton's subsequent libel suit against *The Guardian* ran into an unusual problem. The Parliamentary privilege which defends MPs against the courts made it impossible for *The Guardian* to allege in court that Hamilton had asked Parliamentary questions for money. If *The Guardian* could not raise this issue, its defence was compromised. In July 1995, that was how Mr Justice May saw the situation. He put the case on ice.

An abortive effort was made to get the case heard by Parliament itself. Then Hamilton and his supporters managed to get a clause tacked on to the Defamation Bill. This clause enabled Hamilton to waive his Parliamentary privilege so that his court case could go ahead.

It did not entirely end the difficulty. The other minister who resigned, Tim Smith, refused to waive his privilege: he wanted to keep out of the case. But in mid-August Mr Justice May, summoned back from holiday, took Hamilton's libel suit off ice and put it down for trial on October 1, only six weeks ahead.

That was not a date on which the barristers booked for the trial were going to be available. Geraldine Proudler, *The Guardian*'s solicitor, rang Geoffrey Robertson QC who had led the successful defence of three directors of Matrix Churchill accused of breaking the embargo on arms for Iraq. Robertson was on holiday in Tuscany in the villa of author John Mortimer. Geraldine Proudler (who at a business meeting at Harrods had been presented by Al Fayed with an outsize teddy bear) offered Robertson £30,000 for the brief, plus £2,000 a day during the trial. He accepted.

Tony Blair, also on holiday in Tuscany, commented to Robertson: 'I only hope they've been more accurate about Neil Hamilton than they are about me.'

Having returned to Britain, Robertson gave *Guardian* executives a sober view of their chances of defeating Hamilton and his co-plaintiff Ian Greer. This was partly to get *The Guardian* to put the maximum effort into the few weeks remaining for preparations. The new editor, Alan Rusbridger, said *The Guardian* would fight.

Robertson created a detailed chronology of all that had happened: letters, speeches, Parliamentary questions, payments. Geraldine Proudler sought to guess what papers Hamilton, Greer or the government might hold which could provide useful facts for the case. She could ask for these under the discovery process which allows each side in a court case to see anything relevant which is on record.

Greer was claiming for £10 million of business which he said his firm had lost. This allowed Proudler's team to ask for his accounts. A note in a margin showed that Greer's firm had paid Hamilton a fee in 1989.

From Conservative Central Office, Proudler obtained a document showing that Greer had forwarded £18,000 from Al Fayed and £11,000 from the DHL courier company to 21 MPs to help with their expenses in the 1987 general election.

On September 20, Proudler obtained from Greer records of payments to Hamilton and of bills he had paid for Hamilton, for watercolours and for garden furniture.

On September 26, Charles Gray QC told the High Court that the government would release relevant papers; but anything not relevant would first have to be blacked out. It took the civil servants till about 10 pm to do the blacking-out: some of it had to be done twice. But what remained in the clear included a record of Hamilton's statement to Trade Secretary Heseltine that he had had no financial relationship with Ian Greer. (This meant, authors Leigh and Vulliamy point out, that Heseltine could be confronted in court with evidence that Hamilton had misled him.)

Meanwhile, according to the two authors, Doug Marvin, a lawyer for Al Fayed, had obtained statements from Al Fayed's secretary, his former personal assistant and his doorman. These all backed up what

Al Fayed said about giving Hamilton money in envelopes. Robertson remarked to Marvin that he had asked him for a smoking gun and had been given a Kalashnikov. (The Select Committee on Standards and Privileges, however, later decided that this back-up evidence was not conclusive. None of it was from a witness independent of Al Fayed.)

On Friday September 27, with the trial due to open on the Tuesday, Hamilton's and Greer's QC, Richard Ferguson, asked Robertson if both sides could walk away from the trial, each paying its own costs. He disclosed that a conflict of interests had arisen between Greer and Hamilton. This meant that Greer and Hamilton would each need new lawyers and the trial would have to be put off until mid-1997.

What had happened, Sir Gordon Downey's inquiry was to learn, was that the discovery process had unearthed evidence of payments by Greer to Sir Michael Grylls MP, beyond those Greer had admitted in a 1990 hearing. This torpedoed Greer's, though not Hamilton's, case.

The Guardian decided to offer a deal; but Greer and Hamilton would have to pay towards *The Guardian*'s costs to make it clear who had won. At the last possible moment on the Monday afternoon the deal was done: Greer and Hamilton agreed to pay £15,000. *The Guardian*'s headline next morning read: 'A liar and a cheat'.

THE AFTERMATH

Because the case ended in a deal not a hearing, the evidence which *The Guardian* had gained through the discovery process remained confidential until it was submitted to Sir Gordon Downey's inquiry. *The Guardian* could not use it in support of its reporting. So Greer and Hamilton were able, particularly on television, to dismiss *The Guardian*'s case as all lies. However, in television interviews, Greer admitted making two payments to Hamilton who admitted accepting cash and goods totalling £10,000. This money came from the National Nuclear Corporation and US Tobacco.

Giving evidence to Sir Gordon Downey's inquiry, Hamilton explained why he nevertheless denied to Michael Heseltine that he had had a financial relationship with Greer. What Heseltine wanted to know, he believed, was whether he (Hamilton) had a relationship with Greer which could be misrepresented as a means by which Al Fayed money could get into his pocket. He felt it would have been unwise to mention the money from National Nuclear and US Tobacco.

Concerning Hamilton's controversial stay at the Paris Ritz, Downey set out what he said had been agreed about it: Hamilton and Mrs Hamilton were at the Ritz from September 8 to 14, 1987; no expenditure was charged to Hamilton; Hamilton signed a bill for extras; the Hamiltons stayed in a standard hotel room; Hamilton did not declare the stay in the Parliamentary register.

The Select Committee on Standards and Privileges agreed with Downey that Hamilton had misled Heseltine. It found Hamilton had failed to make several entries in the Parliamentary register which he should have made. But it left the main issue, whether he had received Al Fayed money, open.

CASH FOR ACCESS

For a month or two in 1998, the cash-for-access controversy caused Tony Blair's government the sort of embarrassment which its Conservative predecessor suffered from cash-for-questions. Investigative journalist Antony Barnett of *The Observer* says he had watched people who worked for the Labour Party in Opposition move into lobbying firms when Labour became the government. Lobbyist LLM, for example, was set up by Neil Lawson who worked for Blair on 1997 election strategy, Ben Lucas who ran Blair's political briefing unit and Jon Mendelsohn who handled Blair's contacts with business.

To businessmen seeking help in dealing with the government, these New Labour lobbyists on first-name terms with Tony, Gordon (Brown) and Peter (Mandelson), not to mention the members of Blair's kitchen cabinet, were bound to look to be worth considerable fees.

Barnett says he heard that a lobbyist had promised a businessman an advance look at a government paper. Barnett thought of writing a feature article about it but instead decided to put the lobbyists to the test. With the prospect of a contract with American companies, what would they offer in return?

Barnett persuaded writer Gregory Palast to act as the Americans' representative. Palast, a well-known American expert on energy issues and a campaigner against big companies, agreed that, if the lobbyists were misbehaving, they should be exposed.

Barnett drew up a list of seven or eight lobbying companies. Some responded with complete propriety to Palast's approach. One, however, provided an advance copy of a Select Committee report on energy policy. Others spoke of approaches to Gordon Brown and his adviser Ed Balls of arranging a meeting in the Downing Street dining room and of securing a seat on a government task force.

None offered more or provided more good quotes than Derek Draper, former aide to Labour's chief spin doctor, Peter Mandelson. Draper had not been a main target of the *Observer* investigation. He became the main casualty. 'There are 17 people who count [in government],' Palast quoted Draper as saying. 'And to say I am intimate with every one of them is the understatement of the century.'

Was Draper simply bragging? Palast sought to find this out when Draper invited him to the annual party held by GPC, the lobbying firm that Draper worked for. Peers, MPs and Downing Street officials mixed with the nation's business élite quaffing GPC's champagne, reported Palast.

He asked Draper to point out someone who would vouch for his influence. Seemingly at random, Draper grabbed a short, balding man. It was Roger Liddle of Tony Blair's policy unit. 'Derek,' said Liddle, 'knows all the right people.'

Then, reported Palast, Liddle made his own offer of help in making contacts. 'Just tell me what you want, who you want to meet,' Palast quoted him as saying. 'Derek and I will make the call for you.'

Antony Barnett says that Palast, who could scarcely believe what he had heard, wrote the quote down on the back of Liddle's business card. Liddle told *The Observer* later that he could not remember what he had said but he was simply being friendly. It was nonsense to suggest he was going round offering his services.

Up to that point, says Antony Barnett, *The Observer* had not known of the close connection between Liddle and Draper.

When *The Observer* published the results of its investigation, a storm broke out. Palast came under personal attack from the government side. 'We hit such a sensitive nerve at that time,' says Barnett. 'What I learned is how they went after the messenger. They went after Greg (Palast).'

Palast, government spokesmen told journalists, was an American in a trilby, a lightweight Johnny-come-lately seeking to make some money on the side by selling his scam to *The Observer*. A judge in an American court case, said the spokesmen, had described him as not a credible witness.

In fact, it was *The Observer* which approached Palast, not Palast who approached *The Observer*. Barnett adds: 'We managed to get hold of a senior judge in the States who gave Greg Palast a great reference. He said the judge who criticized Greg was later retired for senility.'

As for Palast the alleged lightweight, Barnett says he was sufficiently heavyweight for Margaret Beckett and John Prescott of the Labour Party to have used his expertise in the past.

The Labour Party was far from united against *The Observer* on the access issue. Barnett was surprised by how much support the paper received from party members critical of Draper and his link to the influential Peter Mandelson. One government minister offered *The Observer* congratulations on its exposé.

David Hencke of *The Guardian* says *The Observer*'s story set him and fellow investigators thinking about the possible source of the money with which Mandelson had bought his expensive house in Notting Hill. Had some come from the lobbying industry? It seemed not. But the *Guardian* team eventually identified the source as a loan from the Paymaster General, Geoffrey Robinson. Both Robinson and Mandelson resigned from the government.

20 Cruelty and corruption abroad

WHY ABROAD NEEDS INVESTIGATION

There are plenty of situations abroad that need investigating. Assertions about faraway countries often go unchallenged or are met with denials which themselves go unchallenged for lack of facts.

Some governments and businessmen have an interest in making the world's beastlier regimes seem less beastly, in order to gain influence and export orders in those countries. Diplomats, companies, charities and journalists have all been tempted to make statements about situations in other countries while leaving important questions unanswered.

DEATH IN MATABELELAND

One of the smartest pieces of overseas investigation was carried out by Donald Trelford, then editor of *The Observer*, in 1983. Zimbabwe had two liberation movements, one backed by the Shona majority, the other by the Matabele minority. It was the Shona movement, led by President Mugabe, which won power in the independence elections of 1980.

Three years later, the Fifth Brigade of the Zimbabwean army set out to subdue Matabeleland. The veteran nationalist, Joshua Nkomo, said people had been massacred, and this was reported in *The Sunday Times*.

Donald Trelford, on a visit to Zimbabwe, flew to Bulawayo, the Matabele capital. A contact of another *Observer* journalist, Neal

Figure 20.1
'All you have to do is point the rifle and press the trigger.' Investigator Roger Cook masquerades in South Africa as a wealthy tourist eager to try canned hunting, the easy but cruel way to shoot big game – trapped in enclosures and drugged, ready for the marksmen. Cook's exposure of the seamy side of game-ranching led to 90 people being prosecuted (picture Carlton TV)

Ascherson, had arranged for him to meet eyewitnesses of the Fifth Brigade's rampage. Trelford slipped out of his hotel at night to meet the eyewitnesses and was back before his minder awoke. His *Observer* article described hundreds of murders under the heading 'Agony of a lost people'.

This shows the importance of advance preparation even when time is, inevitably, limited.

Roger Cook on a *Cook Report* expedition to South Africa exposed canned hunting: trapping lions and other game in enclosures for tourists to shoot. As a result, 90 people were prosecuted by the South African authorities.

USING CONTACTS

Ann Leslie, special correspondent of the *Daily Mail*, says there are three requirements for overseas investigation: curiosity, contacts and research. All three were useful when she looked into the fate of starving North Koreans in 1998.

Teenager Lee's best friend died of hunger at the age of 13. Lee watched his father die of hunger, too. He told Ann Leslie: 'Then my stepmother sold my little brother to a richer family. Then this year she said she couldn't feed me, so she threw me out.'

Lee crossed from North Korea into China where Korean-speaking villagers hid him so he wouldn't be sent back. We know about Lee, and the sufferings of many of his countrymen because Ann Leslie decided to find out what was happening in North Korea, a country shut to the outside world.

When she reached Beijing on her way there, she was told her tourist visa was cancelled:

'Which,' she says, 'enraged me. There I was in Beijing. I thought: "Right. I will do it in another way. I will try to find refugees, find where they get across the border, which isn't hard particularly in winter when the river is frozen." I had a problem, however. I can say "Good morning" and "Thank you" in Korean but don't speak enough to work there.

'I worked quite hard to establish contacts, people in Beijing who took an interest in the North Korean famine and the fact that it wasn't being covered in the Western media because it's a difficult and dangerous story to cover. You have to establish trust so people know they will be protected.'

Her contacts got her to the border. Corruption, she says, is incredibly useful:

'Wherever you are, you can always find an Arthur Daley, ducking and weaving and finding relatives who can get official cars, passes and so on.

'I couldn't pass myself off as a Korean peasant. I never pretend I am somebody I'm not. I dress and behave as I do in London. If you try to

play native, there's a tendency for people to think: "Why is she playing this game?" I am who I say I am. It works.

'*I checked in at a hotel. There's a university there, so there's a slight assumption you're probably an English language teacher. I use my mobile, never the hotel phone.*

'*I wouldn't say it was all that dangerous. There were three bad possibilities: one, you don't get the story; two, people helping you get punished; three, being in militarized border areas which are very sensitive, you might get shot.*

'*No one's life and livelihood is worth two pages in the* Daily Mail. *It's deeply immoral to put the chance of a big byline above the interests of the already suffering people you are writing about.*

'*Local people in the border areas would take more risks than I would. I often think: "Why are they taking this risk?" It's like the dissidents in the old Eastern Europe. They feel passionately that, unless people outside know, what's the point? They may have relatives in Korea, so it's a family matter. They don't want Granny to die of starvation. They want people to know about it.*

'*The fines if they're caught helping Koreans are enormous. But they can't just turn them out to die.*

'*I've never been asked for money. I always say: "This is to help with your costs." In these situations you find extremes of nobility and extremes of wickedness.*'

For a journalist, it's not just a matter of being sympathetic. You have to be sure you are getting the story right. Ann Leslie says:

'*You must start off with: "Why are they lying to me?" Otherwise you end up using rumour.*

'*You have to be precise and use only what they themselves have experienced. You must be wary of becoming a victim of political propaganda. In this case I was convinced I was not. The refugees I spoke to came from a wide range of places. They didn't belong to a highly organized underground transport system.*"'

SECRET PRISON CAMPS

Sue Lloyd-Roberts of the BBC, working with Chinese dissident Harry Wu, established on television that China has a gulag archipelago of prison camps. It is called the Laogai.

'In China,' she says, 'Harry Wu and I travelled in a smart jeep. That intimidated people. They thought: "They must be from Beijing."'

Harry Wu spent years in prison in China. She met him at a London lunch and asked if he knew of anyone who was going there. He told her he had just got an American passport. 'I am going with you,' he said.

They crossed into Xinjiang in Western China where many people are European in appearance, making Sue less conspicuous. They pretended to be academics, studying the ancient Silk Road across the Gobi Desert:

'The prisons are all signposted,' she says. 'Crocodiles of chain-gangs would pass in front of our jeep.

'In the end Harry and I got sentenced to seven years in absentia. The camps are still state secrets; but, before we went, reports of them were called fabrications.'

Journalists can reasonably be apprehensive about going into countries where they don't know the ropes. Sue Lloyd-Roberts sees it the other way round. In such situations, it is she who has the advantage of surprise. 'They are so surprised to see you, no one will stop you.'

She got into solo investigative work because she was uncomfortable with conventional TV reporting with its crew of three, big cameras and big microphones. With an innocuous-looking lightweight camera like a tourist's, you can reach places where a camera crew can't go. And 'people are far more likely to talk to an unintimidating woman'.

She was never, she says, a camera buff but the technicalities are not that daunting. Years of work in an editing suite taught her the sort of pictures that TV wants.

She has been to Tibet five times as a 'tourist', and several times to Burma where she drew attention to British companies doing business with the generals. She says:

'No Western business can do business in Burma without dealing with the military. Burtons announced they were withdrawing.

'I passed myself off as a clothing manufacturer and introduced myself to the Ministry of Foreign Enterprises where I was interviewed by a lieutenant-colonel. He said the wages he paid workers were the lowest in the world.'

Posing as an aid worker, she was the first journalist into Ogoniland, Nigeria, after General Abacha's government murdered the local leader, Ken Saro-Wiwa. In 1998, she was in South-East Turkey, checking on the Turkish Army's use of British-made equipment against the Kurds. Villages, she found, had become ghost communities. 'People were terrified to talk to me.'

She has also been to Indonesia to try to photograph the use of British weapons. Her visit to East Timor, where the local population has suffered at the hands of the Indonesian Army, took weeks to set up. 'I've become a human rights reporter,' she says. 'Somebody has to remind the world that people are suffering.'

She agrees with Ann Leslie that no news item is worth a person's life. Eight years ago a woman TV producer went to Tibet and interviewed eight or ten monks and freedom fighters. A number were arrested. Sue Lloyd-Roberts, when in Tibet, takes pictures of damaged monasteries but is careful not to photograph people.

In Turkey, an old man showed her a house riddled with bullets. She filmed only the back of his head:

'You have to be extremely responsible, even if it makes an item less dramatic. People are unsophisticated and naive. They think that, if it's shown on the BBC, the West will invade tomorrow.'

HOSPITAL HORRORS

Claudia Milne, now head of the independent TV producer Twenty Twenty Vision, read an article in the magazine of Mind, the National

Association for Mental Health, about conditions on the island of Leros, at that time a dumping ground for Greeks classed as mental patients including mentally handicapped people and army refuseniks.

In the Pavilion of the Naked some patients were chained to their beds. There were no knives and forks, baths or showers. People were hosed down.

'Nobody believed we would get in,' says Milne. However, a Channel 4 commissioning editor agreed to pay for a few days' filming. It was just before a general election, when there was no minister in charge, and they were talked in by a freelance producer who spoke Greek.

Also for Channel 4, Brian Woods and Kate Blewett were in Greece in 1997, visiting two institutions where they filmed disabled children tied to cots or locked in cages. They found that if a child was assessed as incurable the child had in effect been given a life sentence.

COMMISSION AND CORRUPTION

While Mrs Thatcher was prime minister, an oil-for-arms deal called al-Yamamah was concluded with Saudi Arabia. At one stage, according to the *Financial Times*, the deal accounted for almost half the annual turnover of British aircraft manufacturer British Aerospace.

A Palestinian businessman, Said Aburish, alleged in *World in Action*'s programme *Jonathan of Arabia* that the Saudi royal family levied commissions on all Western export deals. Did anyone receive commission on al-Yamamah and, if so, how much? The answer to this question is, I am told, the holy grail for British investigative journalists.

A witness in the Aitken libel case (see page 107) said that commissions were paid, but the Conservative government denied it. John Speller, for Tony Blair's government, said in 1997 that UK companies involved in al-Yamamah had operated 'in accordance with the laws and regulations of Saudi Arabia'.

In December 1997, a Panamanian company, with the same address as one set up by a brother-in-law of the Saudi king, issued a writ against Rolls-Royce, seeking payment of commissions allegedly promised on aircraft engines supplied as part of the al-Yamamah deal.

> Payment of commission in return for the placing of a contract is not something peculiar to abroad. The Audit Commission in October 1998 mentioned cases where inducements were offered for local authority contracts in Britain. Councils themselves charge quite openly for what they call planning gain. We give you permission to build a new housing estate: you pay for a new school, road, sports centre.
>
> Alan Doig in his book *Corruption and Misconduct in Contemporary British Politics* gave examples of kickbacks in the former nationalized industries and the Navy.

However, corruption in contracts with poor countries overseas is particularly important because they can ill afford it. George Moody-Stuart, an anti-corruption campaigner who has spent a lifetime in international business, writes in his book *Grand Corruption* (Worldview Publications, Oxford, 1997) that there is a sliding scale for commission payments. Arms contracts attract the biggest commissions, around 25 per cent. As a result, scarce money may be diverted into arms from more useful purchases, to earn the higher commission.

The essential problem is that, where a government is the only purchaser, the signature of whoever signs for that government and will see the contract through is worth money. The commission agent who persuades him to sign and hands him his cut is also worth money. And it may also be worth the commission agent's while to provide a kickback for whoever represents the firm that is paying the money.

Information about commission payments occasionally emerges from court cases. In the 1970s, a case disclosed that commission on a sale of tanks to Iran was paid to a friend of the Shah. In September 1998, a case opened in Belgium alleging payments to two Socialist parties in return for a military aircraft contract.

In late 1998, the Pakistani government alleged corruption in power contracts. Earlier, SGS, a Swiss company employed by many countries to ensure they are not swindled by foreign suppliers, admitted it had paid commission to get a contract with Pakistan. Its chairman said it might in future avoid markets 'where our ethical principles do not enable us to compete on an even basis'.

Tom Bower's interviews with businessmen for his biography *Tiny Rowland, A Rebel Tycoon* (Heinemann, 1993) produced detailed information about Rowland's payments and gifts to leading Africans.

Bower writes that in ten years Rowland's company Lonrho paid out at least £836,000 in what were called special payments. Under the heading 'General Expenses, Africa', Rowland employed a code: 202 was Zambia and 404 its then president, Kenneth Kaunda; 203 was Malawi and 405 its then president, Hastings Banda. Bower shows that Rowland, though generous to Dr Banda, was not so generous to Malawi's railway company. Just before Malawi became independent and Banda took over, Rowland bought a controlling stake in the railway for £140,000. Bower reports that he then cancelled an order for new locomotives and bought shares in a South African company with £5 million which the railway had saved up.

The international organization fighting corruption is Transparency International. The phone number for its British office is 01892-530356.

INTERNATIONAL BODIES

International organizations, whether inter-governmental or sporting, came to the forefront in 1998 and 1999 as targets for investigative journalism. *Panorama* investigated international motor racing and the allocation of its revenues from television. An Olympics official said he had evidence of International Olympic Committee members accepting gifts from Salt Lake City where the winter Olympics of the year 2000 are to be held. Journalists immediately started to inquire who got what.

Neil Buckley alleged in the *Financial Times* in October 1998 that four European Community aid contracts had turned out to be fictitious. Most of the money was spent on additional staff for the European Community Humanitarian Office.

Yet before the autumn of 1998 it was hard to stir much interest in whether international organizations were well run or not.

In November 1997, the *Sunday Times* Insight team headed an article 'Runaway gravy train'. With the help of documents about United Nations agencies from the UN's own monitoring organization, Insight told of extravagant furniture purchases, misuse of aircraft and false claims for refugees. It also told of a conference costing £6 million, run by an agency concerned with housing for poor people. Insight did not, however, follow up with further articles.

In 1998, the *Financial Times* published an interview with Mrs Sadako Ogata, the UN High Commissioner for Refugees. As a result, an e-mail arrived out of the blue. 'There's much more than meets the eye,' wrote the sender of the e-mail. 'We can help you.'

Journalist Jimmy Burns says the *FT* had long wanted to do something about the UN because of American concerns. But first he had to 'check this guy wasn't a complete madman'.

Burns adds: 'He came back with a lot more documents. We had a story contrary to UNHCR's caring image, all based on documents. Editors crave documents. They trust documents more than people, who will lead you up the garden path.'

On July 29, the *FT* gave the story a full page. It made three main allegations. One was that auditors had criticized the UNHCR accounts which, for example, were short of certificates showing that money handed to other agencies was properly spent. Second, UNHCR had failed to protect local staff caring for Rwandan refugees in the Congo. Third, UNHCR acted as a repository for refugees, rather than campaigning for their rights and welfare.

This exposé evoked cries of horror. Mrs Ogata, the UN High Commissioner, is a saintly Japanese. Criticizing her agency was rather like criticizing Mother Teresa.

The *FT* published an account of a meeting at which an official from Britain's Department for International Development berated UNHCR officials over the way they used British money. Foreign Office diplomats listened in embarrassed silence.

UNHCR issued a reply. It said the auditors' report, if critical, had reached a positive and unqualified conclusion on the accounts. It also said it had other mechanisms, besides audit certificates, to vet spending by other agencies.

Jimmy Burns says the *FT* had then to decide what to do. If it did nothing more, UNHCR would think it had got by. But how far do you go on without axe-grinding?

In the event, no other newspapers broached the UNHCR issue; and financial crisis in Russia then seized the attention of the media.

EUROFRAUD

Chris White, who was then writing freelance articles for *The European*, was in a pub in Brussels one evening in 1994 when someone mentioned that two men from the European Commission's tourism department had been accused of fraud. They were being retired on full pensions to get rid of them. 'I was outraged,' says White.

It took him some weeks to find the men's names. He discovered that one was George Tzoanos, head of the tourism unit, and the other Pascal Chatillon, a temporary official in the same unit.

White went to Calais to interview Chatillon at a café run by his wife. Chatillon told him that, although corruption was rife in the unit, he only ever acted on orders. Chatillon was outraged at the way he had been treated. 'I got a lot of detail,' says White, 'despite his wife saying repeatedly: "Don't talk to him. He's a journalist."'

Tzoanos also told White he was innocent. 'There was interference from the top,' he said. 'I was covering for people above me.'

White pursued his inquiries, eventually acquiring an audit report strongly criticizing the award of some consultancy contracts. 'What surprised me,' says White, 'was the number of honest people working for the Commission. I would talk to someone in a pub and next day a brown envelope would come through my door. I built up a huge dossier on corrupt contracts.'

He sought the help of Edward MacMillan-Scott, a member of the European Parliament whom he knew to be interested in what went wrong in the Year of Tourism. MacMillan-Scott put questions to the European Commission on behalf of both these men.

White also approached the Belgian police but they had no way of getting through the Commission's door since it claimed diplomatic immunity for its staff. So White got MacMillan-Scott to lodge a formal complaint with the police, which enabled them to raid the tourism unit, the first time that outside investigators had got into the Commission in 40 years. MacMillan-Scott's complaint alleged that officials had sought illegal commissions on tourism contracts.

At this point Per Brix Knudsen, head of Uclaf, the Commission's anti-fraud unit, unexpectedly gave White an hour-and-a-half interview about his own inquiries into fraud. Unfortunately, Knudsen's complaint about White's report of this interview brought *The European*'s investigation to an end (see page 72). The police inquiries also ran into a problem when the Commission's director-general covering tourism and small business, Heinrich von Moltke, took early retirement.

However, there was a sequel. White got a telephone call from Rosemarie Wemheuer, a German member of the European Parliament's Committee on Budgetary Control. Wemheuer was suspicious about the Commission's reaction to the investigations. She said she had been told that he (White) was inaccurate, that MacMillan-Scott had a financial interest in the matter, and that the Belgian prosecutor in charge of the police inquiries didn't know what he was doing. 'I can believe this,' she said, 'of one of you. But all of you? There has to be something wrong.'

Wemheuer produced a report accusing the Commission of delaying criminal investigations and withholding information from Parliament. This report changed the climate of opinion about malpractice at the Commission and set off the Parliamentary campaign which led to the resignation of all the commissioners in March 1999.

Appendix A
Books for further reading

Eric Barendt, Laurence Lustgarten, Kenneth Norrie and Hugh
    Stephenson: *Libel and the Media* (Oxford 1997)
Wensley Clarkson: *The Valkyrie Operation* (Blake 1998)
Barry Cox, John Shirley and Martin Short: *The Fall of Scotland Yard*
    (Penguin 1977)
Nick Davies: *Dark Heart* (Chatto & Windus 1997; Vintage 1998)
Alan Doig: *Corruption and Misconduct in Contemporary British
    Politics* (Penguin 1984)
Harold Evans: *Good Times, Bad Times* (Weidenfeld 1983)
Ray Fitzwalter and David Taylor: *Web of Corruption* (Granada 1981)
Paul Foot: *Murder at the Farm* (Sidgwick & Jackson 1986)
Paul Halloran and Mark Hollingsworth: *Thatcher's Gold* (Simon &
    Schuster 1995)
Dr Phil Hammond and Michael Mosley: *Trust Me (I'm a Doctor)*
    (Metro 1999)
Luke Harding, David Leigh and David Pallister: *The Liar* (Penguin
    1997)
Christopher Hird: *Challenging the Figures* (Pluto 1983)
Harold Hobson and others: *The Pearl of Days* (Hamish Hamilton
    1972). History of *The Sunday Times* including chapters by Phillip
    Knightley on the early days of Insight
Phillip Knightley: *A Hack's Progress* (Cape 1997)
David Leigh: *The Wilson Plot* (Heinemann 1988)
David Leigh and Ed Vulliamy: *Sleaze* (Fourth Estate 1997)
James Morton: *Bent Coppers* (Warner 1993)

Chris Mullin: *Error of Judgment* (Poolbeg)
David Murphy: *The Stalker Affair and the Press* (Unwin Hyman 1991)
David Northmore: *Lifting the Lid, a Guide to Investigative Research* (Cassell 1996)
Brian O'Kane (editor): *Essential Finance for Journalists* (Oak Tree Press 1993)
Emily O'Reilly: *Victoria Guerin* (Vintage 1998)
Peter Watson: *Sotheby's: Inside Story* (Bloomsbury 1997). This gives a detailed account of how a complex investigation was conducted
Tom Welsh and Walter Greenwood: *McNae's Essential Law for Journalists* (Butterworth)
Brian Whitaker: *News Ltd* (Minority Press 1981)

Appendix B
People who helped with this book

Sam Bagnall, freelance television producer

Martin Banks, chief reporter, *Evening Mail*, Birmingham

Antony Barnett, public affairs editor, the *Observer*

David Bell, municipal reporter, *Evening Mail*, Birmingham

Richard Bettsworth, political editor, *The News*, Portsmouth

David Birkbeck, editor, *Building Homes* magazine

Chris Blackhurst, deputy editor, *The Express*; formerly with *The Independent on Sunday*

Alastair Brett, lawyer, Times Newspapers

Tom Bower, former BBC producer. Author of *Maxwell the Outsider*, *Maxwell the Final Verdict*, *Tiny Rowland*. Has specialized in investigating injustices left over by the war

Jimmy Burns, reporter, the *Financial Times*

Mike Calvin, sports journalist with the *Mail on Sunday*, formerly with *The Times*

Duncan Campbell, crime reporter, *The Guardian*

Bernard Clark runs Clark TV, independent TV production company. Formerly with the BBC for which he launched *Watchdog*

Tony Collins took five years out of journalism to work in his family's business and became interested in computers. Now investigative reporter, *Computer Weekly*

Roger Cook, of *The Cook Report*, came to Britain after the Australian Broadcasting Corporation found his investigative work too hot to handle. He joined *The World at One* on BBC Radio, then embarked on his own programme *Checkpoint* in 1972. To tap into the greater resources of television, he switched to Central TV which has been making *The Cook Report* since the mid-1980s

Nick Davies, investigative reporter, *The Guardian*

Richard Donkin, employment columnist, *Financial Times*. Formerly investigative reporter with the *FT* and the *Yorkshire Post*

Ian Dowell, editor, *Evening Mail*, Birmingham

Geoff Elliott, editor, *The News*, Portsmouth

James Evans, formerly lawyer for *The Sunday Times*

Ray Fitzwalter runs an investigative TV production company, Ray Fitzwalter Associates. Was formerly editor of *World in Action*

Paul Foot, columnist *Private Eye*. Has also contributed extensively to the *Daily Mirror* and *The Guardian*

Michael Gillard, investigative journalist specializing in business, now with *The Express*, formerly with *The Observer*

Jo-Ann Goodwin, former adviser on arts and media to Labour's Shadow Cabinet. Now freelance contributor to the *Daily Mail*

Paul Halloran, freelance investigative reporter in partnership with Mark Hollingsworth with whom he wrote *Thatcher's Gold* (Simon & Schuster, 1995). Was formerly with *Private Eye*

Phil Hammond, doctor and presenter of BBC TV's programme *Trust Me (I'm a Doctor)*. Got into journalism by writing for *Private Eye*

David Hencke, investigative reporter at Westminster for *The Guardian*

Christopher Hird started as a stockbroker but found what interested him was what was wrong with companies. Wrote for *Investors Guardian*, later for *The Economist* and the *Daily Mail*. In 1981 he became editor of Insight at *The Sunday Times*. Joined newly created Channel 4 as a reporter for *Diverse Reports*. Formed independent company Fulcrum Productions with Richard Belfield in 1986

Godfrey Hodgson, former editor of *The Sunday Times'* Insight, is now director of the Reuter Foundation's journalism programme at Green College, Oxford. He has been foreign editor of *The Independent*, a foreign correspondent for *The Observer* and *The Sunday Times* and a reporter and presenter for Thames Television's *This Week* and for *Channel 4 News*

Mark Hollingsworth, freelance investigative reporter in partnership with Paul Halloran. Wrote *MPs for Hire* (Bloomsbury, 1991)

Terry Kelleher, independent TV producer. After university joined an Irish literary magazine which got interested in political investigation. Joined Thames Television as investigative researcher. Made film with Paul Foot about the men convicted of murdering a newspaper boy Carl Bridgewater, which caused the then Home Secretary, Douglas Hurd, to send their case to the Court of Appeal

Mark Killick, producer, *Panorama*, BBC TV. Made *Panorama*'s programme on Robert Maxwell, *The Max Factor*

Paul Lashmar produced the Channel 4 *Dispatches* programme *The Test* which investigated Britain's biggest scanda over cervical smear tests. Worked for eight years with David Leigh at *The Observer* investigating MI5 vetting of BBC staff, arms for South Africa, and Mark Thatcher's lobbying in Oman. Then for *World in Action* he investigated unscrupulous landlords and mortgage brokers, and the killers of Brazil's street children. Now with *The Independent*

David Leigh is comment editor at *The Guardian*. He was previously a contributing editor at *The Observer* and, earlier, the *Observer*'s head of investigations. He has also worked for Thames Television's investigative programme *This Week* and for Granada's *World in Action*. His books include *The Frontiers of Secrecy*, *Chernobyl* and *The Wilson Plot*

David Leppard, editor of Insight, *The Sunday Times*. Got into journalism by freelancing while at Oxford

Ann Leslie, special correspondent for the *Daily Mail*, to which she has contributed since 1967

David Lloyd, head of news and current affairs, Channel 4

Garry Lloyd, one of two *Times* reporters who initiated what became a 30-year fight against corruption in the Metropolitan Police

Sue Lloyd-Roberts, reporter, BBC TV. Demonstrated the existence of prison camps in China

Mazher Mahmood, investigations editor, the *News of the World*. Formerly with *The Sunday Times* and also with TV-am for which he produced *Frost on Sunday*

Peter Marsh, reporter, the *Financial Times*

Martin McGlown, investigative reporter, *Evening Mail*, Birmingham

Donal McIntyre, BBC Documentaries. When with *World in Action* he investigated drug-dealing in Nottingham

Maurice McLeod, *The Voice*

Claudia Milne, executive producer at TV production company, Twenty Twenty Television.

Chris Mullin MP. As a freelance investigative journalist, he did much to destroy the prosecution case against the Birmingham Six. Now parliamentary under-secretary at the Department of the Environment.

Dr David Murphy, School of Management, University of Manchester Institute of Science and Technology. Began working life as a journalist for Tillotson Newspapers, Bolton. Later worked for fringe papers in Manchester

Paul Nuki, consumer affairs editor, *The Sunday Times*. Formerly finance editor

Helen O'Rahilly, editor, *Watchdog*, BBC TV

Bruce Page started in journalism with the *Melbourne Herald*. Worked for *The Sunday Times* 1964–76. Editor of the *New Statesman* 1978–82

Charles Raw, business journalist, formerly at *The Sunday Times*, and *The Observer*. Investigated the financial firm Slater Walker

Bob Satchwell, editor of the *Cambridge Evening News* up to November 1998. Previously with the *Lancashire Evening Post* and the *News of the World*

Jonathan Smith, investigative reporter, *The News*, Portsmouth

John Stonborough, media relations counsel, advises companies on how to counter investigative reporting. After leaving the police, he worked for the *East London Advertiser* and the *Daily Mail* before joining Roger Cook's investigative programme *Checkpoint* on BBC radio. He spent four years exposing fraud for Channel 4's consumer programme *4 What it's Worth*

Jan Tomalin, head of legal services, Channel 4

Stewart Tendler, crime reporter, *The Times*

John Ware, reporter, *Panorama*

Peter Watson, freelance writer on art who led an investigation for Channel 4 into the smuggling of art and antiquities. A former psychiatrist, he joined the *Sunday Times* Insight team and later *The Times*

Chris White, editor of *The Parliament Magazine*, Brussels. He has worked for several national papers, including 14 years with the *Daily Mail*. He freelanced in Bristol then spent five years as press officer for Conservative members of the European Parliament in Brussels. He became a freelance, working for *The European* and ITN, but parted from *The European* when it withdrew from his inquiry into corruption at the European Commission.

Appendix C
Council information open to public view

Under the Local Government (Access to Information) Act, councils have to produce a list of documents and registers which the public (and therefore journalists) have a right to see. The list has also to say where they can be seen (council offices, information centres, libraries, etc.). Here is the list of public documents made available by one council, the London Borough of Redbridge (Redbridge also helps inquirers find in the documents what they are looking for).

LAND MANAGEMENT

Current planning applications
Decided applications
Decision notices and Department of Environment appeal decisions
Property index of planning applications
Tree preservation orders
Register of public bodies' land
Register of statutory listed buildings
Register of enforcement notices
Unitary development plan, plus inspector's reports, register of
    objectors, consideration of objections
Public sewers/drainage records

PERSONAL SERVICES

Housing allocation policy statement/transfers
Sale of council houses and flats
Housing register policy statement
Applications for housing
Register of childminders
Register of private day nurseries, including playgroups
Register of private and voluntary residential care homes
Open inspection reports: residential care homes
Conditions of tenancy
Tenancy/property file
Tenant/leaseholder consultations
Arrears procedure
Community care plan and guide to services
Annual report to tenants

ENVIRONMENT AND CONSUMER PROTECTION

Noise abatement zone register
Register of seized dogs
Register of food premises

ADMINISTRATION AND LEGAL SERVICES

Indexes to register of births, deaths and marriages
Book of notices of marriage (if there is reason to suppose possible
   impediment to a marriage)
Open registers (those on which a registrar is currently working; the
   public have a right to search for a named entry)
Rent register
Council minute books
Local by-laws
Standing orders
Delegated powers
Information about council members
Summary of the public's right to attend council meetings

Register of prescribed information of council members' direct and
indirect pecuniary interests
Council premises: lettings and allocation of tenancies
Index of local charities
Register of notices of motion
Register of dispensations (permissions for councillors to take part in
debates on subjects in which they have a financial interest)
Local land charges register
Register of common land and town and village green

RECREATION AND AMENITIES

Parks and cemetery by laws
Swimming pools by-laws
Swimming pools: opening times and charges
Swimming pools: conditions of hire
Public halls: conditions of hire
Opening times of recreational establishments
Allotment sites

PUBLIC CLEANSING

Refuse collection
Public conveniences: location and opening times
Bulky refuse collection: charges
Trade refuse collection: charges
Street sweeping schedule
Civic amenity sites

TECHNICAL SERVICES

Public footpaths and rights of way
Controlled parking zones
Motorway proposals
Road classification
Rainfall readings
Waiting restrictions

Bridges and level crossings
Street lighting
List of adopted roads
Speed limits
Traffic signs
Road accident statistics
Details of private streets
Removal of abandoned vehicles
Hainault Forest by-laws

FINANCE

Non-domestic rating list
Council tax valuation list
Statutory council tax leaflet
Current estimate book
Current abstract of accounts
Annual report
Annual direct service (formerly labour) organization report
Council members' allowances register

EDUCATION

Ofsted reports on schools
Particulars on schools and admission arrangements
Policy on charging for school activities
Complaints procedure regarding school curriculum
Local management of schools scheme
Budget and out-turn statement under local management of schools
Background papers for reports by the Director of Educational Services
Minutes of school governing bodies
Scale of library charges

DATA PROTECTION

Registrations of new-technology systems made by the council under
the Data Protection Act

Appendix D
Press Complaints Commission – Code of Practice

The Press Complaints Commission is charged with enforcing the following Code of Practice which was framed by the newspaper and periodical industry and ratified by the Press Complaints Commission, November 26, 1997.

All members of the press have a duty to maintain the highest professional and ethical standards. This Code sets the benchmarks for those standards. It both protects the rights of the individual and upholds the public's right to know.

The Code is the cornerstone of the system of self-regulation to which the industry has made a binding commitment. Editors and publishers must ensure that the Code is observed rigorously not only by their staff but also by anyone who contributes to their publications.

It is essential to the workings of an agreed Code that it be honoured not only to the letter but in the full spirit. The Code should not be interpreted so narrowly as to compromise its commitment to respect the rights of the individual, nor so broadly that it prevents publication in the public interest.

It is the responsibility of editors to co-operate with the PCC as swiftly as possible in the resolution of complaints.

Any publication which is criticized by the PCC under one of the following clauses must print the adjudication which follows in full and with due prominence.

1   ACCURACY

i)   Newspapers and periodicals must take care not to publish inaccurate, misleading or distorted material including pictures.

ii) Whenever it is recognized that a significant inaccuracy, misleading statement or distorted report has been published, it must be corrected promptly and with due prominence.

iii) An apology must be published whenever appropriate.

iv) Newspapers, whilst free to be partisan, must distinguish clearly between comment, conjecture and fact.

v)   A newspaper or periodical must report fairly and accurately the outcome of an action for defamation to which it has been a party.

2   OPPORTUNITY TO REPLY

A fair opportunity to reply to inaccuracies must be given to individuals or organizations when reasonably called for.

*3   PRIVACY

i)   Everyone is entitled to respect for his or her private and family life, home, health and correspondence. A publication will be expected to justify intrusions into any individual's private life without consent.

ii) The use of long lens photography to take pictures of people in private places without their consent is unacceptable.

Note – Private places are public or private property where there is a reasonable expectation of privacy.

*4   HARASSMENT

i)   Journalists and photographers must neither obtain nor seek to obtain information or pictures through intimidation, harassment or persistent pursuit.

ii) They must not photograph individuals in private places (as defined in the note to Clause 3) without their consent; must not persist in telephoning, questioning, pursuing or photographing individuals after having been asked to desist; must not remain on their property after having been asked to leave and must not follow them.

iii) Editors must ensure that those working for them comply with these requirements and must not publish material from other sources which does not meet these requirements.

5 INTRUSION INTO GRIEF OR SHOCK

In cases involving grief or shock, enquiries must be carried out and approaches made with sympathy and discretion. Publication must be handled sensitively at such times, but this should not be interpreted as restricting the right to report judicial proceedings.

*6 CHILDREN

i) Young children should be free to complete their time at school without unnecessary intrusion.

ii) Journalists must not interview or photograph children under the age of 16 on subjects involving the welfare of the child or of any other child, in the absence of or without the consent of a parent or other adult who is responsible for the children.

iii) Pupils must not be approached or photographed while at school without the permission of the school authorities.

iv) There must be no payment to minors for material involving the welfare of children nor payment to parents or guardians for material about their children or wards unless it is demonstrably in the child's interest.

v) Where material about the private life of a child is published, there must be justification for publication other than the fame, notoriety or position of his or her parents or guardian.

7 CHILDREN IN SEX CASES

1 The press must not, even where the law does not prohibit it, identify children under the age of 16 who are involved in cases concerning sexual offences, whether as victims or as witnesses.

2 In any press report of a case involving a sexual offence against a child –

    i)   The child must not be identified.

    ii) The adult may be identified.

    iii) The word 'incest' must not be used where a child victim might be identified.

    iv) Care must be taken that nothing in the report implies the relationship between the accused and the child.

8   LISTENING DEVICES

Journalists must not obtain or publish material obtained by using clandestine listening devices or by intercepting private telephone conversations.

9   HOSPITALS

    i)   Journalists or photographers making enquiries at hospitals or similar institutions must identify themselves to a responsible executive and obtain permission before entering non-public areas.

    ii) The restrictions on intruding into privacy are particularly relevant to enquiries about individuals in hospitals or similar institutions.

*10   INNOCENT RELATIVES AND FRIENDS

The press must avoid identifying relatives or friends of persons convicted or accused of crime without their consent.

*11   MISREPRESENTATION

    i)   Journalists must not generally obtain or seek to obtain information or pictures through misrepresentation or subterfuge.

    ii) Documents or photographs should be removed only with the consent of the owner.

    iii) Subterfuge can be justified only in the public interest and only when material cannot be obtained by any other means.

12 VICTIMS OF SEXUAL ASSAULT

The press must not identify victims of sexual assault or publish material likely to contribute to such identification unless there is adequate justification and, by law, they are free to do so.

13 DISCRIMINATION

i) The press must avoid prejudicial or pejorative reference to a person's race, colour, religion, sex or sexual orientation or to any physical or mental illness or disability.

ii) It must avoid publishing details of a person's race, colour, religion, sexual orientation, physical or mental illness or disability unless these are directly relevant to the story.

14 FINANCIAL JOURNALISM

i) Even where the law does not prohibit it, journalists must not use for their own profit financial information they receive in advance of its general publication, nor should they pass such information to others.

ii) They must not write about shares or securities in whose performance they know that they or their close families have a significant financial interest, without disclosing the interest to the editor or financial editor.

iii) They must not buy or sell, either directly or through nominees or agents, shares or securities about which they have written recently or about which they intend to write in the near future.

15 CONFIDENTIAL SOURCES

Journalists have a moral obligation to protect confidential sources of information.

*16   PAYMENT FOR ARTICLES

    i)   Payment or offers of payment for stories or information must not be made directly or through agents to witnesses or potential witnesses in current criminal proceedings except where the material concerned ought to be published in the public interest and there is an overriding need to make or promise to make a payment for this to be done. Journalists must take every possible step to ensure that no financial dealings have influence on the evidence that those witnesses may give. (An editor authorizing such a payment must be prepared to demonstrate that there is a legitimate public interest at stake involving matters that the public has a right to know. The payment or, where accepted, the offer of payment to any witness who is actually cited to give evidence must be disclosed to the prosecution and the defence and the witness should be advised of this.)

    ii) Payment or offers of payment for stories, pictures or information, must not be made directly or through agents to convicted or confessed criminals or to their associates – who may include family, friends and colleagues – except where the material ought to be published in the public interest and payment is necessary for this to be done.

The Public Interest

There may be exceptions to the clauses marked * where they can be demonstrated to be in the public interest.

1   The public interest includes:
    i)   Detecting or exposing crime or a serious misdemeanour.
    ii) Protecting public health and safety.
    iii) Preventing the public from being misled by some statement or action of an individual or organization.
2   In any case where the public interest is invoked, the Press Complaints Commission will require a full explanation by the editor demonstrating how the public interest was served.
3   In cases involving children editors must demonstrate an exceptional public interest to override the normally paramount interests of the child.

Index

INDEX

INDEX

INDEX

www.focalpress.com

Visit our web site for:

- the latest information on new and forthcoming Focal Press titles
- special offers
- our email news service

Join our Focal Press Bookbuyers' Club

As a member, you will enjoy the following benefits:

- special discounts on new and best-selling titles
- advance information on forthcoming Focal Press books
- a quarterly newsletter highlighting special offers
- a 30-day guarantee on purchased titles

Membership is FREE. To join, supply your name, company, address, telephone/fax numbers and email address to:

Elaine Hill
Email: elaine.hill@repp.co.uk
Fax: +44(0) 1865314423
Address: Focal Press, Linacre House, Jordan Hill, Oxford, OX2 8DP

Catalogue

For information on all Focal Press titles, we will be happy to send you a free copy of the Focal Press Catalogue.

Tel: 01865 314693
Email: carol.burgess@repp.co.uk

Potential authors

If you have an idea for a book, please get in touch:

Europe

Beth Howard, Editorial Assistant
Email: beth.howard@repp.co.uk
Tel: +44(0) 1865 314365
Fax: +44(0) 1865 314572

USA

Marie Lee, Publisher
Email: marie.lee@bhusa.com
Tel: 781 9042500
Fax: 781 9042620